THE

GOVERNMENT CLASS BOOK;

DESIGNED FOR

THE INSTRUCTION OF YOUTH

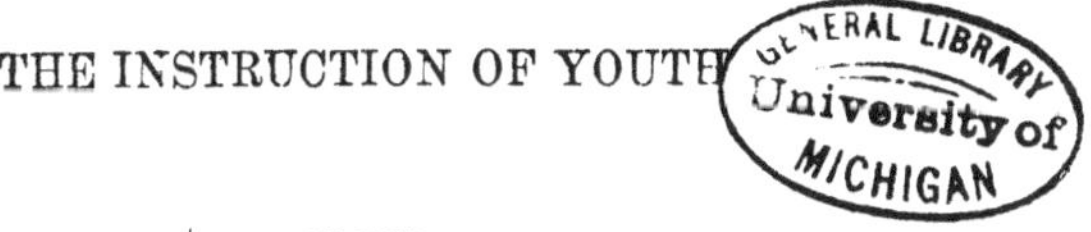

IN THE

Principles of Constitutional Government,

AND

THE RIGHTS AND DUTIES OF CITIZENS.

BY ANDREW W. YOUNG,

Author of "Science of Government," "First Lessons in Civil Government," "American Statesman," "Citizen's Manual of Government and Law."

NEW-YORK:
J. C. DERBY & N. C. MILLER,
5 SPRUCE STREET, TRIBUNE BUILDINGS.
1865.

PREFACE.

The utility of the diffusion of political knowledge among a people exercising the right of self-government, is universally admitted. The form of government established by the people of the United States, though well adapted to promote the general welfare, is highly complicated; and the knowledge requisite to administer it successfully can not be acquired without much study. From the fact that a large portion of the American people are greatly deficient in this knowledge, we may justly conclude that it will never become general, until it shall have been made an object of school instruction.

The administration of the government of this great and rapidly increasing republic, will, in a few years, devolve upon those who are now receiving instruction in the public schools. Yet thousands annually complete their school education, who have never devoted any time to the study of the principles of the government in which they are soon to take a part—who become invested with political power without the preparation necessary to exercise it with discretion. The schools are regarded as the nurseries of our future statesmen. They share largely in the bounty of the state; yet few of them render in return even the rudiments of political science to those who are to become her legislators, and governors, and judges. Not only in the common schools generally, but in a large portion of the high schools and seminaries, this science is not included in the course of instruction.

To many of the most enlightened friends of education and of our free institutions, it has long been a matter of surprise as well as regret, that those to whom the educational interests of the states are more immediately intrusted, should so long have treated the study in question as of minor importance, or have suffered it to be excluded by studies of far less practical utility. The Regents of the University of the State of New York have repeatedly noticed the neglect of this study in the academies and seminaries subject to their visitation ; and they mention it as a remarkable fact, that in many of them preference is given to the study of the Grecian and Roman antiquities. They say : "The constitutions, laws, manners, and customs of ancient Greece and Rome are made subjects of regular study, quarter after quarter, while our own constitutional jurisprudence, and the every day occurring principles of our civil jurisprudence, are not admitted as a part of the academic course !"

To persons who are to engage in any of the industrial or professional pursuits, a preparatory course of training or discipline is deemed indispensable to success. Yet many assume the weighty responsibilities of freemen, and allow their sons to do the same, with scarcely any knowledge of a freeman's duties. On the intelligent exercise of political power, the public prosperity and the security of our liberties mainly depend. Every person, therefore, who is entitled to the rights of a citizen, is justly held responsible for the proper performance of his political duties. And any course of popular instruction which fails to impart a knowledge of our system of government, must be materially defective.

With a view to supply this deficiency, the author, many years since, prepared his "Introduction to the Science of Government." This work soon attained considerable popularity, both as a class book in schools, and as a book for private reading and reference for adults. Not being deem ed, however, sufficiently *elementary* for the children and youth in most of our common schools, another work, entitled, "First Lessons in Civil Government," was written to meet the capacities of younger or less advanced scholars than those for whom the previous work was designed.

The favorable reception of these works by the public, and the assurances of their usefulness to thousands who have studied them, are to the author a source of high gratification, and an ample reward for many years of arduous labor. The value of these works has, however, been in a measure impaired by changes in the government and laws since the time of their first publication. The latter, especially, descending so minutely into the details of the government of the state for which alone it is intended, requires frequent revisions.

It has occurred to the author that a new work, more permanent in the character of its matter, and adapted for use in all the states, is demanded to supply the deficiency in the present course of education. Stimulated by a desire to bear some part in laying a solid foundation for our republican institutions, and encouraged by the success of his former labors in this department of education, he has, after a suspension of several years, resumed his efforts in this enterprise, in the hope that, with the coöperation of teachers, and those having official supervision of the schools, it may be carried forward to an early consummation; when the principles of government shall be made a subject of regular study in the schools, and the elements of a sound political education shall be accessible to the mass of American youth. And he flatters himself, that the attention he has given to this subject has enabled him to prepare a work adapted, in a good degree, to meet the existing want of the schools.

Many words and phrases, as they occur in the course of

the work, have been defined ; and an attempt has been made to explain the several subjects in such a manner as to render them intelligible to youth.

The object which it is the purpose of this work to aid in effecting, claims the earnest attention of parents. Every father, at least, is bound to see that his sons have the means of acquiring a good political education. He can not innocently suffer them to pass from under his guardianship unprepared to discharge their political duties.

The study of this work should not be confined to male pupils. It has long been considered a striking defect in our system of education, that females are not more generally instructed in the principles of civil government, and in matters of business. Although they take no active part in public affairs, the knowledge here commended would enable them to exert a far more powerful and salutary influence upon our national character and destiny. As wives, mothers, teachers, and especially as counselors of the other sex, they could apply this knowledge to valuable purposes. And the question is submitted, whether it would not contribute more to their usefulness than some of those accomplishments which form so large a part of a modern female education, and which are usually lost amidst the cares of married life.

To preserve and transmit the blessings of constitutional liberty, we need a healthful patriotism. But a genuine love of country is hardly to be expected where there is not a proper appreciation of our political institutions, which give it its preëminence among nations. And how can they be duly appreciated if they are not understood ? It has been one of the objects of the writer to bring to view the chief excellencies of our system of government, and thus to lay, in the minds of youth, the basis of an enlightened and conservative patriotism.

That this work, as an elementary treatise on civil government, is not susceptible of improvement, is not pretended. Such as it is, it is submitted to the judgment of a candid public. If it shall prove in any considerable degree useful, the author's highest expectations will have been realized.

TO TEACHERS.

To the meritorious, though often undervalued labors of the instructors of American youth, is our country greatly indebted for the successful working of its system of free government; and upon the labors of their successors rest, in an equal degree, all well-founded hopes of its future political prosperity.

The general introduction and profitable study of this work, depend much upon a hearty and active coöperation of teachers in the enterprise which it is intended to promote. From all who desire to make themselves in the highest degree useful in their profession, such coöperation is confidently anticipated.

The advantage of instructing a class in civil government, is not confined to the pupils. The teacher will find the exercise both interesting and profitable to himself. Although pains have been taken to adapt the work to the capacities of youth, the definition of many terms and phrases, and the further explanation of many subjects, have necessarily been left to be supplied by teachers. The study and investigation which may in some cases be required to qualify them for the task, will be amply rewarded by their own advancement in political knowledge.

No intelligent teacher, it is presumed, will object to the introduction of this study, on the ground that there is not sufficient time or room for an additional exercise. Useful as all the branches now taught may be justly deemed, all of them are not, as is a knowledge of government, indispensable to the security of our liberties. The latter is of far greater importance to an American citizen, than a knowledge of some portions of arithmetic and the higher mathematics ; and in the opinion of some distinguished educators the time now devoted to these, in many schools, is sufficient to acquire a tolerable political education. It is believed, however, that this study need not exclude, or essentially interfere with, any of the studies pursued in the schools generally. By the more advanced scholars in the common schools, the work may be used as a reading book, and thus a two-fold advantage be gained from its use.

To assist the more inexperienced teachers in conducting the exercise, a few questions have been appended to the chapters. Questions may be added by the teachers at pleasure, or to such extent as may be thought necessary. And it is believed the recitations may be made more profitable to pupils, by requiring them, so far as may be, to give answers in their own words. To some of the printed questions, no answers are furnished by the chapters and sections referred to, but may be found in the Synopsis of the State Constitutions, or other parts of the work. Occasionally questions have been inserted to which no part of the work furnishes the answers.

CONTENTS.

PRINCIPLES OF GOVERNMENT.

STATE GOVERNMENTS.

GOVERNMENT OF THE UNITED STATES.

CHAPTER XLII.

CHAPTER XLIII.

CHAPTER XLIV.

CHAPTER XLV.

CHAPTER XLVI.

COMMON AND STATUTORY LAW.

CHAPTER XLVII.

CHAPTER XLVIII.

CHAPTER XLIX.

CHAPTER L.

CHAPTER LI.

CHAPTER LII.

CHAPTER LIII.

CHAPTER LIV.

CHAPTER LV.

CHAPTER LVI.

CHAPTER LVII.

CHAPTER LVIII.

CHAPTER LIX.

CHAPTER LX.

CHAPTER LXI.

CHAPTER LXII.

LAW OF NATIONS.

CHAPTER LXIII.

CHAPTER LXIV.

CHAPTER LXV.

CHAPTER LXVI.

CHAPTER LXVII.

SYNOPSIS OF THE STATE CONSTITUTIONS.

GOVERNMENT CLASS BOOK.

PRINCIPLES OF GOVERNMENT.

CHAPTER I.

Mankind fitted for Society, and for Civil Government and Laws.

§ 1. MANKIND are social beings. They are by nature fitted for society. By this we mean that they are naturally disposed to associate with each other. Indeed, such is their nature, that they could not be happy without such association. Hence we conclude that the Creator has designed men for society. It can not, therefore, be true, as some say, that the savage state is the natural state of man.

§ 2. Man is so formed that he is dependent upon his fellow men. He has not the natural strength of other animals. He needs the assistance of creatures like himself to protect and preserve his own being. We can hardly imagine how a person could procure the necessaries of life without such assistance. But men have the gifts of reason and speech. By conversation they are enabled to improve their reason and increase their knowledge, and to find methods of supplying their wants, and of improving their social condition.

§ 3. But, although men need the assistance of each other, they are so formed that each must have the care of him-

---

CHAPTER I.—§ 1. What is the natural state of mankind? § 2. What renders them mutually dependent? By what means are they enabled to supply their wants?

self. If every man were fed and clothed from a common store, provided by the labor of all, many, depending upon the labor of others, would be less industrious than they now are. By the present arrangement in society, which obliges every man to provide for his own wants, more is earned, a greater number are cared for, and the general welfare is better promoted than would be done if each labored for the benefit of all.

§ 4. From this arrangement comes the right of property. If each man's earnings should go into a common stock for the use of all, there would be nothing that any one could call his own. But if each is to provide for himself, he must have a right to use and enjoy the fruits of his own labor.

§ 5. But all men in society have the same rights. Therefore, in laboring to supply our wants, and to gratify our desires, we can not rightfully do so any further than is consistent with the rights of others. Hence we see the necessity of some established rules for securing to every member of society the free enjoyment of what justly belongs to him, and for regulating his conduct toward his fellow-members.

§ 6. These rules for regulating the social actions of men, are called laws. *Law*, in a general sense, is a rule of action, and is applied to all kinds of action. But in its limited and proper sense, it denotes the rules of human action prescribing what men are to do, and forbidding what they are not to do.

§ 7. We have seen that man is fitted for society, and that laws are necessary to govern the conduct of men in the social state. We see also that mankind are fitted by nature for government and laws. Man is also a moral being. The word *moral* has various significations. Sometimes it means only virtuous, or just; as, a moral man; that is, a man of moral character, or who lives a moral life; by which is meant that the conduct of the man is just and right.

§ 8. But in a wider sense, the word moral relates to the

---

§ 3. Why should every man labor for himself? § 4. What comes from this arrangement? § 5. How are the rights of men secured to them? § 6. What is *law*? § 7. For what else than society are mankind fitted by nature? Define *moral*.

social actions of men, both right and wrong. Thus, in speaking of the character of a man, we say, his morals are good, or his morals are bad. And of an action, we say, it is morally right, or it is morally wrong. Man's having a moral nature implies that he has a sense of right and wrong, or at least the power or faculty of acquiring it; and, being a moral agent, he is accountable for his actions.

§ 9. Thus we have seen that men are social, reasonable, and moral beings. They have power to discern their own wants and the wants of their fellow men; to perceive what is right and what is wrong; and to know that they ought to do what is right and to forbear to do what is wrong. Their reason enables them to understand the meaning of laws, and to discover what laws are necessary to regulate the social actions of men. Hence we conclude that they are fitted and designed for society, and for government and law.

§ 10. The youngest reader probably knows, that in speaking of society, we do not refer to any of those associations usually called societies, but to *civil* society, composed of the people of a state or nation. A *nation*, or *state*, is a large number of persons united under some form of government; as, the French nation; the British nation; or the state of New-York; the state of Virginia. Sometimes it signifies the ruling or governing power of a state or nation, as, the state has provided for educating its citizens, and for supporting the poor.

§ 11. The object of the people in forming a state association, or, as is sometimes said, of entering into civil society, is to promote their mutual safety and happiness. In uniting for this purpose, they agree to be governed by certain established rules and principles; and the governing of the people of a state or nation according to these rules, is called *civil government*. The word *government* also signifies the rules and principles themselves by which the people are governed; and sometimes the persons who administer the government—that is those who make the laws of a state and carry them into effect—are called *the government*.

---

§ 8. What is implied in man's having a moral nature? § 9. What qualities or faculties in mankind fit them for government and law? § 10. What is a state or nation? § 11. What is the object of forming state associations? What is meant by *civil government*?

CHAPTER II.

Rights and Liberty, defined.

§ 1. We have spoken of the rights of men, and of laws as designed to secure to men the free enjoyment of their rights. But a more particular definition of rights and laws will be useful to young persons just commencing the study of civil government.

§ 2. A *right* means ownership, or the just claim or lawful title which a person has to anything. What we have acquired by honest labor, or other lawful means, is rightfully our own; and we are justly entitled to the free use and enjoyment of it. We have a right also to be free in our actions. We may go where we please, and do what ever we think necessary for our own safety and happiness; provided we do not trespass upon the rights of others; for it must be remembered that others have the same rights as ourselves.

§ 3. The rights here mentioned are *natural* rights. They are so called because they are ours by nature or by birth; and they can not be justly taken from us or alienated. Hence they are also called *inalienable*. We may, however, forfeit them by some offense or crime. If, for example, a man is fined for breaking a law, he loses his right to the money he is obliged to pay. By stealing, he forfeits his liberty, and may be justly imprisoned. By committing murder, he forfeits his right to life, and may be hanged.

§ 4. Rights are also called personal, political, civil, and religious. *Personal rights*, or the *rights of persons*, are rights belonging to persons as individuals, and consist of the right of *personal security*, or the right to be secure from injury to our bodies, or persons, or our good names; the right of *personal liberty*, or the liberty of moving, acting, or speaking without unjust restraint; and the *right of property*,

---

Chap. II. § 2. Define the word *right*. May we do whatever we please? § 3. Why are rights called *natural?* Why *inalienable?* How may they be lost? § 4. What are *personal* rights? Define rights of person and right of property. State the distinction between personal rights and the rights of person.

or the right to acquire and enjoy property. The terms *rights of person* and *rights of persons*, or *personal rights*, have not the same meaning. The rights of person, as the term is generally used, does not include the right of property; personal rights include both the right of property and the rights of person.

§ 5. *Political rights* are those which belong to the people in their political capacity. The word *political*, in a general sense, relates to government. The whole body of the people united under one government, is called the political body, or body politic. The right of the people to choose and establish for themselves a form of government, or constitution, and the right to elect persons to make and execute the laws, are political rights. The right of voting at elections is therefore a political right.

§ 6. *Civil rights* are those which are secured to the citizens by the laws of the state. Some make no distinction between civil rights and political rights. In a proper sense—that in which the terms are here used—there is this difference: political rights are those secured by the political or fundamental law, called the constitution; civil rights are more properly those which are secured by the civil or municipal laws. The difference will more clearly appear from the definition elsewhere given of the political and civil laws. (Chap. III. § 5, 6.)

§ 7. *Religious rights* consist in the right of a man to make known and maintain his religious opinions, and to worship God in that way and manner which he believes in his conscience to be most acceptable to his Maker. This right is called also the *right of conscience*. But in exercising this right, a man may not abuse it by violating the rights of others, or disturbing the peace and order of society.

§ 8. Now, although human rights are thus divided into classes and differently defined, they are all natural rights. It is generally held in this country as a truth, that "all men are created equal;" that is, born with the same rights. And if men, as social and moral beings, are fitted by *nature* and designed for government and laws, we conclude

---

§ 5. Define *political* rights. What particular rights are political? § 6. What e *civil* rights? § 7. *Religious* rights? What else are they called? § 8. Under what general term are the different rights embraced?

that their political, civil, and religious rights, and all other rights to which they are entitled by the law of nature, are natural rights.

§ 9. *Liberty* is the being free to exercise and enjoy our rights, and is called natural, political, civil, or religious, according to the particular class of rights referred to. Thus the exercise of rights guarantied by the constitution or political law, is called political liberty. The free enjoyment of rights secured by the civil or municipal laws, is called civil liberty. And freedom of religious opinion and worship is called religious liberty.

§ 10. Hence liberty itself is a natural right. The words *right* and *liberty*, however, have not the same meaning. We may have a right to a thing when we have not the liberty of using it. John has a pencil which is justly his own; but James takes it from him by force. John's liberty to enjoy the use of his pencil is lost, but his right to it remains. James has no right to the use of the pencil, though he enjoys the use of it.

§ 11. This example serves also to explain further the use of the different terms applied to rights and liberty. John's right to his pencil, being guarantied to him by the laws of civil society, is a *civil* right. It is with equal propriety called a *natural* right, because, by the law of nature, he has a right to the use of his pencil.

CHAPTER III.

Laws, defined.

§ 1. Law has been briefly defined. (Chap. 1. § 6.) As in the case of rights and liberty, laws are distinguished by different names; as, the law of nature, or natural law; the moral law; the law of revelation, or revealed law; the political law; the civil or municipal law.

§ 2. The *law of nature* is of the highest possible authority,

---

§ 9. What is *liberty?* Political, civil, and religious liberty? § 10. What is the difference between *right* and *liberty?* § 11 What does this example further explain? Chapter III.—§ 1. Define *law.*

being established by the supreme Lawgiver himself. It is called the law of nature, because it is right in itself—right in the nature of things, and ought to be obeyed, though no positive command had ever been given to men. It is a perfect rule of right for all moral and social beings. It is that eternal rule of right to which God himself conforms.

§ 3. The law of nature, as a rule of human action, arises out of man's relation to his Maker and to his fellow men. As a creature, he must be subject to the laws of his Creator, on whom he is dependent. He is also in a measure dependent upon his fellow beings. All being created equal, each is bound by the principles of natural justice to render to others that assistance which is necessary to make them as happy as himself, or which they justly owe to him in return.

§ 4. The *moral law* is that which prescribes to men their duties to God and to each other. As a rule of human conduct therefore, it corresponds exactly to the law of nature. The moral law is briefly expressed in the decalogue or ten commandments, and is still more briefly summed up in the two great commandments, to love God with all our heart and to love our neighbor as ourselves. God being its author, it is called the *divine law;* and, being found in the Holy Scriptures, in which his will is revealed to mankind, it is called the *revealed law*, or *law of revelation.*

§ 5. *Political law*, as has been observed, is that system or form of fundamental rules, called the constitution, by which the people in their political capacity, or as a body politic, agree to be governed. The nature of this law will more clearly appear from a more particular definition of constitution, and from a description of the manner in which a constitution is made. (Chap. V.)

§ 6. The word *municipal* was used by the Romans to designate that which related to a *municipium*, which was a free town, or city. The rights of a citizen of such free city or town were called *municipal rights*, and its officers were called *municipal officers.* In this country, the word is not only used in this limited sense, but is extended to what

---

§ 1. By what names are laws distinguished ? § 2. Define the *law of nature* § 3. From what does the law of nature arise ? § 4. What is meant by the *moral law ?* § 5. Define *political law.*

pertains to a state. Hence the body of laws which prescribe the duties of the citizens of a state, are called the *municipal* or *civil law.* And the term is used to distinguish the laws made by the legislature, or law-making power of the state, from the constitution, or political law, adopted by the people in their political capacity.

§ 7. If, as has been said, the laws of the Creator form a perfect rule of conduct for all mankind, and ought in all cases to be obeyed, then all human law ought to agree with the divine law. If a human law is contrary to the divine law, or if it requires us to disobey the commands of God, it is not binding, and should not be obeyed. So the Scriptures teach. They speak approvingly of men who disobeyed human authority, and who gave as the reason, that it was their duty to obey God rather than men; and they furnish many examples of good men who submitted to severe punishment, even to death, rather than do what they knew to be contrary to the divine will.

§ 8. But although the divine will as revealed in the Scriptures, is a perfect rule or law for all mankind, and although human laws ought to conform to the divine law, yet it would be impossible to govern the people of a state by that law alone. The divine law is broad, and comprehends rules to teach men their whole duty; but it does not specify every particular act of duty. Much of it consists of general principles to which particular acts must be made to conform. It requires men to deal justly with each other; but men do not always agree as to what is right. Human laws, therefore, become necessary to declare what shall be considered just and right between man and man.

§ 9. It may be observed, further, that all the divine precepts could not be carried into effect in civil government. They are spiritual, and reach to the thoughts and intents of the heart. They require us to love our Creator supremely, and our neighbor as ourselves; in other words, to do to others as we would that they should do to us. But as the omniscient God only knows when men fail in these duties, no human authority could enforce such a law.

---

§ 6. Define *municipal.* How are municipal or civil laws distinguished from political? § 7. Ought the divine law in all cases to be obeyed? § 8. Why then are human laws necessary?

Human laws, therefore, have respect chiefly to the outward acts of men, and are designed to regulate their intercourse with each other.

§ 10. Although the laws of the state can not compel men to fulfill the great law of love, it is nevertheless morally binding upon all. A perfectly holy Creator could consistently require of his moral and accountable creatures nothing less than supreme love to himself, and equal love to one another. This, as has been remarked, is in accordance with the law of nature, which is right in the nature of things. (Chap. III. § 2, 3.)

§ 11. While the divine law accords perfectly with the principles of natural justice, the giving of it to mankind manifests the wisdom and benevolence of the supreme Lawgiver. Man is so formed, that it is for his highest happiness strictly to obey this law. The generous man, in relieving the wants of others, contributes to his own happiness. The boy who divides an apple with his fellow, is more happy than he would be if he retained the whole to himself. It is generally true, that, in performing acts of kindness and charity to others, we most effectually promote our own happiness, and feel the saying to be true, "It is more blessed to give than to receive."

CHAPTER IV.

Different Forms of Government. Monarchy; Aristocracy; Democracy; Republic.

§ 1. Governments have existed in a great variety of forms. The earliest governments of which we have any knowledge, are the patriarchal. *Patriarch*, from the Greek, *pater*, father, and *arkos*, chief, or head, means the father and ruler of a family. This kind of government prevailed

---

§ 9. Can you give any other reason? § 10. What measure of love is due to the Creator and our fellow men respectively? § 11. What are the characteristics of this law of love? Chap. IV. § 1. What were the earliest governments? Define *patriarch*.

in the early ages of the world, and in a state of society in which the people dwelt together in families or tribes, and were not yet formed into states or nations. The patriarchal government existed before the flood, and for a long period afterward. Abraham, Isaac, and Jacob, the fathers of the Hebrew race, as also the sons of Jacob, the heads of the twelve tribes, were called patriarchs.

§ 2. After their departure from Egypt, the government of the Hebrews was a *theocracy*. This word is from *theos*, God, and *kratos*, power, and signifies a government by the immediate direction of God. The laws by which they were governed were given to them on Mount Sinai by God himself, their leader and king. This theocratic form of government, with some changes, existed until the coming of the Messiah.

§ 3. But the forms of government which have most prevailed, are designated by the terms, monarchy, aristocracy, and democracy, or republic. These words severally indicate by what persons, and in what manner, the governing power of a state is exercised. This power is usually called the *sovereign*, or *supreme* power. Where kings rule, they are called sovereign ; and where the power is in the hands of the people, the people are sovereign. In the strict sense of the term, however, entire sovereignty, or supreme power, exists only where power is exercised by one man, or a single body of men, uncontrolled or unrestrained by laws or by any other power. But in a more general sense, it is that power in a state which is superior to all other powers within the same.

§ 4. A form of government in which the supreme power is in the hands of one person, is called a monarchy. The word *monarch* is from two Greek words, *monos*, sole or only, and *arkos*, a chief ; and is a general name for a single ruler, whether he is called king, emperor, or prince. A government in which all power resides in or proceeds from one person, is an *absolute* monarchy. If the power of the monarch is restrained by laws or by some other power, it is called a *limited* monarchy.

---

§ 2. What was the government of the Hebrews called? Define *theocracy* § 3. What is *sovereign* or *supreme power?* § 4. What is a *monarchy?* An absolute monarchy? A limited monarchy?

§ 5. A monarchy is called *hereditary* in which the throne passes from father to son, or from the monarch to his successor, by inheritance. On the death of a sovereign, the eldest son is usually heir to the crown; or if there is no son, it falls to the daughter, or some other relative. A monarchy is *elective*, where, on the death of the ruler, his successor is appointed by an election. A few such monarchies have existed.

§ 6. An absolute monarchy is sometimes called *despotism*. The word *despot* is from the Greek, and means *master*, or *lord*. It has nearly the same meaning as *tyrant*, which also is from the Greek, and signifies *king*. These words at first meant simply a single ruler. They are now applied, for the most part, to rulers who exercise authority over their subjects with severity. In an absolute despotism, the monarch has entire control over his subjects. They have no law but the will of the ruler, who has at command a large force of armed men to keep his people in subjection. The governments of Russia and Turkey are highly despotic.

§ 7. An *aristocracy* is a form of government in which the power is exercised by a privileged order of men, distinguished for their rank and wealth. The word *aristocracy* is from the Greek word *aristos*, best, and *kratos*, power, or *krateo*, to govern; and means a government of the best. It is also used for the nobility of a country under a monarchical government. *Nobles* are persons of rank above the common people, and bear some title of honor. The titles of the English nobility are those of duke, marquis, earl, viscount, and baron. These titles are hereditary, being derived from birth. In some cases they are conferred upon persons by the king.

§ 8. A *democracy* is a government of the people; the word democracy being from the Greek *demos*, the people, and *krateo*, to govern. In a government purely democratic, the great body of freemen meet in one assembly to make and execute the laws. There were some such governments in ancient Greece; but they necessarily comprised small territories, scarcely more than a single town. The freemen of a state could not all meet in a single assembly.

---

§ 5. A hereditary monarchy? An elective monarchy? § 6. A *despotism*? Define *despot* and *tyrant*. § 7. What is an *aristocracy*? Define the word. § 8. What is a *democracy*? Define the word.

§ 9. The government of this country, though a government of the people, is not one of the kind just described; it is a republic. A *republic* is a government in which the power to enact and execute the laws is exercised by representatives, who are persons elected by the people to act for them. Yet, as not only the election of representatives, but the adoption of the constitution or form of government itself is the act of the people; and as, therefore, all power comes from the people, the government is also democratic; and is properly called a *democratic republic*, or a *representative democracy*.

§ 10. A republic is sometimes also called a *commonwealth*. *Common* signifies general, and is applied to what belongs to or is used by the people generally. *Weal* means welfare or happiness. *Wealth* also was formerly sometimes used for weal. Hence *commonwealth* means strictly the *common good*, or the *common happiness*. In a general sense it signifies a state; but it is properly applied to a free state, one in which the people enjoy common rights and privileges. Hence every state in the union is a commonwealth or republic.

STATE GOVERNMENTS.

CHAPTER V.

The Nature and Objects of a Constitution, and the Manner in which it is made.

§ 1. Of all the different forms of government which have existed, a republican government, on the plan of that which has been established in this country, is believed to be best adapted to secure the liberties of a people, and to promote the general welfare. Under the reign of a wise and virtuous ruler, the rights of person and property may be

---

§ 9. What is a *republic?* Wherein do a democracy and a republic differ? § 10. What is a *commonwealth?* Chap. V.—§ 1. What is the object of civil government? § How is this object best secured?

fully enjoyed, and the people may be in a good degree prosperous. But the requisite virtue and wisdom have seldom been found in any one man or a few men. And experience has proved that the objects of civil government may be best secured by a written constitution founded upon the will or consent of the people.

§ 2. The word *constitute* is from the Latin, and signifies *to set*, to fix, to establish. *Constitution*, when used in a political sense, means the established form of government of a state. In a free government, like ours, it is properly called the *political law*, being established by the people as a body politic, or political body. (CHAP. III, § 5.) It is also called the *fundamental law*, because it is the *foundation* of all other laws of the state, which are enacted by the legislature for regulating intercourse between the citizens, and are called the *municipal* or *civil* law, and must conform to the fundamental, or political law.

§ 3. A constitution is in the nature of an agreement between a whole community or body politic and each of its members. This agreement or contract implies, that each one binds himself to the whole, and the whole bind themselves to each one, that all shall be governed by certain laws and regulations for the common good.

§ 4. The nature of a constitution will further appear from the manner in which it is made. It is evident that a people, in establishing a constitution, must have some right or authority to act in the business. Whence this right is derived, we will not now stop to inquire. There is, however, somewhere power to enact a law authorizing the people to make a constitution and prescribing the manner in which it is to be made.

§ 5. In forming a constitution, the people must act collectively. But their number is too large to meet in a single assembly. Therefore they choose a small number to act for them. One or more are chosen in each county, or smaller district, and are called delegates. A *delegate* is a person appointed by another with power to transact business as his representative. The assembly composed of the

---

§ 2. What is a constitution? By what name is it called? § 3. What is it's nature? § 4. By what authority is a constitution made? § 5. By whom is a constitution formed? § What is the assembly called?

delegates so elected, is called *convention;* a name given to most public meetings other than legislative assemblies. Delegate and representative are words of nearly the same meaning. The latter, however, usually designates a person chosen to assist in making the laws of the state.

§ 6. The rules agreed upon by the convention as a basis of government, are arranged in proper form. The several portions relating to the different subjects are called articles, and numbered; and the articles are divided into sections, which also are numbered. But what has been thus prepared by the convention is not yet a constitution. It is only a draft of one, and can not become a constitution without the consent of the people to be given at an election. If a majority of the persons voting at such election vote in favor of the proposed constitution, it is adopted, and becomes the constitution of the state.

§ 7. One of the most valuable rights of the people under a free government, is the right to have a constitution of their own choice. Indeed it is in this right that their freedom principally consists. It is by the constitution that their rights are secured. All the people join in establishing the constitution; but they do not all unite in making and executing the laws; in other words, they do not themselves administer the government; this is done by their representatives. But if these should enact unjust and oppressive laws, the people, having by their constitution reserved the right to displace them, may do so by electing others in their stead.

§ 8. In an absolute monarchy the people have no political rights—the right to establish a form of government for themselves, and the right to elect those who are to make and administer the laws. The monarch has entire control over his subjects. He can take their lives and property when he pleases. His will is their law; and he has at command a large force of armed men to keep his people in subjection.

§ 9. In a limited monarchy, the people have some political rights. Such a monarchy is Great Britain. The king

---

§ 6. How is a constitution adopted? § 7. How are the rights of the people secured by a constitution? § 8. What is the condition of the people in an absolute monarchy? § 9. Describe briefly the government of Great Britain. What political rights have the people?

or sovereign is in a measure restrained by laws ; and he can not make laws alone. The laws are framed and agreed to by parliament, and must be approved by the king or queen. Parliament consists of two bodies of men, the house of lords and the house of commons. The members of the latter are elected by the people, who, in such election, exercise a political right.

§ 10. But the political right of establishing a constitution or form of government, is not enjoyed by the people of that country. They have no written instrument, like ours, called constitution, adopted by the people. What is there called the constitution, is the aggregate or sum of laws, principles, and customs, which have been formed in the course of centuries. There is therefore no restraint upon the power of parliament; hence no law which may be enacted is contrary to the constitution ; and the people have not the same security against the enactment of unjust laws as the people of the United States.

CHAPTER VI.

Qualifications of Electors; or, by whom Political Power is exercised in the States of this Union.

§ 1. One of the first provisions usually inserted in a constitution of a free state, is that which declares who shall be allowed to take a part in the government ; that is, to whom the political power shall be intrusted. As this power is exercised by voting at elections, the constitution very properly prescribes the qualifications of electors, or, in other words, declares what shall be necessary to entitle a man to the right of voting, or the right of suffrage. When, therefore, we speak of the people politically, we mean those only who are qualified electors.

§ 2. To be competent to exercise the right of suffrage, a person must be a freeman, or, as we sometimes say, he

---

§ 10. Of what does the constitution of Great Britain consist ? Chap. VI. § 1. By what are the qualifications of voters prescribed ? § 2. Who are freemen ?

should be his own master. While under the control of a parent or guardian, he might be constrained to act contrary to his own judgment. All our state constitutions, therefore, give this right only to free male citizens of the age of twenty-one years and upwards; twenty-one years being the age at which young men become free to act for themselves.

§ 3. But even if this freedom were obtained at an earlier age, it would not be expedient to bestow this right upon persons so young. They have not the necessary knowledge and judgment to act with discretion. Some are competent at an earlier age; but a constitution can make no distinction between citizens. It has therefore, in accordance with the general opinion, fixed the time at the age of twenty-one, when men shall be deemed capable of exercising the rights and performing the duties of freemen.

§ 4. That a man may vote understandingly, he must have resided long enough in the state to have become acquainted with its government and laws, and to have learned the character and qualifications of the persons for whom he votes. State constitutions therefore require, that electors shall have resided in the state for a specified period of time, varying, however, in the different states from three months to two years. In most of the states, they must also have resided for some months in the county or district, and be residents of the town in which they offer to vote.

§ 5. But in giving the right of suffrage to all free male citizens twenty-one years of age, it is not given to every *man*, because all *men* of that age are not citizens. Persons born in foreign countries and residing here are *aliens*, and are not entitled to the political rights of persons born in this country. They are presumed to have too little knowledge of our government, and to feel too little interest in public affairs, on their first coming hither, to be duly qualified for the exercise of political power. Laws, however, have been enacted for naturalizing aliens after they shall have resided here long enough to become acquainted with and attached to our government. By naturalization they

---

§ 3. Why should none but freemen vote? § 4. Why is a term of residence required? § 5. Why are not aliens immediately allowed to vote?

become citizens, entitled to all the privileges of native or natural born citizens. (Chap. XXXIV, § 3, 4.)

§ 6. The constitutions of most of the states confer the rights of an elector on *white* male citizens only. Maine, New Hampshire, Vermont, Massachusetts, and Rhode Island, are the only states in which colored men have the same electoral rights as white citizens. In New York, men of color owning a freehold estate (an estate in lands) of the value of $250, are qualified voters.

§ 7. It is provided also in state constitutions, that electors committing infamous crimes are disfranchised. *Franchise* is a right or privilege enjoyed by the citizens of a state. Hence the right of voting at elections is called the *elective franchise;* and an elector, when deprived of this privilege, is *disfranchised.* An *infamous crime* is one which is punishable by imprisonment in a state prison. Men guilty of high crimes are deemed unfit to be intrusted with so important a duty as that of electing the persons who are to make and execute the laws of the state. It is provided, however, that if such persons are pardoned before the expiration of the term for which they were sentenced to be imprisoned, their forfeited rights are restored.

§ 8. By the earliest constitutions of many of the old states, electors were required to own property, or to have paid rents or taxes, to a certain amount. In the election of the higher officers, freeholders only were entitled to vote. A *freeholder* is an owner of real estate, (property in lands,) which he holds in his own right, and may transmit to his heirs. In the constitutions of the newer states, property has not been made a qualification of an elector ; and in the amended constitutions of the old states this restriction upon the elective franchise has been removed, until it has nearly ceased to exist in the United States. It is now enjoyed by all white male freemen, with few exceptions, in almost every state of the Union.

---

§ 6. In what state do colored men vote? § 7. How are electors sometimes disfranchised? What is an infamous crime? § 8. What is said of property as a qualification?

CHAPTER VII.

Elections.

§ 1. For the convenient exercise of political power, as well as for the purposes of government generally, the territory of a state is divided into districts of small extent. It has been remarked, that the people of a state, being too numerous to meet in one assembly to make laws and transact the public business, elect a small number to represent them. But to elect these representatives and other officers, and to adopt the constitution, or fundamental law of the state, are political duties, which must be performed by the people in person, and in a *collective* capacity. Hence the necessity of small territorial divisions, in which the people may assemble for political purposes.

§ 2. A state is divided into counties, and these are divided into towns or townships. The people of every county and every town have power to manage their local concerns. The corporate powers of counties and towns, and the election and the powers and duties of county and town officers, will be given in subsequent chapters.

§ 3. The electors of the state meet every year in their respective towns for the election of officers. Meetings for electing town officers are, in a majority of the states, held in the earlier part of the year. Most officers elected by the people, other than town officers, are chosen at the general state election, which, in most of the states, is held in October or November.

§ 4. Elections are conducted by persons designated by law, or chosen by the electors of the town for that purpose. It is their duty to preserve order, and to see that the business is properly done. They are usually called *judges of elections*, or *inspectors of elections*. Persons also, (usually two,) serve as clerks. Each clerk keeps a list of the names of the persons voting, which is called a *poll-list*. *Poll*, which

---

Chap. VII. § 1. For what purpose is the territory of a state divided? § 2. What are the territorial divisions of a state called? § 3. When are state elections generally held? § 4. By whom are elections conducted? Define *poll*.

is said to be a Saxon word, signifies *head*, and has come to mean person. Thus, so much a head means so much for every *person* By a further change it has been made to signify an election, because the persons there voting are numbered. Hence, "going to the polls" has obtained the same meaning as going to an election.

§ 5. When the inspectors are ready to receive votes, one of them makes it known by proclaiming with a loud voice, that "the polls are now open." The inspectors receive from each voter a ballot, which is a piece of paper containing the names of the persons voted for, and the title of the office to which each of them is to be elected. *Ballot*, from the French, means a little ball, and is used in voting. Ballots are of different colors; those of one color signifying an affirmative vote, or *yes;* those of another color a negative vote, or *no.* From this has come the application of the word ballot to the written or printed ticket now used in voting.

§ 6. If no objection is made to an elector's voting, the ballot is put into the box, and the clerks enter his name on the poll-list. If the inspectors suspect that a person offering to vote is not a qualified elector, they may question him upon his oath in respect to his qualifications as to age, the term of his residence in the state and county, and citizenship. Any bystander also may question his right to vote. This is called *challenging*. A person thus challenged is not allowed to vote until the challenge is withdrawn, or his qualifications are either proved by the testimony of other persons, or sworn to by himself.

§ 7. In a few states, the voters are registered. A list is kept of the names of all who have, upon examination, been ascertained to be qualified electors; and those only whose names are on the register are allowed to vote. Thus many interruptions to voting by the examination of voters at the polls, and much illegal voting, are prevented. Voters in some states are also required to take what is called the "elector's oath," in which they promise to be true and faithful to the state and its government, and to the constitution of the United States; and to give their votes as

§ 5. Describe the manner of voting. Define *ballot*. § 6. Who may challenge voters? § 7. How and why are voters registered? Are they registered in this state?

they shall judge will conduce to the best good of the same.

§ 8. After the polls are closed, the box is opened, and the ballots are counted. If the number of ballots agrees with the number of names on the poll-lists, it is presumed no mistake has been made, either in voting or in keeping the lists. If the election is one for the choosing of town officers, it is there determined who are elected, and their election is publicly declared.

§ 9. The election of county and state officers can not be determined by the town canvassers. A statement of the votes given in each town for the persons voted for, is sent to the county canvassers, who, from the returns of votes from all the towns, determine and declare the election of the officers chosen for the county. To determine the election of state officers, and of such others as are elected for districts comprising more than one county, a statement of the votes given for the several candidates, is sent by the several boards of county canvassers to the state canvassers, who, from the returns of votes from the several counties, determine the election of the state officers.

§ 10. In a few states, voting at elections is done *viva voce.* These words mean by word of mouth. In voting in this manner, the elector speaks the name of the person for whom he votes.

§ 11. In most of the states, persons are elected by a plurality of votes. An election by *plurality* is when the person elected has received a higher number of votes than any other, though such number be less than a majority of all the votes given. Suppose, for example, three candidates receive 1000 votes: One receives 450; another, 300; the third, 250 votes. The first, having the highest number, though not a majority, is elected. In the New England, or eastern states, a *majority*, that is, more than one-half of all the votes given, is necessary to the election of many of the higher officers. The least number of votes out of 1000, by which a person can be elected by this rule, is 501.

§ 12. Either of these modes is liable to objection. When a simple plurality effects an election, 1,000 votes may be

---

§ 8, 9. How is it determined what persons are elected? § 10. What is *viva voce* voting? § 11. What is an election by plurality? By majority? § 12 What objections are there to either of these modes?

so divided upon three candidates as to elect one by 334 votes; or of four candidates, one may be elected by 251 votes, and against the wishes of nearly three-fourths of the electors. An objection to the other mode is, that if no person receives a majority of all the votes, another election must be held. Numerous trials have, in some instances, been necessary to effect a choice; and the people of a district have remained for a time without a representative in the state or national legislature.

CHAPTER VIII.

Division of the Powers of Government.

§ 1. Having shown the nature of a constitution and the manner in which it is made and adopted, it will next be shown how the powers of government under a state constitution are divided. As the excellence of a form of government consists much in a proper separation and distribution of power, this subject deserves special attention.

§ 2. We notice first the separation of the political and civil powers. The words *political* and *civil* are often used as having the same meaning. Thus, speaking of the system of government and laws of a country, we use the general term, "political institutions," or "civil institutions;" either of which is deemed correct. But these words have also a particular signification, as has already been shown in the distinction made in preceding chapters between political rights and civil rights, and between the political law and the municipal or civil laws. (Chap. II, and III.) Hence it appears, that what we mean by political power is the power exercised by the people in their political capacity, in adopting their constitution and electing the officers of the government; and that, by the civil power is meant the power exercised by these officers in administering the government.

Chap. VIII. § 1, 2. What division of power is first mentioned? Give the distinction between the political and civil powers.

§ 3. In an absolute government, no such distinction exists ; all power is centered in the supreme ruler. There is no political law binding on him. Being himself restrained by no positive laws or regulations that have been adopted by the people, or that may be altered by them, the people have no political rights. In a mixed government, or limited monarchy, political power is exercised to some extent. Although there is no written constitution adopted by the people, as in a republic, the members of one branch of the law-making power are elected by the people. In such election they are said to exercise political power.

§ 4. We notice next the division of the civil power. This power, in well constructed governments, is divided into three departments, the legislative, the executive, and the judicial. The legislative department is that by which the laws of the state are made. The legislature is composed of two bodies, the members of which are elected by the people. In limited monarchies where one branch of the legislature is elective, the other is an aristocratic body, composed of men of wealth and dignity, as the British house of lords.

§ 5. The executive department is intrusted with the power of executing, or carrying into effect, the laws of the state. There is in this department a governor, assisted by a number of other officers, some of whom are elected by the people ; others are appointed in such manner as the constitution or laws prescribe. The powers and duties of the governor of a state will be more particularly described in another place.

§ 6. The judicial department is that by which justice is administered to the citizens. It embraces the several courts of the state. All judges and justices of the peace are judicial officers ; and they have power, and it is their business to judge of and apply the law in cases brought before them for trial. A more particular description of the powers and duties of judicial officers, and the manner of

---

§ 3. What is said of political power in absolute and mixed governments ? § 4. How is the civil power divided ? What is the business of the legislature ? How is a legislature constituted ? § 5. What is the executive department ? In whom is the power vested ? § 6. What is the business of the judicial department ? Of what does it consist ?

conducting trials in courts of justice, will be given elsewhere. (Chap. XVII—XX.)

§ 7. Experience has shown the propriety of dividing the civil power into these three departments, and of confining the officers of each department to the powers and duties belonging to the same. Those who make the laws should not exercise the power of executing them ; nor should they who either make or execute the laws sit in judgment over those who are brought before them for trial. A government in which the different powers of making, executing, and applying the laws should be united in a single body of men, however numerous, would be little better than an absolute despotism.

§ 8. Again, the legislative department of the civil power is divided. Under all our state constitutions, the legislature consists of two branches, both of which must agree to a proposed measure before it becomes a law ; and in many of the states, it must also be approved by the governor. This is making the chief executive officer a third branch of the law-making power ; and is not in accordance with the principle of keeping the several departments of the civil power separate and distinct from each other. The reason for this departure from the general principle mentioned, will be stated in another chapter. (Chap. XI. § 16.)

CHAPTER IX.

State Legislatures—how constituted.

§ 1. The legislature of every state in the union is composed of two houses—a senate and a house of representatives. The latter, or, as it is sometimes called, the lower house, in the states of New York, Wisconsin, and California, is called the assembly ; in Maryland and Virginia, the house of delegates ; in North Carolina, the house of commons ; and in New Jersey, the general assembly. In

---

§ 7. Can you give any reasons for this division of the civil power ? § 8. How is the legislative power divided ? CHAP. IX. § 1. Of what branches is a legislature composed ?

most of the states, the two houses together are called *general assembly.*

§ 2. The senate, as well as the other house, is a representative body ; its members being elected by the people to represent them. Why, then, is only one of the two branches called the house of representatives? Perhaps for this reason : Under the governments of the colonies, while yet subject to Great Britian, there was but one representa tive assembly. The other branch of the legislature was called a *council*, consisting of a small number of men who were appointed by the king. After the colonies became free and independent states, a senate was substituted for the old council, and although it is an elective body, the other house, being much more numerous, is called, by way of distinction, the *house of representatives.*

§ 3. Senators are chosen annually in the six New England states, namely, Maine, New Hampshire, Vermont, Massachusetts, Rhode Island, and Connecticut. In the other states they are elected for terms of two, three, or four years. In most of the states in which senators are elected for longer terms than one year, they are not all elected at the same time. They are divided into classes ; and those of one class go out of office one year, and those of another class another year ; so that only a part of the senators are elected every year, or every two, or three, or four years.

§ 4. The senate, as distinguished from the house of representatives, is sometimes called the upper house. It was designed to be a more select body, composed of men chosen with reference to their superior ability, or their greater experience in public affairs.

§ 5. Senators are differently apportioned in different states. In some states they are apportioned among the several counties, so that the number to be elected in each county shall be in proportion to the number of its inhabitants. In others they are elected by districts, equal in number to the number of senators to be chosen in the state, and a senator is elected in each district. The districts are

---

§ 2. Why is only one called house of representatives? § 3. For how long terms are senators chosen? How long in this state? § 4. Why is the senate called upper house? § 5 How are senators apportioned? How in this state?

to contain, as nearly as may be, an equal number of inhabitants; and sometimes they comprise several counties.

§ 6. Representatives are apportioned among the counties in proportion to the population in each. In some states they are elected in districts of equal population, counties being sometimes divided in the formation of districts. In the New England states, representatives are apportioned among the towns. In about one-half of the states, they are elected annually; in the others, (including most of the southern and western states,) they are elected every two years.

§ 7. The different modes of apportioning members of the legislature have in view the same object—equal representation; that is, giving a member to the same number of inhabitants in one county or district as to an equal number in another. But in some counties the population increases more rapidly than in others. The representation then becomes unequal, being no longer in proportion to population.

§ 8. In order to keep the representation throughout the state as nearly equal as possible; in other words, to secure to the people of every county or district their just proportion of the representatives, the constitution requires that, at stated times, the people of the state shall be numbered, and a new apportionment of senators and representatives be made among the several counties according to the number of inhabitants in each county; or if the state is one in which members of the legislature are chosen in districts, a new division of the state is made into districts.

§ 9. But the periods of time between the enumerations of the people, are not the same in all the states. In some states the enumerations are made every ten years; in others, shorter periods have been fixed, from eight down to four years. This enumeration or numbering of the people is called taking the census. *Census* is from the Latin, and was used by the ancient Romans to signify a declaration or statement made before the censors by the citizens, con-

---

§ 6. How are representatives apportioned? For what terms elected? How apportioned, and for what term elected in this state? § 7. What is the general object of apportionment? § 8. How in an equal representation provided for? § 9. How often are enumerations made? How often in this state? Define *census*?

taining an enumeration or register of themselves, their wives, children, servants, and their property and its valuation. In the United States, although the census sometimes includes a similar register, the word usually means simply an enumeration of the people.

§ 10. The constitution also prescribes the qualifications of senators and representatives. If, as qualifications for an elector, full age, citizenship, and a considerable term of residence in the state and county, are properly required, as we have seen, (Chap. VI. § 2–5,) they must be at least equally necessary for those who make the laws. In no state, therefore, are any but qualified electors eligible to the office of senator or representative. In some states, greater age and longer residence are required ; and in some, the age and term of residence have been still further increased in the case of senators. The property qualification formerly necessary for members of the legislature, as well as for voters, has been almost entirely abolished. (Chap. VI. § 8.)

§ 11. If a member of the legislature dies, or resigns his office before the expiration of the term for which he was chosen, the vacancy is filled by the election of another person at the next general election, or at a special election called for that purpose, or in such other manner as the constitution may provide. But a person chosen to fill a vacancy, holds the office only for the remainder of the term of him whose place he was chosen to supply.

CHAPTER X.

Meetings and Organization of the Legislature.

§ 1. The legislature meets as often as the constitution requires, to enact such laws as may be necessary to promote the public welfare, and to perform such other duties

---

§ 10. What are the qualifications of senators and representatives in this state? § 11. How are vacancies filled in the senate? Chap. X. § 1. How often do legislatures meet? How often in this state? What is meant by *session?*

as are assigned to it by the constitution and the laws. In about half of the states, sessions are held annually ; in the others biennially, or once in two years. A legislative session includes the daily meetings of a legislature from the time of its first assembling, to the day of final adjournment. Thus we say the session commenced in January and ended in March. The word *session* has reference also to a single sitting, from the hour at which the members assemble on any day, to the time of adjournment on the same day. Thus we say, the legislature holds a daily session of four hours ; or, it holds two sessions a day, as the case may be.

§ 2. Meetings of the legislature are held at a place permanently fixed by the constitution ; at which place the principal state officers keep their offices. Hence it is called the *seat of government*, or perhaps more frequently, the *capital* of the state. *Capital* is from the Latin *caput*, the head, and has come to mean chief, or the highest. A capital city is therefore the chief city of a state or kingdom. But the word *capital*, applied to a city, now generally indicates the seat of government.

§ 3. When the two houses have assembled in their respective chambers, some person designated for that purpose administers to the members of each house the oath of office, in which they solemnly swear (or affirm,) that they will support the constitution of the United States, and the constitution of the state, and faithfully discharge the duties of their office.

§ 4. Each house then proceeds to *organize* for business, by appointing proper officers, and determining the right of members to seats in the house. In organizing a legislative body, the first thing done is the election of a presiding officer, or chairman, who is usually called *speaker*. The lieutenant-governor, in states in which there is one, presides in the senate, and is called *president of the senate*. In the absence of the presiding officer, a temporary speaker or president is chosen, who is called speaker or president *pro tempore*, commonly abbreviated, *pro tem.*, which is a Latin phrase, meaning *for the time*.

§ 5. The duty of the person presiding is to keep order,

§ 2. Where do legislatures meet? What is the place called? § 3. To what are members bound by their oath of office? § 4. How are the houses organized? What are the presiding officers called? § 5. What are their general duties?

and to see that the business of the house is conducted according to certain established rules. When a vote is to be taken, he puts the question, which is done by requesting all who are in favor of a proposed measure, to say *aye*, and those opposed to say *no*. And, when a vote has been taken, he declares the question to be carried or lost. This part of a speaker's business is similar to that of the chairman of an ordinary public meeting.

§ 6. The other officers chosen by each house are, a *clerk* to keep a record or journal of its proceedings; to take charge of papers, and to read such as are to be read to the house; and to do such other things as may be required of him; a *sergeant-at-arms*, to arrest members and other persons guilty of disorderly conduct, to compel the attendance of absent members, and to do other business of a like nature: also one or more *door-keepers*. The officers mentioned in this section are not chosen from the members of the house.

§ 7. The constitution does not prescribe to either house the order of business, or the particular manner in which it shall be done; but authorizes each house to determine for itself the rules of its proceedings. But there are sundry things which it expressly enjoins. It determines what portion of the members shall constitute a quorum to do business. *Quorum* is the Latin of the English words, *of whom*, and has strangely come to signify the *number* or *portion* of any body of men who have power to act for the whole. Thus with reference to a legislative body consisting of a certain number of members, instead of saying, A majority *quorum* shall have power to act; or, A majority *of whom* shall have power to act, our constitutions generally say, A majority shall constitute a quorum to do business. In some states, more than a bare majority is required for a quorum.

§ 8. Constitutions generally require also that the proceedings of legislative bodies shall be open to public inspection. The doors may be closed against spectators only when the public good shall require secrecy. And that the people may be fully informed of what is done, each house is required to keep and publish a journal of its proceedings.

---

§ 6. What other officers are chosen? and what are their duties? § 7. Define *quorum*. What number is a quorum in this state? § 8 Are the proceedings ever secret?

§ 9. Provision is also made, either by the constitution or by law, against injury or interruption to the business of the legislature. Members may not, by any prosecution at law, except for crimes and misdemeanors, be hindered during their attendance at the sessions of the legislature, nor in going to or returning from the same. Each house may compel the attendance of absent members. It may for good cause expel a member, and punish, not only its members and officers, but other persons, for disorderly conduct, or for obstructing its proceedings.

CHAPTER XI.

Manner of Enacting Laws.

§ 1. When the two houses are duly organized and ready for business, the governor sends to both houses a written communication called *message*, in which, as the constitution requires, he gives to the legislature information of the condition of the affairs of the state, and recommends such measures as he judges necessary and expedient. The message is read to each house by its clerk.

§ 2. But the measures to which the governor calls the attention of the legislature, are but a small portion of those which are considered and acted upon. Many are introduced by individual members. Others are brought into notice by the petitions of the people in different parts of the state. *Petition* generally signifies a request or prayer. As here used, it means a written request to the legislature for some favor—generally for a law granting some benefit or relief to the petitioners. Petitions are sent to members, usually to those who represent the counties or districts in which the petitioners live, and are by these members presented to the house.

---

§ 9. What provision is made to prevent interruption? Chap. XI. § 1. When is the governor's message communicated? What does it contain? § 2. In what other way are measures introduced?

§ 3. Now it is evident, that a proper consideration of the numerous subjects pressed upon the attention of the legislature—some of them of very great importance—must require much labor. If the necessary investigation of so many subjects should occupy the time of the whole house, there would not be time enough to act upon one-half of them. Therefore, in order to dispatch business, the labor of the house must be divided, that the investigation of all the different subjects may be going on at the same time.

§ 4. Hence arises the practice which prevails in all legislative bodies, of the appointment of committees. As soon as may be, after a house is organized, committees are appointed on all subjects usually acted on in the legislature. A legislative committee is generally composed of three, five, or seven members, who examine the subjects referred to them, and report the result of their examination to the house. Committees are appointed by the presiding officer of each house. Occasionally, though very rarely, they are elected by the house itself.

§ 5. Some or all of the following committees are appointed in every legislature: a committee on finance, or the funds, income, and other money matters of the state, sometimes called the committee of ways and means; a committee on agriculture; a committee on manufactures; committees on the incorporation of cities and villages; on banks and insurance companies; on railroads; on canals; on education; on elections; on public printing, besides many others. So numerous are these subjects, that in constituting the committees, every member may be put on some committee.

§ 6. All matters relating to these subjects of a general nature, which arise during the session, are referred to their appropriate committees. Thus, a question or proposition relating to banks, is referred to the committee on banks; matters relating to rail-roads, are referred to the committee on rail-roads; those relating to schools, are referred to the committee on education, &c. As these committees continue during the session, they are called *standing* committees. When a question arises having no relation to any

§ 3, 4. What is done to expedite business? How are committees appointed? and what do they do? § 5. Name some of the committees. § 6. What are *standing* committees? *Select* committees?

subject on which there is a standing committee, it is usually referred to a *special* or *select* committee appointed to consider this particular matter.

§ 7. Committees meet in private rooms, during hours when the house is not in session ; and any person wishing to be heard in favor of or against a proposed measure, may appear before the committee having it in charge. Having duly considered the subject, the committee reports to the house the information it has obtained, with the opinion whether the measure ought or ought not to become a law. Measures reported against by committees, seldom receive any further notice from the house.

§ 8. From what has been said, the utility of committees is readily seen. Although no proposed measure can become a law unless acted on and approved by the two houses, its necessity may be inquired into, and the information necessary to enable the house to act understandingly upon the question, may be obtained, as well by a few members as by the whole house. By the daily examination of so many subjects in committee, a large amount of business is soon prepared for the house to act upon, and much of its time is saved.

§ 9. If a committee reports favorably upon a subject, it usually brings in a bill with its report. A *bill* is the form or draft of a law. Not all bills, however, are reported by committees. Any member of the house desiring the passage of a law, may give notice that he will, on some future day, ask leave of the house to introduce a bill for that purpose ; and if, at the time specified, the house shall grant leave, he may introduce the bill. But at least one day's previous notice must be given of his intention to ask leave, before it can be granted.

§ 10. The different steps in the progress of a bill, or the different forms of action through which it has to pass, are numerous. A minute description of them in a work designed chiefly for youth, will scarcely be expected. A thorough knowledge of the proceedings of legislative assemblies, can be practically beneficial, in after life, to but few of those who shall study this elementary treatise.

---

§ 7. How do committees discharge their duties? § 8. Wherein does the utility of committees appear? § 9. What is a bill? § 10. By whom, and how, are bills introduced?

Those who shall hereafter have occasion for this knowledge, will find works adapted to a more mature age, in which the subject is fully treated.

§ 11. A bill, before it is passed, must be read three times ; but it may not be read twice on any one day without unanimous consent, that is, the consent of the whole house ; or, as is believed to be the rule in some bodies, the consent of three-fourths, or two-thirds of the house. In some legislatures, the rule allows the first and second readings to be on the same day. A bill is not to be amended until it shall have been twice read. Nor is it usual for it to be opposed until then ; but it may be opposed and rejected at the first reading.

§ 12. After a bill has been twice read, and fully debated and amended, it is proposed to be read on a future day the third time. If the question on ordering the bill to a third reading is not carried, the bill is lost, unless revived by a vote of the house to reconsider. But if the question to read the third time is carried, the bill is accordingly read on a future day, and the question taken on its final passage.

§ 13. When the final vote is to be taken, the speaker puts the question : "Shall the bill pass ?" If a majority of the members present vote in the affirmative, (the speaker also voting,) the bill is passed ; if a majority vote in the negative, the bill is lost. Also if the ayes and noes are equal, it is lost, because there is not a majority in its favor. In a senate where a lieutenant-governor presides, not being properly a member, he does not vote, except when the ayes and noes are equal ; in which case there is said to be a *tie ;* and he determines the question by his vote, which is called the *casting* vote. In some states, on the final passage of a bill, a bare majority of the members present is not sufficient to pass it, in case any members are absent. The constitutions of those states require the votes of a majority of *all the members elected* to each house.

§ 14. When a bill has passed one house it is sent to the other, where it must pass through the same forms of action ; that is, it must be referred to a committee ; reported by the committee to the house ; and be read three times before

§ 11. How often must a bill be read ? When is it amended ? § 12. After the second reading and amendment, what follows ? § 13. Describe the proceedings on the final passage of a bill. § 14. How is it acted on in the other house ?

a vote is taken on its passage. This vote having been taken, the bill is returned to the house from which it was received. If it has been amended, the amendments must be agreed to by the first house, or the second must recede from their amendments, or the amendments must be so modified as to secure the approval of both houses, before the bill can become a law.

§ 15. Some young reader may inquire why a bill should take so long and slow a course through two different houses; and why one body of representatives is not sufficient. The object is to secure the enactment of good laws. Notwithstanding bills go through the hands of a committee and three different readings in the house; yet through undue haste, wrong information, or from other causes, a house may, and often does, commit serious errors. Legislatures are therefore divided into two branches; and a bill having passed one house is sent to the other where the mistakes of the former may be corrected, or the bill wholly rejected.

§ 16. But in many of the states, a bill, when passed by both houses, is not yet a law. As the two houses may concur in adopting an unwise measure, an additional safeguard is provided against the enactment of bad laws, by requiring all bills to be sent to the governor for examination and approval. If he approves a bill, he signs it, and it is a law; if he does not sign it, it is not a law. In refusing to sign a bill, he is said to *negative*, or *veto* the bill. *Veto*, Latin, means, *I forbid.*

§ 17. But no governor has full power to prevent the passage of a law. If he does not approve a bill, he must return it to the house in which it originated, stating his objections to it; and if it shall be again passed by both houses, it will be a law without the governor's assent But in such cases greater majorities are generally required to pass a law. In some states, a majority of two-thirds of the members present is necessary; in others, a majority of *all the members elected.* In a few states, only the same major-

---

§ 15. Why is a legislature divided into two branches? § 16. Why are bills submitted to the governor for his approval? Define *veto*. § 17. What if a governor refuses to sign a bill? Are bills presented to the governor in this state? If so, and he disapproves them, by what majorities must they be again passed? Within how many days is he to return bills in this state?

ities are required to pass a bill against the veto as in the first instance. Or if the governor does not return a bill within a certain number of days, it becomes a law without his signature, or without being considered a second time. In some states, bills are not sent to the governor, but are laws when passed by both houses and signed by their presiding officers.

CHAPTER XII.

Executive Department. Governor and Lieutenant-Governor.

§ 1. The chief executive power of a state is, by the constitution, vested in a governor. The governor is chosen by the people at the general election; in South Carolina by the legislature. The term of office is not the same in all the states. In the six New England states, the governors are chosen annually; in the other states, for the different terms of two, three, and four years.

§ 2. The qualifications for the office of governor are also different in the different states. To be eligible to the office of governor, a person must have been for a certain number of years a citizen of the United States, and for a term of years preceding his election a resident of the state. He must also be above a certain age, which, in a majority of the states, is at least thirty years; and in some states he must be a freeholder.

§ 3. The powers and duties of a governor are numerous. He communicates by message to the legislature, at every session, information of the condition of the state of its affairs generally, and recommends such measures as he judges necessary and expedient. He is to take care that the laws be faithfully executed, and to transact all necessary business with the officers of the government. He may convene the legislature on extraordinary occasions:

Chap. XII. § 1. For what terms are governors chosen? For what term in this state? § 2. What are the qualifications for governor in this state? § 3. What are his general powers and duties?

that is, if, at a time when the legislature is not in session, a matter should arise requiring immediate attention, the governor may call a special meeting of the legislature, or as it is usually termed, an extra session.

§ 4. A governor has power to grant reprieves and pardons, except in cases of impeachment, and, in some states, of treason. To *reprieve* is to postpone or delay for a time the execution of the sentence of death upon a criminal. To *pardon* is to annul the sentence by forgiving the offense and releasing the offender. A governor may also *commute* a sentence; which is to exchange one penalty or punishment for another of less severity; as, when a person sentenced to suffer death, is ordered to be imprisoned.

§ 5. The governor has power also, in some of the states, with the consent of the senate, to appoint the higher officers of the militia of the state, and the higher civil officers in the executive and judicial departments. In a few of the states, there are executive councils whose advice and consent are required in such cases. In making such appointments, the governor nominates, that is, he *names* to the senate, in writing, the persons to be appointed. If a majority of the senators consent, the persons so nominated are appointed. Many other duties are by the constitution devolved upon the governor.

§ 6. A lieutenant-governor has few duties to perform. He presides in the senate, in which he has only a casting vote. In the state of New York, he serves in some of the boards of executive officers. In nearly one-half of the states the office of lieutenant-governor does not exist. The chief object of electing this officer seems to be to provide a suitable person to fill the vacancy in the office of governor in case the latter should die, resign, be removed, or otherwise become incompetent.

§ 7. When the lieutenant-governor acts as governor, the senate chooses from its own number a president. If the offices of both the governor and lieutenant-governor should become vacant, the president of the senate must act as

---

§ 4. In what cases has he power to grant reprieves and pardons? Define these words. What is *commute?* § 5. Are any officers in this state appointed by the governor? Is there a council? § 6. What are the duties of a lieutenant-governor? Is there one in this state? § 7. When he acts as governor, who takes the chair of the senate?

governor. If there should be neither a governor, a lieutenant-governor, nor a president or speaker of the senate, then the speaker of the house of representatives would become the acting governor. This is believed to be the rule for supplying vacancies in most if not all of the states.

CHAPTER XIII.

Assistant Executive State Officers.

§ 1. Among the executive officers who assist in the administration of the government, there are in every state, some or all of the following: a secretary of state, a controller or auditor, a treasurer, an attorney-general, a surveyor-general. The mode of their appointment and the terms of their respective offices, are prescribed by the constitution or by law. In some states they are appointed by the governor and senate; in others by the legislature; and in others they are elected by the people. They keep their offices at the seat of government of the state.

§ 2. The *secretary of state* keeps a record of the official acts and proceedings of the legislature and of the executive departments, and has the care of the books, records, deeds of the state, parchments, the laws enacted by the legislature, and all other papers and documents required by law to be kept in his office. He causes the laws passed by the legislature to be published in one or more newspapers, as directed by law; and also to be printed and bound in a volume, and distributed among the state officers for their use, and among the county and town clerks, to be kept in their offices for the use of the people who wish to examine the laws. Also one or more copies are exchanged with each of the other states for copies of their laws to be kept in the state library. Various other duties are performed by the secretary.

Chap. XIII. § 1. What assistant executive officers are there in this state? Are they appointed or elected? § 2. What are the duties of the secretary of state?

§ 3. The *state auditor*, in some states called *controller*, manages the financial concerns of the state ; that is, the business relating to the money, debts, land and other property of the state. He examines and adjusts accounts and claims against the state, and superintends the collection of moneys due the state. When money is to be paid out of the treasury, he draws a warrant (a written order,) on the treasurer for the money, and keeps a regular account with the treasurer of all moneys received into and paid out of the treasury. And he reports to the legislature or other proper officers, a statement of the funds of the state, and of its income and expenditures during each year.

§ 4. The *treasurer* has charge of all the public moneys that are paid into the treasury, and pays out the same as directed by law ; and he keeps an accurate account of such moneys, specifying the names of the persons from whom they are received, to whom paid, and for what purposes. He also exhibits annually a statement of moneys received and paid out by him during the year, and of the balance in the treasury.

§ 5. Auditors, treasurers, and other officers intrusted with the care and management of money or other property, are generally required, before they enter on the duties of their offices, to give bonds, in sums of certain amount specified in the law, with sufficient sureties, for the faithful performance of their duties. The sureties are persons who bind themselves to pay the state all damages arising from neglect of duty on the part of the officers, not exceeding the sum mentioned in the bond.

§ 6. The *attorney-general* is a person learned in the law, appointed to act for the state in law-suits in which the state is a party. He prosecutes persons indebted to the state, and causes to be brought to trial persons charged with certain crimes. He also gives his opinion on questions of law submitted to him by the governor, the legislature, and the executive officers. In some states there is no attorney-general. In such states prosecutions in behalf of the state are conducted by the state's attorney for each county.

---

§ 3. Of an auditor or controller ? § 4. Of a treasurer ? § 5. Of what officers are sureties required ? § 6. What are the duties of an attorney-general ? Is there one in this state ?

§ 7. The *surveyor-general* superintends the surveying of the lands belonging to the state. He keeps in his office maps of the state, describing the bounds of the counties and townships; and when disputes arise respecting the boundaries, he causes surveys to be made, if necessary, to ascertain such bounds. He performs certain other duties of a similar nature. In many of the states there is no surveyor-general, the duties of that office being done by a county surveyor in each county.

§ 8. There is also, in many of the states, a *superintendent of schools,* called in some states, *superintendent of public instruction,* whose principal duties are described in a subsequent chapter. (Chap. XXII, § 10.)

§ 9. There is also a printer to the state, or *state printer,* whose business it is to print the journal, bills, reports, and other papers and documents of the two houses of the legislature, and all the laws passed at each session. State printers are either chosen by the legislature, or employed by persons authorized to make contracts for the public printing; or the printing is let to the lowest bidder.

§ 10. There are other officers employed by the state, among whom are the following: a *state librarian,* who has charge of the state library, consisting of books containing matter of a public nature, such as the laws of all the states, and of the United States, with a large collection of miscellaneous books; persons having the care of the public buildings and other property of the state; superintendents of state prisons, lunatic asylums, and other state institutions, whose duties are indicated by their titles, and need no particular description.

---

§ 7. The duties of surveyor-general? Is there one in this state? § 8. A superintendent of schools? § 9. What is the business of state printer? § 10. What other state officers are there?

CHAPTER XIV.

Counties and County Officers. Powers and Duties of County Officers.

§ 1. Some of the purposes for which a state is divided into small districts have been mentioned. (Chap. VII, § 1.) There are other reasons, equally important, for these territorial divisions. Laws for the whole state are made by the legislature ; but certain regulations may be necessary for the people in some parts of the state which are not needed in others, and which the people of these places can better make for themselves. It is the business of the governor and his assistant executive state officers to execute or carry into effect the laws of the state ; but they could not see this done in every place, or in every minute portion of the state. Again, for the convenience of those who may be obliged to go to law to obtain redress for injuries, courts of justice must be established near the residence of every citizen.

§ 2. But in order to carry out these objects, a state must be divided into small districts with fixed boundaries, that it may be known what persons come under certain regulations, and over whom these local officers are to exercise authority. The smallest territorial divisions of a state are called *townships*, or *towns*, which contain generally from twenty-five to one hundred square miles, and which, if in a square form, would be from five to ten miles square. But for certain purposes larger districts than townships have been found necessary. These are formed by the union of several townships, and are called *counties*. These divisions are the same as those of England, the country from which the colonies (now states) were chiefly settled.

§ 3. Counties in England were formerly districts governed by *counts* or earls ; from which comes the name of *county*. A county was also called *shire ;* and an officer was appointed by the count or earl to perform certain acts in the principal town in the county, which was called

---

Chap. XIV. § 1. For what reasons is a state divided into counties and townships ? § 2. How large are townships ? § 3. From what comes the name of *county ?* Of *shire*, and *sheriff ?*

shire town, and the officer was called *shire-reeve*, or *sheriff*, whose powers and duties were similar to those of the sheriff of a county in this country. The shire town is that in which the court-house and other county buildings are situate, and where the principal officers of the county transact their business. In a few counties there are two towns in which the courts are held alternately. Hence each division is called a *half-shire.*

§ 4. Counties and towns are bodies politic, or bodies corporate. *Corporate* is from the Latin, *corpus*, which means *body.* A *corporation*, or body politic, is an association of persons authorized by law to transact business under a common name, and as a single person. The laws of the state give such authority to the inhabitants of counties and towns. The people of a town or county have power, to some extent, to manage their own internal affairs, and to make rules and regulations for their government; and they may buy, hold, and sell property, and sue and be sued, as an individual. Similar powers are given to rail-road, banking, insurance, and other incorporated companies. But there is in some respects a difference between these corporations and those which are created for purposes of government, as states, counties, towns, cities, and villages, which will be noticed in another place. (Chap. XVI.)

§ 5. As a county possesses various corporate powers, there must be among its officers some in whose name these powers are to be exercised. In some states there is a board of *county commissioners*, (usually three,) who exercise corporate powers. In a few, these powers are exercised by and in the name of the *board of supervisors*, which is composed of the supervisors of the several towns in the county, of whom there is one supervisor in each town. These boards, or such officers in other states as exercise these powers, have generally the power also to examine and settle the accounts against the county, and to make orders and contracts in relation to the building or repairing of the court-house, jail, and other county buildings; and to perform such other acts as the laws require.

§ 6. There is in each county a *treasurer* to receive and

---

§ 4. Define *corporation.* What powers have town and county corporations? § 5. In what officers are these powers vested? In whom in this state? § 6. What are the duties of a county treasurer?

pay out the moneys required to be collected and paid out in the county. There is also, in some states, a county *auditor* to examine and adjust the accounts and debts of the county, and to perform certain other duties. The business of county treasurers and auditors in their respective counties, is of the same nature as that of state auditors and treasurers. In states in which there is no county auditor, the duties of auditor are performed by the treasurer, and some other county officer or officers.

§ 7. There is also in each county a *register* or *recorder*, who records in books provided for that purpose, all deeds, mortgages, and other instruments of writing required by law to be recorded. In New York, and perhaps in some other states, the business of a register or recorder is done by a county clerk, who is also clerk of the several courts held in the county, and of certain boards of county officers. In some states, deeds, mortgages, and other written instruments, are recorded by the town clerks of the several towns.

§ 8. Another county officer is a *sheriff*, whose duty it is to attend all the courts held in the county; to execute all warrants, writs, and other process directed to him by the courts; to apprehend persons charged with crime; and to take charge of the jail and of the prisoners therein. It is his duty, also, to preserve the public peace; and he may cause all persons who break the public peace within his knowledge or view, to give bonds, with sureties, for keeping the peace, and for appearing at the next court to be held in the county, and to commit them to jail if they refuse to give such bonds. A sheriff is assisted by deputies.

§ 9. There are in each county one or more *coroners*, whose principal duty is, to inquire into the cause of the death of persons who have died by violence, or suddenly, and by means unknown. Notice of the death of a person having so died is given to a coroner, who goes to the place of such dead person. A jury is summoned to attend the examination; witnesses are examined; and the jury give their opinion in writing as to the cause and manner of the death. Such inquiry is called a *coroner's inquest*. In one or two

---

§ 7. Of a register or recorder? Where are deeds, &c., recorded in this state? § 8. What are a sheriff's duties? § 9. What is the business of a coroner?

states, the office of coroner, it is believed, does not exist; in which case the inquest is held by a justice of the peace, or some other officer.

§ 10. An attorney, elected or appointed for that purpose, attends all courts in which persons are tried in the county for crimes committed therein, and conducts the prosecutions in the trial of the offenders. In states where there is no attorney-general for the state, the prosecuting attorney for each county serves in this capacity, in trials in which the state is a party. As all crimes and breaches of the peace are considered as committed against the state, and prosecuted in its name, this attorney is sometimes called *state's attorney.*

§ 11. In some states there is a *county-surveyor,* whose duties within his county are similar in their nature to those of a state surveyor-general.

§ 12. County officers are generally elected by the people of the county. Some of them are, in some of the states, appointed by some authority prescribed by the constitution or laws of the state.

CHAPTER XV.

Towns and Town Officers. Powers and Duties of Town Officers.

§ 1. The districts of territory into which counties are divided, are, in some states, called *towns.* In others they are called, and perhaps more properly, *townships;* and the name of *town* is given to an incorporated village, or a city. We shall, however, in this work, apply to these territorial divisions the shorter name of *towns,* as they are called in most of the old states.

§ 2. The electors of the several towns meet once a year for the election of town officers, and for certain other business purposes. The electors of a town have power, at their

---

§ 10. Are there state's attorneys in the counties of this state? § 11. Is there a county surveyor? § 12. Are county officers elected by the people in this state? Chap. XV. § 1. Into what are counties divided? § 2. What is done at the annual town meetings?

annual town meetings, to order money to be raised for the support of the poor, for the building and repairing of bridges, and for other town purposes ; to make regulations concerning fences ; to fix the compensation of town officers in certain cases ; and to perform such other duties as come within the usual powers of towns. The powers of towns, however, are not precisely the same in all the states.

§ 3. Among the town officers elected at town meetings, are the following; not all of them, however, are elected in any one state : One or more persons who have the general oversight and direction of town affairs, called by some name corresponding to the nature of their duties ; a town clerk ; one or more assessors ; justices of the peace ; overseers of highways ; overseers of the poor ; school officers ; constables ; a collector of taxes ; a treasurer ; fence-viewers ; pound-keepers, &c. In some states there are also sealers of weights and measures ; persons to measure and inspect wood, lumber, bark, and other commodities.

§ 4. The officers first mentioned in the preceding section, are, in the New England states, called *selectmen*, of whom there are at least three, and may in no state be more than nine, in each town. In a few states they are called *trustees of townships*, and are three in number. In a few other states, there is in each town one such officer, called *supervisor*. The powers and duties of these officers are more numerous in some states than in others. They have power to lay out roads, and lay out and alter road districts ; to do certain acts relating to roads, bridges, taxes, common schools, the support of the poor, &c. ; and to examine and settle all demands against the town. In some of the states, some of these duties are performed by other officers.

§ 5. The *town-clerk* keeps the records, books, and papers of the town. He records in a book the proceedings of town meetings, the names of the persons elected, and such other papers as are required by law to be recorded. In some states, deeds and other conveyances are required to be recorded by the clerks of towns.

[For a description of the duties of *assessors* and *justices of*

---

§ 3. What officers are elected? Are all these elected in the towns of this state? § 4. What are those officers called who direct town affairs? What in this state? § 5. What are the duties of a town clerk?

the peace, see Assessment and Collection of Taxes, and Justices' Courts.]

§ 6. For the repairing of *highways,* a town is divided by the proper officers into as many road districts as may be judged convenient ; and a person residing in each district is chosen, called *overseer* or *supervisor,* or *surveyor* of *highways,* whose duty it is to see that the roads are repaired and kept in order in his district. In some states a tax is laid and collected for this purpose ; and each person assessed may perform labor or furnish materials to the amount of his tax. In other states, road taxes are assessed upon the citizens in days' labor, according to the value of their property ; every man, however, being first assessed one day for his head, which is called a *poll-tax.* Persons not wishing to labor, may pay an equivalent in money, which is called *commuting.*

§ 7. *Overseers of the poor* provide for the support of the poor belonging to the town who need relief, and have no near relations who are able to support them. In some states there is in each county a poor-house, to which the poor of the several towns are sent to be provided for ; the expense to be charged to the towns to which such poor persons belonged.

§ 8. The principal duties of a *constable* are, to serve all processes issued by justices of the peace in suits at law for collecting debts, and for arresting persons charged with crimes. The business of a constable in executing the orders of a justice of the peace, is similar to that of a sheriff in relation to the county courts.

§ 9. The town *treasurer* receives all moneys belonging to the town, and pays them out as they may be wanted for town purposes ; and accounts yearly to the proper officers. The office of town treasurer does not exist in all the states.

§ 10. The duties of *fence-viewers* relate chiefly to the settling of disputes between the owners of adjoining lands concerning division fences ; and examining or viewing of fences when damage has been done by trespassing animals ; and the estimating of damages in such cases.

---

§ 6. What officers in this state have the care of highways? What is a poll-tax? § 7. By whom are the poor provided for? Are there county poor-houses in this state? § 8. The duties of constables? § 9. Of treasurer? Are there town treasurers in this state? § 10. The duties of fence-viewers? § 11. Of town-sealer?

§ 11. The town *sealer* keeps correct copies of the standard of weights and measures established by the state. Standard copies are furnished by the state sealer to each county sealer, at the expense of the county, and the county sealer furnishes each town sealer a copy at the expense of the town. The town sealer compares the weights and measures brought to him with the copy in his possession, and sees that they are made to agree with it, and seals and marks them. A person selling by a weight or measure that does not agree with the standard, is liable to the purchaser for damages—generally to several times the amount of the injury.

For a particular description of the duties of town officers, reference must be had to the laws of the several states.

CHAPTER XVI.

Incorporation and Government of Cities, Villages, &c.

§ 1. Cities and incorporated villages have governments peculiar to themselves. Places containing a large and close population need a different government from that of ordinary towns or townships. Many of the laws regulating the affairs of towns thinly inhabited, are not suited to a place where many thousand persons are closely settled. Besides, the electors in such a place would be too numerous to meet in a single assembly for the election of officers or the transaction of other public business.

§ 2. Whenever, therefore, the inhabitants of any place become so numerous as to require a city government, they petition the legislature for a law incorporating them into a city. The law or act of incorporation is usually called a *charter*. The word *charter* is from the Latin *charta*, which means paper. The instruments of writing by which kings or other sovereign powers granted rights and privileges to individuals or corporations, were written on paper or

Chap. XVI. § 1. Why is the incorporation of cities, &c., necessary? § 2. How are city charters obtained? Define *charter?*

parchment, and called *charters.* In this country, it is commonly used to designate an act of the legislature conferring privileges and powers upon cities, villages, and other corporations.

§ 3. The chief executive officer of a city is a *mayor.* A city is divided into wards of convenient size, in each of which are chosen one or more *aldermen,* (usually two,) and such other officers as are named in the charter. The mayor and aldermen constitute the *common council,* which is a kind of legislature, having the power to pass such laws, (commonly called *ordinances,*) and to make such orders and regulations, as the government of the city requires. The mayor presides in meetings of the common council, and performs also certain judicial and other duties. There are also elected in the several wards, assessors, constables, collectors, and other necessary officers, whose duties in their respective wards are similar to those of like named officers in country towns, or townships.

§ 4. The inhabitants of cities, however, are not wholly governed by laws made by the common council. Most of the laws enacted by the legislature are of general application, and have the same effect in cities as elsewhere. Thus the laws of the state require, that taxes shall be assessed and levied upon the property of the citizens of the state to defray the public expenses ; and the people of the cities are required to pay their just proportion of the same ; but the city authorities lay and collect additional taxes for city purposes.

§ 5. In cities there are also courts of justice other than those which are established by the constitution or general laws of the state. There is a court for the trial of persons guilty of disturbing the peace, and of such other minor offenses as are usually punishable by imprisonment in the county jail, called *police court.* It is held by a *police justice,* elected by the people, or appointed in such manner as the law prescribes. In some of the larger cities, there are courts of *civil* as well as criminal jurisdiction, differing from those which are common to counties generally.

---

§ 3. What are the principal city officers called? What inferior officers are elected? § 4. Are the citizens governed wholly by their own laws? § 5. What criminal court is peculiar to cities? § 6.

§ 6. The government of incorporated *villages* is not in all respects like that of cities. The chief executive officer of such a village is, in some states, called *president.* The village is not divided into wards ; the number of its inhabitants being too small to require such division. Instead of a board of aldermen, there is a board of *trustees* or *directors,* who exercise similar powers. The president of a village is generally chosen by the trustees from their own number. In some states, incorporated villages are called *towns ;* and their chief executive officer is called *mayor.*

§ 7. The necessity and effect of incorporating a village may not yet clearly appear to every reader. Let us illustrate. By a general law of the state, or by a vote of the electors of a township in pursuance of such law, cattle may run at large in the highways. This might be to many persons in a village, a great annoyance, which can be prevented or abated only by confining the cattle. Or, sidewalks may need to be made. Or, it may be deemed necessary to provide means for extinguishing fires, by purchasing fire-engines and organizing fire companies. In an unincorporated village there is no power to compel the citizens to do these things. Those, therefore, who desire that the citizens should have power to make all needful regulations for the government of the village, petition the legislature for an act of incorporation granting the necessary powers.

§ 8. The constitutions of some states require the legislature to pass a general law prescribing the manner in which the people of any village may form themselves into a corporation, with the necessary powers of government, without a special law for that purpose.

§ 9. Besides these *territorial* corporations for purposes of government, as counties, towns, cities, &c., there are *incorporated companies* for carrying on business of various kinds, as turnpike and rail-road companies, and companies for the purposes of banking, insurance, manufacturing, &c. These kinds of business, to be carried on successfully, sometimes require a larger amount of money than one man possesses. A number of persons, therefore, unite their

---

§ 6. What are village officers usually called ? § 7. Illustrate, by example, the necessity of a village incorporation ? § 8. Are corporations always formed by special laws ? § 9. What is said of incorporated *companies ?*

capital under an act of incorporation granting them power to manage their business which they could not have in an ordinary business partnership. Besides, a common partnership must end on the death of any one of the partners; but an incorporated company is not thus affected by the death of its members.

§ 10. It is in the nature of corporations to have a perpetual existence. A corporation may live after the persons who first composed it are all dead; for those who come after them have the same powers and privileges. A town or city incorporated a hundred years ago, is the same town or city still, although none of its first inhabitants are living. So a railroad or banking corporation may exist after the death of many, or even all of the original corporators.

§ 11. But there are certain particulars in which all corporations are not the same. A state has been defined to be a body politic, or corporation. (Chap. I. § 10; III, § 5.) But it differs from other government corporations, as counties, towns, cities, &c., in this: the latter are formed by acts of the legislature; but a state is formed by the people in their political capacity in establishing the constitution.

§ 12. Again, all these government corporations differ from incorporated business companies. In forming a town or city, many persons are brought into the corporation against their wishes or consent; because, in governments, all who live within certain prescribed bounds must come under the same laws; but of an incorporated business association, as of a common business partnership, none become members but by their own act or choice. There is another difference: The latter are what are called *stock* companies; and although they may be continued after the death of the first corporators, those who afterward come into the association, do so by becoming owners of the capital stock of those who preceded them. This latter difference will more clearly appear from the more particular description, elsewhere given, of the incorporated companies, and of the manner in which the stock is transferred. (Chap. XXIII., § 11—15.)

---

§ 10. What is peculiar in the nature of corporations? § 11 In what does a state differ from other government corporations? § 12. Wherein do all government corporations differ from incorporated business companies?

CHAPTER XVII

Judicial Department. Justices' Courts.

§ 1. Having seén how the legislative and executive departments of a state government are constituted, and how the laws are made and executed, the manner in which the local affairs of counties and towns are conducted, and the powers and duties of their respective officers; we proceed to describe the *judicial* department, the powers and duties of judicial officers, and the manner in which justice is administered.

§ 2. It is the business of the legislature to determine what acts shall be deemed public offenses, or crimes, and to make laws for securing justice to the citizens in their dealings and general intercourse with each other; but to judge of and apply the laws; that is, to determine what the law is and whether it has been broken, and to fix the just measure of damage or of punishment, and to order such decision to be carried into effect, are duties which, as has been observed, have been wisely assigned to a separate and distinct department. (Chap. VIII. § 7.)

§ 3. A government without some power to decide disputes, to award justice, and to punish crime according to the laws of the state, would not be complete. To allow every man to be his own judge in cases of supposed injury, and to redress his own wrongs, would endanger the rights of others. Justice is best secured to the citizens by establishing courts for the redress of injuries and the punishment of crimes; and that no person may suffer unjustly, it is provided that every person charged with crime or any other wrong, is entitled to a fair and impartial trial.

§ 4. For the convenience of persons who may be compelled to seek relief at law, courts are established in every

---

Chap. XVII. § 2. What is the business of the judicial department? § 3. If there were no courts of justice, what would be the result? § 4. What are the lowest courts called? Why? Define *jurisdiction?*

town. These are courts of the lowest grade, and are called *justices' courts*, being held by justices of the peace who are, in most of the states, elected by the people of the several towns. They are called the lowest courts, because they have jurisdiction only in cases in which the smallest sums or damages are claimed, or in which only the lowest offenses are tried. The word *jurisdiction* is from the Latin *jus*, law, or *juris*, of the law, and *dictio*, a pronouncing or speaking. Hence the *jurisdiction* of a court means its power to pronounce the law.

§ 5. Although justices of the peace are generally elected in the towns, their jurisdiction extends over the county; that is, they have power to try causes arising in any part of the county, or between citizens residing in other towns. The jurisdiction of justices of the peace is generally prescribed by law. The law prescribes the sum that may be sued for, or the amount of damage that may be recovered in a justice's court, and the grade of offenses that may be tried in it. In some states justices of the peace may try suits only in which the sum in controversy does not exceed $50; but in most of them, the jurisdiction of a justice extends, it is believed, to sums of $100 or more.

§ 6. Causes, in which money is claimed for damage or for debt, are called *civil* causes; those for the trial of persons charged with crime, or some misdemeanor, are called *criminal* causes. All crimes, strictly speaking, are misdemeanors. In common usage, however, the word *misdemeanor* denotes a smaller offense, such as is usually punishable by fine, or by imprisonment in a county jail, and not in a state prison. Causes, actions, and suits, are words of similar meaning in law language, being generally used to signify prosecutions at law, or lawsuits. The party that sues is called *plaintiff*; the party sued is the *defendant*.

§ 7. Prosecutions at law are conducted in nearly the same manner in the different states. The following is a sketch of the proceedings in an ordinary civil suit in a justice's court: The justice, at the request of the plaintiff, issues a *summons*, which is a writ or precept addressed to a constable of the town, in some states to any constable of

---

§ 5. To what extent has a justice jurisdiction? § 6. What are civil causes? Criminal? Misdemeanors? § 7. How is a suit in a justice's court commenced?

the county, commanding him to summon the defendant to appear before the justice on a day and at an hour specified, to answer the plaintiff (naming him) in a suit, the nature of which is stated in the summons.

§ 8. The constable serves the summons by reading it or stating the substance of it to the defendant; and if requested, gives him a copy of it. If he does not find the defendant, he leaves a copy at his place of residence with some one of the family of proper age. At or before the time named for trial, the constable returns to the justice the summons with an indorsement stating the day on which it was served, and whether served personally or by copy. If served by copy, and the defendant does not appear at the time named for trial, a new summons is issued, as the practice is in some states—perhaps all of them; and the trial may not proceed unless a summons has been personally served.

§ 9. The parties may appear in person, or by attorney. An *attorney* is any person lawfully appointed to transact business for another; hence the word attorney does not always mean an attorney at law, or lawyer, who is properly an officer of a court of law. When the parties have appeared and answered to their names, they make their *pleadings;* that is, the plantiff declares for what he brings his suit; and the defendant states the nature of what he has to *offset* against the demand of the plaintiff, or denies the demand altogether. These acts of the parties are called *joining issue.*

§ 10. If the parties are ready for trial, the justice proceeds to try the issue. If the witnesses have not been subpœned and are not in attendance, the cause is adjourned to a future day; and the justice, at the request of either party, issues a *subpæna,* which is a writ commanding persons to attend in court as witnesses. The witnesses on both sides are examined by the justice, who decides according to law and equity, as the right of the case may appear, in which he is said to *give judgment.* To the amount of the judgment, whether against the plaintiff or the defendant, are added the costs; for it is considered to

§ 8. How is a summon served? § 9. Describe the manner of joining issue
§ 10. How are witnesses procured? and how is the issue tried?

be just that the party in default shall pay the expense of the suit. The costs consist of the *fees* or compensation to be paid the justice, constable and witnesses for their services.

§ 11. If a defendant does not appear at the time of trial, the justice may proceed to try the cause, and decide upon the testimony of the plaintiff's witnesses. If a plaintiff does not answer or appear when his name is called in court, the justice enters judgment of *nonsuit*. A plaintiff may, at any time before judgment is rendered, discontinue or withdraw his action, in which case also judgment of nonsuit is given. In cases of nonsuit, and also when no cause of action is found, judgment is rendered against the plantiff for the costs.

§ 12. A debtor may avoid the expense of a lawsuit by *confessing judgment*. The parties go before a justice, and the debtor acknowledges or confesses the claim of the creditor, and consents that the justice enter judgment accordingly. In some states, the confession and consent must be in writing, and signed by the debtor. The amount for which judgment may be confessed is limited by law, but is, in some states at least, and perhaps in most if not all of them, larger than the sum to which the jurisdiction of a justice is limited in ordinary suits.

CHAPTER XVIII.

Trial by Jury; Execution; Attachment; Appeals; Arrest of Offenders.

§ 1. The administration of justice in courts of law is not left entirely to the justices and judges. Parties may not always have sufficient confidence in the ability, honesty, and impartiality of the justice by whom a suit is to be tried, to intrust their interests to his judgment. Therefore the constitutions of all the states guaranty to every person the right of trial by a jury. This right has been enjoyed

---

§ 11. What if a defendant or plaintiff does not appear? § 12. How is judgment confessed? Chap. XVIII. § 1. Why are juries instituted?

in England many centuries. It was established here by our ancestors, who were principally from that country.

§ 2. A *jury* is a number of men qualified and selected as the law prescribes, and sworn to try a matter of fact, and to declare the truth on the evidence given in the case. This declaring of the truth is called a *verdict*, which is from the Latin *verum dictum*, a true declaration or saying. A jury in a justice's court consists in most or all of the states, as is believed, of six men; in the higher courts, of twelve men, who are generally required to be freeholders. The manner of selecting the jurors is not the same in all the states.

§ 3. After issue has been joined, and before testimony has been heard, either party may demand that the cause be tried by a jury. Whereupon the justice issues a *venire*, which is a writ or precept directing a constable to summon the required number of duly qualified men to appear before the justice, to make a jury to try the cause.

§ 4. The testimony and arguments on both sides having been heard, the jurors are put under the charge of the constable, who is sworn to keep them in some convenient place, without meat or drink, except such as the justice may order, until they shall have agreed on their verdict, or have been discharged by the justice; and not to allow any person to speak to them during such time, nor to speak to them himself, except by order of the justice, unless to ask them whether they have agreed on their verdict.

§ 5. All the jurors must agree in a verdict; and when so agreed, they return in charge of the constable, and, in open court, deliver their verdict to the justice, who enters judgment according to the finding of the jury. If the jurors, after having been out a reasonable time, do not all agree upon a verdict, the justice may discharge them, and issue a new venire, unless the parties consent to submit the cause to the justice.

§ 6. If a judgment is not paid within the time prescribed by law, the justice issues an *execution*, which is a precept directing a constable to collect the amount of the judgment; and authorizing him to take and sell the goods and

---

§ 2. What is a *jury*? A *verdict*? § 3. A *venire*? § 4. How are jurors kept during their deliberations? § 5. What is done if they agree? If they disagree? § 6. What is an *execution*? What if it is not satisfied?

chattels of the debtor, and to make his returns to the justice within the time required. *Goods* and *chattels* are personal or movable property, or property other than freehold, or real estate. If the money can not be collected, the execution is returned as not satisfied. If a constable does not faithfully obey the directions contained in the execution, he and his sureties become liable to pay the judgment.

§ 7. Laws have been passed in all the states for the benefit of poor men, who are allowed to retain, for the use and comfort of themselves and their families, certain articles of personal property, which may not be sold on execution ; such as necessary household furniture, apparel, beds, tools and implements of trade, &c. The practice which formerly prevailed, of imprisoning debtors who were unable to satisfy executions, has been abolished, except for fines and penalties.

§ 8. The foregoing description of the proceedings of a justice's court is that of a prosecution in ordinary cases. But there are other modes of prosecution in certain cases, one of which is by attachment. An *attachment* is a writ directing the property of a debtor to be taken, and kept till a trial can be had, and judgment obtained. This mode of proceeding is adopted when the plaintiff has reason to believe that a debtor conceals himself to avoid being prosecuted by summons, or is about to remove his property or himself from the county, or intends in some other way to defraud his creditors.

§ 9. In case of an absent or concealed debtor, the constable, (as is supposed to be the common practice,) leaves a copy of the attachment, with an inventory or list of the articles of property attached, at the defendant's last place of abode, or, if he had none in the county, the copy and inventory are to be left with the person in whose possession the property is found. If the defendant does not appear on the day of trial, the plaintiff may proceed to prove his demand and take judgment. An execution is then issued against the property attached.

§ 10. If either party is dissatisfied with a judgment rendered in a justice's court, he may *appeal* to a higher court

§ 7. Is all personal property liable to be sold on execution ? § 8. What is an *attachment?* In what cases is it used ? § 9. How is it served ? § 10. What if a party is dissatisfied with a judgment ?

for trial, or for a review of the judgment. The party appealing is called *appellant;* the adverse party is the *appellee* or *respondent.*

§ 11. An important part of the duties of a justice of the peace relates to the arrest and trial of persons charged with crimes and misdemeanors. Although they have not power to try high offenses usually called crimes, they may order the apprehension of persons charged with such offenses, and cause them to be committed for trial.

§ 12. A person knowing or suspecting another to have committed an offense, may make complaint to a judge or justice of the peace, who examines the complainant on oath, and witnesses, if any appear; and if he is satisfied that an offense has been committed, he issues a *warrant*, directing the person accused to be brought before him. The complainant and witnesses for the prosecution, and next the prisoner and his witnesses, are examined. If the offense is one of which the magistrate has jurisdiction, he may proceed to try the prisoner, who, it will be recollected, is entitled to be tried by a jury.

§ 13. If the offense is one which the magistrate has not power to try, he binds the prosecutor or complainant and all material witnesses to appear and testify against the prisoner at the next court having power to indict and try him. And if the offense is one for which the prisoner may be bailed, the magistrate takes bail for his appearance at court. If the offense is not bailable, or if no satisfactory bail is offered, the magistrate orders him to be committed to jail to await his trial. But, as will be seen hereafter, he must be indicted by a grand jury before he can be tried. (Chap. XIX., § 7–9.) And were there no danger of an offender's escape before he could be brought to trial, his previous arrest and examination might be unnecessary.

§ 14. The obligation or bond given by a prosecutor and witnesses for their appearance at court, is sometimes called a *recognizance.* They bind themselves, with sureties, to forfeit and pay a certain sum of money in case of their non-appearance. A similar bond or recognizance is given in case of bail. The person accused binds himself, with

---

§ 11. What power have justices in cases of crime? § 12. How are offenders arrested and examined? § 13. How is the prisoner disposed of if the justice can not try him? § 14. Define *recognizance* and *bail?*

sureties, in such sum as the justice requires, which is to be paid if he shall not appear for trial. The word *bail* is from a French word meaning *to deliver*, or *to release*. Hence, the justice *bails*, sets free, or delivers to his sureties, the party arrested. Also the sureties are said to bail a person when they procure his liberation.

CHAPTER XIX.

Courts other than Justices' Courts; Grand and Petit Juries, &c.

§ 1. THE court next higher than a justice's court, is a court held in each county, generally called a *county court*, or *court of common pleas*. This court is usually held by a county judge elected by the electors of the county in most of the states; in some, appointed by the legislature; and in others, by the governor, with the advice and consent of the senate. In a few of the states this court consists of more than one judge. In some states, county courts are held by judges of the circuit courts.

§ 2. In this court are tried civil causes in which are claimed sums of greater amount than a justice of the peace has jurisdiction of, and criminal causes in which are charged the lower crimes committed in the county. Also causes removed by appeal from a justice's court are tried in this court; in which cases it is said to have *appellate* jurisdiction. Courts are also said to have *original* jurisdiction; which means that suits may *originate* or commence in such courts.

§ 3. There is in every state at least one court, and in most of the states there are two or more courts of higher grade than a county court. They are called in the different states by different names; as *circuit court*, *superior court*, *supreme court*, and *court of appeals*. A *circuit* court probably obtains its name thus: A state is divided into judicial districts, in each of which one or more judges are elected,

---

CHAP. XIX. § 1. How are county courts constituted? How in this state? § 2. What causes are tried in them? What is *appellate* and what *original* jurisdiction? § 3. Name the courts of this state. What jurisdiction has a circuit court?

who go around holding a court once a year or oftener in each of the counties composing a judicial district. This court usually has both original and appellate jurisdiction; it being a part of its business to try appeals from the county courts. It also tries such of the higher crimes as a county court has not the power to try. Courts in which crimes are tried are sometimes called courts of *oyer and terminer*.

§ 4. Every county court, and every circuit having like jurisdiction, has a jury to try issues of fact, and a grand jury. An *issue of fact* is when the *fact* as to the indebtedness or the guilt of the party charged is to be determined from the testimony. An *issue of law* is one in which it is to be determined what is the *law* in the case, which is done by the judge instead of the jury. The jury by which issues of fact are tried, as distinguished from a grand jury, is called a *petty* or *petit jury*. It consists of twelve men, all of whom must agree in a verdict.

§ 5. The manner of selecting grand and petit jurors is prescribed by law. A number of judicious men in each town are selected by some person or persons lawfully authorized; and the names of the men so selected are written on separate pieces of paper, and put into a box in each town, and kept by the town clerk; or as is the practice in some states, the names of the men designated as jurors in the several towns are sent to the county clerk, and by him kept in a box. Previous to the sitting of the court, the requisite number is drawn out the box; and the men whose names are drawn, are summoned to attend as jurors.

§ 6. It is the business of a *grand jury* to inquire concerning crimes and misdemeanors committed in the county; and if there appear just grounds of accusation against any person, they make to the court a presentment or formal charge against him, upon which he is to be put upon trial. The number of grand jurors is not always the same. In some states there may not be more than twenty-three nor less than twelve. It is not required that they shall all agree in order to put a person upon trial

---

§ 4. What juries have county and circuit courts? What is an issue of fact? An issue of law? § 5. How are the jurors selected? § 6. What is the business of a grand jury? Of what number does it consist in this state?

§ 7. On the opening of the court, the grand jurors are sworn to make a true presentment of all things given them in charge. The judge then gives them a charge, and appoints one of them foreman ; and the jurors retire to a private apartment to attend to their duties. They hear all complaints brought before them against persons for crimes and breaches of the peace, and examine witnesses who appear to testify ; and when it is requested, they have the assistance and advice of the state's attorney ; or as he is called in some states, the *district attorney*, or *prosecuting attorney*. If they think any person complained of ought to be tried, they draw up a writing, in which they charge him with the offense of which they think him guilty. This is called an *indictment*. It is signed by the foreman, indorsed "a true bill," and carried by the jury into court. If the person accused has not before been arrested, he may now be arrested, and put upon trial. (See Chap. XVIII., § 12–14.)

§ 8. As grand juries do not try crimes, but merely make inquiry into them, some may not readily perceive the necessity of such juries. Innocent persons might be subjected to great inconvenience and expense in defending themselves in court against the slanderous reports or false accusations of evil minded persons. It is to prevent this that grand juries are instituted, who make careful examinations into the cases brought before them, and do not often charge persons with crime unless there is a strong probability of their being found guilty on trial.

§ 9. So important was the institution of grand juries considered, that the constitution of the United States, to which the constitutions and laws of the states must conform, was made to provide, that "no person shall be held to answer for a capital or other infamous crime, unless on a presentment or indictment of a grand jury," except in certain cases. (Con. U. S., Amend. Art. V. For the definition of "infamous crime," see Chap. VI., § 7.)

§ 10. It is the opinion of many that this requirement of a previous indictment by a grand jury has reference only to the courts of the United States ; and that the states

---

§ 7. Describe the proceedings of a grand jury. What is an indictment ? § 8. Why are grand juries instituted ? § 9. By what instrument are grand juries required ? § 10. What is the opinion of some on this subject ?

may dispense with it. Hence, efforts are now making in some states to abolish grand juries. It is supposed that an examination at all times before a justice or a judge, when the prisoner can be present with his witnesses, is more likely to protect him against being unnecessarily subjected to the trouble and expense of a trial, than before a grand jury, where complaints are often made by malicious persons, and sustained by the testimony of partial or corrupt witnesses.

§ 11. The *supreme court* is generally the next higher, and in most of the states, the highest state court. This court differs somewhat in the different states, both in the manner of its formation and in its jurisdiction. It is believed, however, to have, in the states generally, both original and appellate jurisdiction, civil and criminal. In the state of New York and a few other states, there is one higher court, called *court of appeals*, which has appellate power only. Its business is to review cases from the supreme court.

§ 12. Suits in the county, circuit, and supreme courts, are commenced by a *writ*, (in some states a summons or a declaration,) which is served by the sheriff of the county in which the suit is to be tried. He also serves warrants and executions issued by these courts. A sheriff is to these courts what a constable is to a justice's court. His powers and duties have been elsewhere described. (Chap. XIV., § 8.)

CHAPTER XX.

Chancery or Equity Courts; Probate Courts; Court of Impeachment.

§ 1. It might be supposed, that in instituting the courts which have been described, all necessary provision had been made for securing justice to the citizens. But many cases arise in which justice and equity can not be obtained in these courts. To afford relief in such cases, a

---

§ 11. Is there a supreme court in this state? Describe it. Is there a higher court? § 12. How are suits commenced in county and other higher courts? Chap. XX. § 1. What is the object of a court of chancery?

court has been established called a *court of equity*, or *court of chancery*. What often renders it impossible to get justice in ordinary courts of law, is the want of witnesses; but in a court of equity the parties may themselves be put on oath.

§ 2. A debtor, to avoid the payment of his debts, may conceal his property or his money; but this court may compel him to disclose and give up the same to satisfy an execution; and it may prevent persons indebted to him from making payment to him. A person refusing to fulfill a contract may, in courts of common law, only be sued for damage; but this court may in certain cases compel him to fulfill the contract itself. It may also restrain individuals and corporations from committing fraudulent acts, and prevent persons from committing wastes on land and certain other injuries, until the right at law can be tried.

§ 3. Courts of chancery were established, it is believed, in a majority of the old states. But separate and distinct organizations called chancery courts, now exist in but a few states; the power to try suits in equity having been given to the judges of the common law courts.

§ 4. Suits *in equity* are not commenced as suits *at law*. The plaintiff prepares a bill of complaint, the facts stated in which are sworn to by himself. The bill, which contains a petition or prayer that the defendant may be summoned to make answer on oath, is filed with the clerk of the court, who issues a subpœna commanding the defendant to appear before the court on a day named. A trial may be had on the complaint and answer alone; or witnesses may be introduced by the parties. The case is argued by counsel, and a *decree* is pronounced by the court, which the court has power to carry into effect.

§ 5. There is another kind of courts which are in their nature different from ordinary law courts, and are called *probate courts*. There is in every county a probate court held by a *judge of probate*, whose duties relate to the proving of wills and the settling of the estates of persons deceased. A *will* is a writing in which a person gives directions concerning the disposal of his property after his

---

§ 2. Mention some of its powers. §3. Are there separate and distinct chancery courts in this state? § 4. How are suits commenced and tried in these courts? § 5. What is the business of a probate court?

death. The Latin word *probatus* means proof; from which *probate* has come to be applied to the proving of a will. (See Wills and Testaments.) In the state of New York the judge of this court is called *surrogate*, and the court is called *surrogate's court*.

§ 6. There is still another court in every state, which is not a common law court. It is the *court of impeachment*. The name is applied to the senate when sitting on a trial of impeachment. An *impeachment* is a charge or accusation against a public officer for corrupt conduct in his office; as if a governor, for money offered him, should approve and sign a law; or a judge should, for money or from some other selfish or personal motive, give a wrong judgment. The constitution gives to the house of representatives the power to impeach, and to the senate the power to try the persons impeached. This practice has come from Great Britain, where the impeachment is made by the house of commons, and the house of lords is the high court of impeachment.

§ 7. The house of representatives, in a case of impeachment, acts in nearly the same manner as a grand jury in a court of law. A complaint is made to the house; and if, upon examination, there appear to a majority of the members present sufficient grounds for the charge, an accusation in writing is prepared, called *articles of impeachment*, and delivered to the senate. In some states, a majority of the members elected is necessary to impeach. The president of the senate orders the court to be summoned. The accused is brought before the court to answer to the charge, and has counsel assigned him. The senators are sworn truly to try and determine the impeachment according to evidence; and a day is fixed for trial.

§ 8. The house of representatives usually choose from their number a committee of managers to conduct the trial, the proceedings in which are the same as in law courts. The senators retire and deliberate as jurors in such courts. Two-thirds of the senators—in some states two-thirds of all the senators elected—must concur in order to convict the person accused. If a person is convicted,

---

§ 6. What is a court of impeachment? Its business? What is an impeachment? By whom made? § 7. How is it done? § 8. Describe the mode of trial. What follows conviction?

the court may remove him from office, or disqualify him to hold any office in the state, for a time, or for life ; or may both remove and disqualify him. This court can pronounce no other sentence. But if the act committed is a crime, the offender may also be indicted, tried, and punished in a court of justice.

§ 9. Judicial officers may also be removed by the governor on address of the legislature. If a judge is suspected of corrupt conduct in his office, or of being incompetent to discharge its duties, complaint is made to the legislature, and the party complained of is notified, and an opportunity is given him of being heard in his defense. If both branches, by the required majorities, concur in the opinion that he ought to be removed, they address the governor, setting forth their reasons for the removal. If the governor considers the reasons sufficient, the officer is removed. This mode of removal does not exist in all the states. In New York, and perhaps in a few other states, the legislature makes the removal without the concurrence of the governor ; and in that state some of the lower judicial officers may be removed by the senate on the recommendation of the governor. In a few states, judges are not removable by impeachment.

CHAPTER XXI.

Assessment and Collection of Taxes.

§ 1. Every government must have the power of providing means for its support. The money which is needed to pay the expenses of administering the government, if the state has no permanent source of revenue, or income, must be raised by taxation. A *tax* is a rate or sum of money assessed upon the person or property of a citizen for the use of the state. When assessed upon the person, it is called a *poll-tax*, or *capitation tax*, being a certain sum on

---

§ 9. By what other modes are judicial officers removed ? Chap. XXI. How is money raised for government purposes ? What is a poll-tax ?

every poll, or head. But as persons ought generally to contribute to the public expenses according to their ability, taxes are more just and equal when laid upon the property of the citizens. Few poll-taxes are levied in this country.

§ 2. There are certain kinds of property which are exempt from taxation; such as the corporate property of the state, of counties, and of towns, including the buildings in which the public business is done, the prisons, jails, asylums, &c., and the lands attached to them; school-houses and meeting-houses, with the lands attached; burying-grounds, and the property of literary and charitable institutions. But the property of business corporations, as rail-road, banking, insurance, manufacturing, and other stock companies, like that of individuals, is liable to taxation. *Real estate*, or *real property*, is land with the buildings and other articles erected or growing thereon. *Personal estate*, or *personal property*, consists of movables, as goods, chattels, money, and debts due from solvent debtors.

§ 3. As the property of every person is to be assessed in proportion to its value, it is necessary, first, to make a correct valuation of all the taxable property. For this purpose, the assessor or assessors pass through the town, and make a list of the names of all the taxable inhabitants, and the estimated value of the property, real and personal, of each; and returns of the same are made to the proper county officers, who cause the tax-list for each town to be made out, and order the taxes to be collected.

§ 4. In some states, persons liable to taxation are themselves required to furnish lists of all their taxable property, printed blank lists having been previously distributed among them for this purpose. To secure an accurate valuation, the assessors, (called also *listers*,) may require persons to make oath that they have made a true statement of their property and its value. In states where the polls of the tax-payers are assessed, these also are set down in the lists at such sums as the law directs to be affixed to each poll.

§ 5. Before a tax-list can be made out, it must be known what amount is to be collected in each town. This amount

---

§ 2. What property is exempt from taxation? What is real, and what personal property? § 3–4. By whom, and how, is property valued? How in this state? § 5. Of what three items does the tax consist?

is made up of three parts: First, the sum wanted to pay the expenses of the town for the preceding year; secondly, the town's share of the county expenses; and thirdly, its proportional share of the expenses of the state government, or of what is to be raised for state purposes.

§ 6. The apportionment of the amount of the state and county expenses among the several towns, is made according to the amount of property in each as valued by the assessors. The state auditor or controller, having received from the several counties returns of the value of the property in each county, is enabled to determine its quota of the amount to be raised for state purposes. To each county's share of the state expenses is added the sum to be raised in the county for county purposes; and the amount is apportioned among the towns in proportion to the value of the assessed property of each. Then adding to each town's share of the amount of the state and county expenses, the amount to be raised for town purposes, gives the sum to be collected in the town.

§ 7. Having thus ascertained the sum to be raised in each town, the officers whose duty it is, cause a tax-list to be made out, in which the amount of each person's tax is set opposite his name and the estimated value of his property. The tax-list of each town, certified and signed by the proper persons, is put into the hands of the collector, with a warrant ordering the same to be collected.

§ 8. The money collected for county and state purposes is paid to the county treasurer, who pays to the state treasurer the amount raised in the county for state expenses, and retains the remainder to be expended in the county. The money collected for town purposes is paid to such persons in the town as are by law authorized to receive the same.

---

§ 6. How is it ascertained? § 7. Who in this state cause the tax-list to be made out, and order the taxes to be collected? § 8. To whom is the money paid when collected?

CHAPTER XXII.

Education. School Funds; Schools, &c.

§ 1. The proper object of government is to promote the welfare and happiness of its citizens. For this purpose, it must provide for making and properly administering laws to protect the people in the enjoyment of life and the fruits of their labor. But it should go further, and make express provision for improving the condition of the people, especially the less fortunate portions of them.

§ 2. The prosperity of a state or nation depends essentially upon the education of its citizens. This is seen by comparing the condition of the people of this country with the condition of the people of those countries where the benefits of education are not enjoyed. Ignorance tends to make men idle, vicious, and miserable. On the other hand, learning is not only a means of enjoyment in itself, but of improving the social condition of a people.

§ 3. Again, a free government is better adapted than any other to promote the welfare of a nation. But if the people are not properly educated, they are incapable of self-government. And as many persons are unable to pay for the tuition of their children, the safety of the government itself requires the establishment of a system of education, by which the great body of the people may be fitted to discharge their social and political duties. The states have accordingly instituted school systems for the instruction of children and youth of all classes at the public expense.

§ 4. In most of the states, the schools are supported only in part, in a few of them wholly, at the expense of the states. Some states have provided funds, the income of which is annally applied to this object. *Fund* generally signifies the money or capital stock employed in carrying on trade or any other business operation. *State funds* are the moneys and other property of the state which

---

Chap. XXII. § 1. What is the proper object of government? How is it to be done? § 2. What is the effect of education upou a people? Of ignorance? § 3. Why should government provide the means of education? § 4. To what extent is this done? By what means?

are set apart for paying the expenses of the government, or for the construction of canals, roads, and other public improvements. The interest of these funds, and the income from other sources, are called the *revenue.*

§ 5. In some states, school funds are created by appropriating the public lands, which are lands owned by the state as a body corporate. The proceeds of these lands, from sales or rents, constitute a part or the whole of the school fund, the interest of which is annually applied to the support of schools. If the income from the school fund is insufficient for this purpose, the deficiency may, as is done in some states, be supplied, in whole or in part, by taxation, or from the state treasury.

§ 6. Many of the new states have large school funds. At an early period, while most of the territory from which these states have been formed was yet the property of the United States, and uninhabited, Congress passed an act by which a particular section of land (number sixteen) in every township is reserved for the support of schools therein. By this act, one-thirty-sixth part of the lands within each of these states has been thus appropriated, besides smaller portions granted for the benefit of a university in each state. These lands are in the charge of proper officers, who dispose of them, and apply the proceeds as the law directs.

§ 7. The school funds of many of the states have been largely increased by certain moneys received from the United States. In 1837, there had accumulated in the national treasury about thirty millions of dollars over and above what was needed for the support of the government. By an act of congress, this surplus revenue was distributed among the states then existing, to be kept by them until called for by congress. Although congress reserved the right to recall the money, it was presumed that it would never be demanded. That it never will be, is now almost certain. Many of the states have appropriated large portions of their respective shares for school purposes. From its having been said to be only *deposited* with the states, this fund is sometimes called the *United States deposit fund.*

---

§ 5. How is the deficiency in the income of the school fund supplied? § 6. How, and to what extent, are school funds provided in the new states? § 7. In what way, and to what extent, were the school funds increased in 1837?

§ 8. School moneys coming from the state treasury, or state fund, are usually apportioned among the several towns of the state ; and each town's share of such moneys, together with what may come to the town by taxation or from its school lands, is divided among the several districts according to the number of children between certain ages in each district, or in such other manner as may be directed by law. If the moneys thus received are insufficient to pay the wages of teachers, a rate bill is made out in each district for the deficiency, and collected from the persons whose children have been taught in the schools.

§ 9. The towns, or townships, are divided into districts of suitable size for schools, which are called *district schools.* From their being supported by a common fund, and designed for the common benefit, or from the lower or more common branches being taught in them, they are also called *common schools.* One or more *trustees* or *directors* are chosen in each district to manage its affairs ; a *clerk* to notify meetings and record the proceedings of the same ; and a *collector* to collect taxes for building and repairing school-houses, and all rate bills for the payment of teachers.

§ 10. The highest school officer is the *state superintendent of common schools,* or, as he is sometimes called, *superintendent of public instruction.* The superintendent collects information relating to the schools ; the number of children residing in each district, and the number taught ; the amount paid for tuition ; the number of school-houses, and the amount yearly expended in erecting school-houses ; and other matters concerning the operation and effects of the common school system. If there is no other officer whose duty it is, the superintendent also apportions the money arising from the state funds among the several counties. He reports to the legislature at every session the information he has collected, and suggests such improvements in the school system as he thinks ought to be made.

§ 11. There is in every county an officer who receives from the state superintendent the money apportioned to

---

§ 8. How are school moneys from the state treasury apportioned ? How is the deficiency in the public moneys to pay teachers made up ? § 9. Why are schools called *district* schools, and *common* schools ? What officers are elected in districts ? § 10. What is the state superintendent in this state called ?

the county, and apportions the same among the towns; reports to the state superintendent the number of children in the county; and performs such other duties as the law requires. In some states, there is no such county officer; but the money is apportioned by the state superintendent among the towns; and the reports from the towns are made directly to the state superintendent.

§ 12. In the towns are officers whose duties are to examine teachers, visit schools, apportion the school moneys among the districts, and to collect the lists of the number of children in the several districts, with such other information as the law requires, and report the same to the county officer, or, if there is none, to the state superintendent. In some states, there is in each county an officer or a board of officers, for examining teachers, and performing certain other duties relating to the schools of the county.

§ 13. Academies and colleges also receive aid from the state, to a limited extent. A distinct fund is created in some states for their benefit; in others, they are aided by special appropriations from the state treasury.

CHAPTER XXIII.

Canals and Rail-Roads.

§ 1. In carrying out the purposes of government, provision ought also to be made to secure to the people the means of obtaining a suitable reward for their industry, and to render the labor of all, as nearly as may be, equally profitable.

§ 2. The people of some states do not possess the same advantage as those of others; nor do all the people of the same state enjoy equal advantages. Those who reside at a great distance from market, or from navigable waters

---

Chap. XXIII. § 1. What other duty does the government owe to the citizens? § 2. What portion of the people of a state are most favored?

and good roads, are not so well rewarded for their labor as those who reside near them, because of the greater cost of the transportation, both of what they have to sell, and of the goods they buy. Hence the necessity of good roads, canals, or other means of facilitating trade between the different parts of the state.

§ 3. Among the works intended to effect this object, *canals* are perhaps the most useful, and are to be preferred wherever their construction is practicable. Canals are sometimes constructed by incorporated companies ; but generally these works, especially those of great magnitude, are made by the state, and are the property of the state. Although there are some states in which are no canals of this kind, it may be interesting to young persons generally to know how so important a state work is made.

§ 4. To raise the money necessary to make a canal, the legislature might levy a general tax upon the property of the citizens. But this would not be expedient or just ; because, first, the payment of so large a sum by the people within the time in which it would be desirable to complete the work, would be inconvenient and burdensome ; and secondly, the expense must fall alike upon the people of all parts of the state ; whereas, those residing most remotely from the line of the work, would derive from it little or no benefit.

§ 5. When, therefore, a great enterprise of this kind is undertaken by a state, the law authorizing the work usually provides a *fund*, the income of which is to be applied to this object. This fund consists of such lands, property, and moneys as the legislature may grant for this purpose. Funds were thus constituted in some of the western states, to which funds congress made grants of the public lands of the United States lying within those states.

§ 6. These funds, however, furnish but a part, some of them but a small portion of the money necessary to complete the work ; and some states undertaking public improvements may not have the lands or other property to constitute such a fund. The state therefore borrows the

---

§ 3. By whom are canals made ? Is there such a public work in this state ? § 4. Why should not the money to make them be raised by a general tax ? § 5. How are funds sometimes provided for this purpose ? § 6. For the want of such funds, how is the money obtained ? How is it to be repaid ?

money for a long term of years, and depends upon the income of the canal fund and the tolls to be collected on the canals, for the repayment of the money borrowed. Should the revenues of the canal and of the canal fund be insufficient, the deficiency may be supplied by taxation.

§ 7. The business of borrowing the money is done on the part of the state, by persons duly authorized, who give for the money borrowed the bonds of the state, which are written promises to pay the money at the times specified, with interest at the rate agreed on; the interest generally to be paid semi-annually. These bonds are usually given in sums of $1,000 each, or less. The debts of a state thus contracted by issuing bonds, are called *state stocks*, as the capital, or stock required to construct a state work is obtained by the sale of its bonds. These bonds, like the certificates of stock in a rail-road or other corporate business company, are transferable, and may be bought and sold as promissory notes, and constitute an important article of trade.

§ 8. These stocks are taken by men who have large sums of money to lend, and who consider the state a responsible debtor; because, if it has no other sufficient means of paying its bonds, the legislature has power to raise the money by taxation. Most of the states have contracted debts in this manner for various purposes. State stocks are purchased and held not only by capitalists in this country, but by many in Europe.

§ 9. Officers are appointed to manage the canal fund, and others to superintend the canals. There are also officers, called *canal collectors*, at suitable distances along the canals, to collect the *tolls*, which are charges paid by the masters or owners of boats for the use of the canal.

§ 10. The states of New York, Pennsylvania, Ohio, and some other western states, have prosecuted the canal enterprise on a large scale. Although large debts have been contracted for the construction of canals in these states, the benefits derived from them more than compensate for the vast expense of their construction.

§ 11. *Rail-roads*, although they are of public utility, are

---

§ 7. How is the business of borrowing done? What are *state stocks*? § 8. What renders the purchase of state stocks a safe transaction? § 9. By whom are canal affairs managed? § 10. What states are most noted for their canals?

not properly public works, being constructed by companies incorporated for that purpose. The necessity for an act of incorporation is readily seen. Rail-roads pass through the lands of private individuals; and without the authority of law, the land of no person can be taken for such purpose; nor can a law authorize it to be taken, unless the work is one of general advantage; nor even in such case, without compensation to the owner for his land; for it is declared by the state constitutions, that "private property shall not be taken for public use without just compensation."

§ 12. If, therefore, the legislature deem a proposed rail-road to be of public utility, they pass an act to incorporate a company with the requisite powers to construct the road, on making compensation for the land, the value of which is to be estimated in such manner as the law prescribes. The law also prescribes the manner in which the affairs of the road are to be conducted.

§ 13. The amount of capital to be employed by the company, is mentioned in the act of incorporation, or charter, and is raised in this way: The amount of the capital, or stock, is divided into shares of $100, or less. Persons wishing to invest money in the road, subscribe the number of shares they will respectively take. When all the shares are thus sold and the money is paid in, the company is ready to proceed to the construction of the road. The owners of these shares are called *stockholders*, who choose from among themselves such number of *directors* as the charter authorizes. The directors elect from their number a *president*.

§ 14. Persons buying shares receive certificates signed by the proper officers, stating the number of shares for which each certificate is given. The holders of these certificates, if they wish to make other use of the money they have invested in the business, may sell their stock to others, to whom they pass their certificates, which are evidence of the amount of stock purchased. Thus these certificates are bought and sold as promissory notes.

§ 15. Stockholders depend, for the reïmbursement of their capital, upon the money to be received for the trans-

---

§ 11. By whom are rail-roads usually constructed? Why is an act of incorporation necessary? § 12. What does the act provide? § 13. How is the capital, or stock, raised? What officers are chosen, and by whom? § 14. What is the nature of these certificates of stock?

portation of passengers and freight. Such portion of the income of the road as remains after paying all expenses of running and repairs, is divided semi-annually among the stockholders. Hence the sums thus divided are called *dividends.* The earnings of some roads are so large as to make the investment a profitable one ; so that the holder of shares is enabled to sell them at an advance. When shares in the stock of any institution are sold at their nominal value, the price named in the certificates, the stock is said to be at *par.* When they are sold for more or less than their nominal value, they are said to be above or below *par.* In large commercial cities, as New York, Boston, Philadelphia, and others, the purchase and sale of state stocks, and stocks in rail-roads, banks, &c., is a regular and extensive business of capitalists.

CHAPTER XXIV.

Banks and Insurance Companies.

§ 1. Banks, we are told, were first instituted in Italy, where certain Jews assembled, seated on benches, ready to lend money, and to exchange money and bills ; and *banco* being the Italian name for bench, banks took their title from this word. The first banks are said to have been only places where money was laid up or deposited for safe-keeping. But banks at the present day are not used for depositing alone.

§ 2. Banks in this country can be established only by authority of law. They are incorporated by an act of the legislature. The capital stock is raised by the sale of shares, and issue of certificates, as in the case of rail-roads. (Chap. XXIII., § 13.) The stockholders elect of their number (usually) thirteen *directors,* who choose one of themselves as *president.* The president and directors choose a cashier and clerks.

---

§ 15. How do stockholders expect to be refunded ? What are dividends ? When are stocks at par ? When above or below par ? Chap. XXIV. § 1. Where were the first banks ? and whence is the name derived ? § 2. By what authority are our banks established ? How is the capital stock raised ?

§ 3. Merchants and others in commercial places, deposit in banks, for safe-keeping, the money they receive in the course of business, and then draw it out on their written orders as they have occasion to use it. An order of this kind is called a *check*.

§ 4. Persons depositing money only once, or very seldom, and intending to draw for the same at once, usually receive from the cashier a *certificate of deposit*, which states the name of the depositor, the sum deposited, and to whose order it is to be paid. For the use of money deposited for any considerable period, banks agree to pay interest, usually less, however, than the rate established by law. Certificates of deposit may, by indorsement, be made transferable as promissory notes and other negotiable paper, (Chap. LX., § 2,) and are often remitted, instead of money, to distant places, where, by presenting them at a bank, they may, for a trifling compensation, be converted into money.

§ 5. A material part of the business of banks is to assist merchants and others in transmitting money to distant places. Thus: A, in New York, wishing to send $1,000 to B, in Philadelphia, puts the money into a bank in New York, takes for it an order, called *draft*, on a bank in Philadelphia, for that amount, to be paid to B. The draft is sent by mail to B, who presents his draft at the bank, and receives the money; and the bank charges the amount to the New York bank.

§ 6. But persons unacquainted with commercial business, especially young persons, may not know how the bank in Philadelphia is to be repaid. In the course of trade between the two cities, business men are constantly remitting money both ways through the banks, which thus receive the money and draw upon each other. Thus millions of dollars may be annually transmitted between the two cities, without any expense except the small charge of the banks for doing the business, and without the risk of loss by accident or robbery which attends the conveyance of money in person.

---

§ 3. How do business men deposit and draw out their money? § 4. What is a *certificate of deposit?* How is it made transferable? and convertible into money? § 5. Describe the manner of transmitting money through banks. § 6. How are banks repaid? What is saved to business men by this mode of remittance?

§ 7. Banks also lend money. The borrower gives a note for the sum wanted, signed by himself, and indorsed by one or more others as sureties. The cashier pays the money for the note, retaining out of it the interest on the sum lent, instead of waiting for it until the note becomes due. This is called *discounting* a note.

§ 8. The bills of banks pass as money. A bank bill or note is a promise of the bank to pay the bearer a certain sum on demand, signed by the president and cashier. It passes as money, because the bank is bound to pay it in specie if it is demanded. Paying notes thus is *redeeming* them. When a bank is unable to redeem all its bills, it is said to have failed, or to be broken ; and the bill holders suffer loss, unless some security has been provided. This has been done in some states by making the stockholders individually liable for the redemption of the bills ; that is, the property owned by them as individuals may be taken and sold on execution for that purpose. Such security, however, has never been generally provided.

§ 9. But a system of banking, sometimes called *free banking*, has more recently been adopted in some states. It is so called, because the business of banking is thrown open to all by a *general law*. Any person, or any number of persons, may, by complying with the provisions of this general law, establish a bank without a special law for this purpose. Hence it is also called the *general banking* system.

§ 10. Persons, before commencing business under this law, must put into the hands of the proper state officers ample securities for the redemption of their bills ; and they may not issue bills to a greater amount than the amount of their securities. These securities must consist of approved state stocks, or United States stocks, or partly of public stocks, and partly of real estate. When a bank fails, the lands and stocks held in pledge by the state are sold, and the avails are applied to the redemption of the

---

§ 7. Describe the operation of lending money by a bank. § 8. Describe a bank bill. What if a bank is unable to redeem its bills ? How are bill-holders secured against loss ? § 9. What is the nature of the free banking system ? § 10. How does this law provide for the security of bill-holders ? § 11. What is the business of insurance companies ? What do they insure ? Define *policy*. *premium.*

bills. This system of banking seems to be growing into public favor.

§ 11. *Insurance companies* also are authorized by law. Their business is to insure persons against loss by fire. The corporators, on being paid a small sum, consisting generally of a certain percentage on the amount for which the property is insured, promise to pay such amount if the property shall be destroyed by fire. There are companies also for insuring vessels at sea ; and *life* insurance companies, that agree to pay, in case of the death of the person insured, a certain sum for the benefit of his family, or of some other person named in the policy. The word *policy* as here used, means the writing containing the terms or conditions on which the company agrees to indemnify the person insured in case of loss. The money paid to obtain insurance, is called *premium.*

§ 12. The profits of the stockholders consist of the excess of money received for premiums over the amount paid out for losses. Thus, if a company has issued 2,000 policies, each covering property of an average amount of $1,000, the amount of risk is $2,000,000 ; and if the rate of insurance is one per cent., the amount received in premiums is $20,000. Hence, if none of the 2,000 buildings is burned within the time the insurance is to run, the $20,000 are gained. If ten of them should be burned, there would still be a gain of $10,000. If twenty should be destroyed, there would be no gain, but an actual loss to the amount of the expenses of the concern.

§ 13. But from the average number and amount of losses annually for many years, companies are enabled so to fix the rates of insurance as to give the stockholders a fair profit on their capital. The rates are not the same on all kinds of property ; a higher per centage is charged on that which is deemed hazardous, or more exposed to fire, than on that which is less exposed. The profits on the business of the company, or the *dividends,* as they are called, are annually or semi-annually divided among the stockholders, in proportion to the amount of their respective shares.

---

§ 12. Of what consist the profits of stock insurance companies ? Show this by an example. § 13. How are companies enabled to fix proper rates of insurance ? Is all property insured at the same rate ? Why not ? § 14. Describe the character of mutual insurance companies. How is money raised for paying losses ?

§ 14. There is another kind of insurance companies, which differ materially from the *stock* companies described in the preceding sections. They are *mutual* insurance companies. They are so called because the members unite in insuring each other. Every person having his property insured by such a company is a member of it. He has his buildings and the property in them valued; and pays a certain rate per cent. on such valuation. A fund is thus raised out of which any member suffering loss by fire is paid the amount for which the property was insured. When the fund is exhausted, it is again supplied by a tax assessed upon the members in proportion to the amounts for which they are respectively insured.

CHAPTER XXV.

The Militia.

§ 1. It is the practice of governments to keep their respective countries prepared to defend themselves against foreign enemies. For this purpose all men liable to do military duty are enrolled, and are required to meet on certain days every year for instruction in the art of war, in order to be ready for actual service whenever it shall be required. The body of soldiers thus enrolled are called the *militia*. There are other words which are sometimes applied to bodies of soldiers; as *infantry*, which means the soldiers or troops who serve on foot; *cavalry*, the troops on horses; *artillery*, those who manage the cannon and other heavy weapons of war. But all troops are comprehended in the general term, *militia*.

§ 2. The militia of a state, or a portion of them, may also be needed to aid in executing the laws of the state, and in suppressing insurrection or rebellion. An *insurrection* is a rising against the public authority, or the attempt of persons to prevent the execution of a law. *Rebellion* generally

---

Chap. XXV. § 1. What preparation is made for the public defense? What does the word *militia* include? § 2. For what other purpose may portions of the militia be wanted? Define *insurrection* and *rebellion*.

means nearly the same as *insurrection;* but more properly it signifies a revolt, or an attempt to overthrow the government to establish a different one. As it is the duty of an executive to see the laws executed, power is given by the constitution to the governor to call out a sufficient military force for this purpose.

§ 3. All able-bodied white male citizens of the United States, between the ages of eighteen and forty-five years, are liable to perform military service in the states in which they reside, except such as are exempt by the laws of the states and of the United States. Persons exempt by the laws of the states are generally the following: Ministers of the gospel; commissioned officers of the militia having served a certain number of years; members of uniformed companies having served for a specified time; members of fire companies; certain public officers while in office; and in some states teachers and students of colleges, academies, and common schools; and a few others.

§ 4. Persons exempt by the laws of the United States are the vice-president, the subordinate executive and all the judicial officers of the government of the United States; members of congress and its officers; custom-house officers and their clerks; post-officers and drivers of mail stages; ferrymen employed at ferries on post-roads; pilots and mariners.

§ 5. By the constitutions of the several states, the governors are made the commanders-in-chief of the militia of their respective states; and by the constitution of the United States, the president is made commander-in-chief of the army and navy of the United States, and also of the militia of the states when called out into actual service. It has already been remarked, (§ 2,) that the military force of the state is at the command of the executive to protect the government and its citizens. So the president was thought the proper person to have command of the public forces, to execute the laws of the United States, to repel invasion, and to carry on war. Hence the governors and the president are not among the public officers who are exempt from military duty.

---

§ 3. Who are liable to do military service? Who are exempt by the laws of the states generally? § 4. Who by the laws of the United States? § 5. What military authority have the governors and the president? Why have they this power?

§ 6. Persons who, having been duly notified, refuse to appear at military parades, or, appearing without being equipped as the law directs, are tried by a military court, called *court martial*, consisting usually of three military officers, or of such other persons as may be appointed according to the law of the state. If the persons tried do not show good cause for their delinquency, they are fined in such sums as the law prescribes. In certain cases courts may consist of more than three members.

§ 7. The highest militia officer, except the governor, is the *adjutant-general* of the state; who keeps a list of all the higher commissioned officers, containing the dates of their commissions, their rank, the corps (pronounced *core*) they belong to, the division, brigade, and regiment, and their places of residence. He distributes all orders from the commander-in-chief (the governor,) to the several divisions; attends public reviews where the commander-in-chief reviews the militia; and obeys all orders from him relative to carrying into execution the system of military discipline established by law.

§ 8. There is also in some states a *commissary-general*, who has the care of the arsenals and magazines, and the articles deposited in them. An *arsenal* is a building in which are kept cannon, muskets, powder, balls, and other warlike stores; all of which are to be kept in repair and ready for use.

§ 9. There are persons who, believing all wars to be wrong, can not conscientiously do military service. As it is the object of our government to secure to every person the liberty of conscience as well as other rights, the constitutions of many of the states provide, that those who are averse to bearing arms, may be excused by paying annually a sum of money instead of rendering the service. But it may well be doubted whether compelling a man to pay the money is not itself a violation of the right of conscience. Many persons conceive it to be no less morally wrong to commute for the service than to perform it. In some states, all persons belonging to the society of Friends,

---

§ 6. How are persons dealt with for non-attendance and delinquency at parades? § 7. What are the duties of the adjutant-general? § 8. What is the business of a commissary-general? Is there one in this state? Define *arsenal*. § 9. What is done in the case of persons averse to bearing arms? Are any exempt in this state without commuting?

usually called Quakers, are exempt without the payment of an equivalent in money.

§ 10. In the states of New York and Ohio, the rank and file of the militia are not required to train in time of peace. Persons liable to perform military service, except those connected with the uniformed companies, are enrolled in the militia; but instead of doing duty, they pay annually a small tax, which is in New York fifty cents, and in Ohio fifty cents, or a day's highway labor.

§ 11. Laws abolishing trainings and musters of the great body of the militia, are, it is believed, growing into favor, and for these among other reasons: First, the militia system produces no material improvement in discipline; secondly, the expenditure of time and money in these useless exercises, and for arms and equipments, are burdensome to many citizens; and thirdly, there is no probability of an occasion requiring a large portion of the militia to be so suddenly called into service as to allow no time for preparation. Volunteer companies like those kept up and disciplined in the states above named, and the standing army of the nation, are deemed sufficient for any supposable emergency.

§ 12. Happily the practice of settling disputes between nations by war, is becoming less popular in civilized and Christian communities. War is a dreadful evil, and ought to be discouraged, and, if possible, avoided. Were governments so disposed, they might in most cases settle their differences as individuals do, by submitting them to the judgment of a third party. If the love of military honor were less encouraged, and the principles of peace duly inculcated, the time would be hastened when "nations shall learn war no more."

---

§ 10. What regulations exist in New York and Ohio? § 11. For what reasons is the drilling of the whole militia deemed unnecessary? § 12. What is your opinion of war? What is a better way of settling disputes between nations?

GOVERNMENT OF THE UNITED STATES.

CHAPTER XXVI.

Causes of the Revolution.

§ 1. The plan of government in this country is peculiar. To a person previously unacquainted with our political institutions, it might seem strange, after having read the foregoing description of the state governments, to be told that there is still another and a different government to which the people are subject. How the people of more than thirty states, all having complete and distinct governments, can at the same time be subject to another government, also complete in all its parts, he would not immediately understand. He would not know what is meant by the government of the United States. How the states, all having governments of their own, can be *united* in one government, he would not readily perceive.

§ 2. We shall therefore proceed to a description of the government of the United States, from which will appear the relation between that government and the state governments. It will also appear that the state governments, each of which has in itself a great deal of machinery, all move in harmony with the great political machine—the government of the United States. It is easy to see that a knowledge of these governments is important to the people who live under them, as every freeman exercises a part of the governing power, both in the government of his own state, and in the general government.

§ 3. To assist the reader in understanding the constitution and government of the United States, we shall first give a sketch of the governments which preceded, and of the principal causes which led to the revolution in the gov-

Chap. XXVI. § 2. What is there in our government that renders a knowledge of it important to the people? § 3. To what country were the American colonies subject? What is a *colony?*

ernment of this country. Most of the youth who are of sufficient age to study this work, probably know that our present forms of government were not established by the early settlers in this country. The first inhabitants were *colonists.* A *colony* is a settlement of persons in a distant place or country, who remain subject to the government of the state or country from which they removed. The American colonies which have become the "United States," were chiefly settled from Great Britain, and were under her jurisdiction.

§ 4. The political rights and privileges enjoyed by the colonists as British subjects, were very limited, and were conferred by the charters of the king. The people had not then, as now, constitutions of their own choice. There were colonial governments; but they were such as the king was pleased to establish, and might be changed at his pleasure. These governments were in *form* somewhat similar to that of our state governments. There was what might be called a legislature; also an executive or governor; and there were judges.

§ 5. But of the officers of these departments of the government, only the members of one branch of the law-making power were elected by the people. The other branch was composed of a small number of men, called a council; but they were appointed by the king and subject to his control, as was also the governor, who had the power of an absolute negative or veto to any proposed law. And laws after having received the assent of the governor, must be sent to England and approved by the king, before they could go into effect.

§ 6. Hence we see that the colonists had no security for the passage of such laws as they wanted. And the consequence was, that they were often denied good and wholesome laws, by the refusal of the king to sanction them. Not only so; many laws enacted by parliament were very unjust and oppressive. The object of these laws was to secure to Great Britain alone the trade of the colonies. One law declared that no goods should be imported by the col-

---

§ 4. Whence did the people derive their rights and privileges? What was the *form* of the colonial governments? § 5. From whom did the officers derive their power? Were any elected? On whose approval did the laws finally depend? § 6. What was the effect of this upon the colonists? What was the object of the laws of parliament relating to the colonies?

onists but in English vessels ; if brought in other vessels, both the goods and vessels were to be forfeited to the British government.

§ 7. Another law required such articles as England wanted, to be transported to that country and other countries belonging to Great Britain. The colonists were permitted to ship to foreign markets such products only as English merchants did not want. They were prohibited from selling abroad any wool, yarn, or woolen manufactured goods. This was done to keep the markets open for British wool and manufactures. Another law declared that no iron wares of any kind should be manufactured here. Thus was it attempted to suppress manufactures in the colonies.

§ 8. Hence we see that it was the policy of the British government to compel the colonists to buy of England all the goods they wanted which they did not themselves produce, and to sell to England the surplus productions of the colonies. For this purpose, heavy duties were laid upon goods imported into the colonies from other countries than Great Britain and her possessions. These duties were taxes levied upon goods brought into the colonies from abroad, and were collected by officers here from the persons importing the goods.

§ 9. The following facts will explain to the young reader more clearly the nature and effects of these duties : The colonists traded with the West India islands, some of which belonged to Great Britain, some to France, and some to Spain. To secure the whole trade, the British government imposed high duties upon the molasses, sugar and other articles imported into the colonies from the French and Spanish islands. The people of the colonies could therefore avoid the payment of these duties only by importing the above mentioned goods from the British islands.

§ 10. Not satisfied with these acts, parliament claimed the right to tax the colonies, "in all cases whatsoever ;" and an act was passed accordingly, laying duties upon all

---

§ 6, 7. What did some of these laws require ? § 8. By what particular means did that government secure the colonial trade ? Define *duty*. § 9. Explain the nature and effect of these duties. § 10. What right did parliament claim ? What act was accordingly passed ? What did the colonists do ? What was the final result ?

tea, glass, paper, &c., imported into the colonies ; and the money thus collected was put into the British treasury. The colonists petitioned the king and parliament to repeal these obnoxious laws ; but their petitions were denied. Having given up all hope of relief, congress, which was a body of delegates from the several colonies, declared the colonies to be free and independent states, no longer subject to the government of Great Britain. This declaration was maintained by a war which lasted about seven years, when Great Britain gave up the contest, and acknowledged the independence of the states ; and the *revolution* was accomplished.

CHAPTER XXVII.

Nature of the Union under the Confederation.

§ 1. As early as the year 1774, the colonies united in the plan of a congress, to be composed of delegates chosen in all the colonies, for the purpose of consulting on the common good and of adopting measures of resistance to the claims of the British government. The first great continental congress met on the 4th of September, 1774. Another congress assembled in May, 1775. This congress adopted sundry measures having reference to war, and finally made the declaration of independence, July 4th, 1776. The continental congress, the members of which were chosen by the state legislatures, conducted the affairs of the nation until near the close of the war.

§ 2. With a view to a permanent union of the colonies under a general government, the congress, in November, 1777, agreed upon a frame of government, contained in certain articles, called, "Articles of Confederation and perpetual Union between the States." These articles were to go into effect when they should have received the assent of all the states. But as the consent of the last state (Maryland)

Chap. XXVII. § 1. When did the first continental congress meet? How were its members chosen? What great act did it do in 1776? § 2. What did it in November, 1777? When did the confederation go into effect?

was not obtained until March, 1781, they went into operation only about two years before the close of the war.

§ 3. As a plan of national government, the confederation was soon found to be very defective. The union formed under it was a very imperfect one. Having been framed in time of war, it had respect to the operations of war rather than to a state of peace. Although it answered some good purpose in carrying on the war, it was not well adapted even to the condition of the country then existing. Its defects appeared almost as soon as it went into effect; and after the return of peace, it was found that the union, instead of being strengthened and perpetuated by it, could be preserved only by a radical change in the system of government.

§ 4. The leading defect of the confederation was its weakness. Congress could do little more than to recommend measures. As it could not legislate directly upon persons, its measures were to be carried into effect by the states; but the states were not in all cases willing, and some of them did at times refuse to do so, and congress could not compel them. It belonged to congress to determine the number of troops and the sums of money necessary to carry on the war, and to call on each state to raise its share; but congress could not enforce its demands. It borrowed money in its own name, but it had not the means of paying it. It had no power to lay and collect taxes; this power was reserved to the states.

§ 5. Hence we see that congress was dependent for every thing upon the good will of thirteen independent states. It is a wonder that a government of such inherent weakness should bring the war to a successful issue. It was a sense of danger from abroad, rather than any power in the government, that induced a sufficient compliance with the ordinances of congress to achieve the independence of the states.

§ 6. On the restoration of peace, new difficulties arose. We have already spoken of the want of power in congress

---

§ 3. How did the union formed by it prove? What was the probable cause of its imperfections? § 4. What was its leading defect? Mention some instances of its weakness? § 5. What probably aided in inducng compliance with the ordinances of congress? § 6. What new difficulties arose after peace? What difficulty attended the laying of duties by the states?

to lay and collect taxes for war purposes. Money was now wanted to discharge the public debt, and to pay the current expenses of the government; yet congress had no power to raise it, either by a *direct tax* upon the persons or property of the citizens, or *indirectly* by duties on goods imported, as at present under the constitution. The power to lay and collect duties was with the states; but it was of little use so long as each state could impose such duties as it chose. The states being unable to agree upon a uniform rate of duties, the goods would be imported into states which levied the lowest duties. It was expedient, if it had been possible, to borrow more money on the credit of the union, as the heavy debt contracted during the war remained unpaid, and congress had no means of paying it.

§ 7. But the inability to raise money was not the only difficulty that attended the want of power by congress to lay duties. This power was necessary also to regulate the foreign trade. We have already remarked, that it was the policy of Great Britain before the revolution to secure in the colonies a market for her manufactures. (Chap. XXVI.) Not only so; she had by her navigation acts, for more than a hundred years, imposed heavy duties upon foreign vessels coming into her ports, in order to secure the carrying trade to her own shipping. In addition to this, she also levied high duties upon the produce of the states sent to pay for the goods we were obliged to buy of her, our own people not having as yet the means, nor having had time, to establish manufactories, and to manufacture for themselves.

§ 8. Another of the numerous troubles which arose from this imperfect union was the want of peace and harmony between the states. Laws were enacted in some states with a view to their own interests, which operated injuriously upon other states. This induced the latter states to retaliate, by passing laws partial to themselves and injurious to the former. The states soon became disaffected toward each other; and their mutual jealousies and rivalries and animosities at length became so great as to cause

---

§ 7. For what other purpose did congress need the power to lay duties? How had Great Britain secured the carrying trade? § 8. What other trouble arose from this imperfect union?

fears that some of the states would become involved in war among themselves, and that the union would be broken up.

§ 9. In the hope of remedying the difficulty last mentioned, an attempt was made to procure the insertion, into the articles of confederation, of a provision giving to congress the power to regulate trade; but the attempt failed. In January, 1786, the legislature of Virginia proposed a convention of commissioners from all the states, to take into consideration the situation and trade of the United States, and the necessity of a uniform system of commercial regulations.

§ 10. A meeting was accordingly held at Annapolis, in September, 1786; but as commissioners from only five states attended, viz., New York, New Jersey, Pennsylvania, Delaware, and Virginia, the commissioners deemed it unadvisable to proceed to business relating to an object in which all the states were concerned; but they united in a report to the several states and to congress, in which they recommended the calling of a general convention of delegates from all the states, to meet in Philadelphia on the 2d Monday of May, 1787, with a view not only to the regulation of commerce, but to such other amendments of the articles of confederation as were necessary to render them "adequate to the exigencies of the union."

§ 11. In pursuance of this recommendation, congress, in February, 1787, passed a resolution for assembling a convention. All the states, except Rhode Island, appointed delegates, who met pursuant to appointment; and framed the present constitution of the United States. They also recommended it to be laid by congress before the several states, to be by them considered and ratified in conventions of representatives of the people. Conventions were accordingly called for this purpose in all the states, except Rhode Island, and the constitution was ratified by all of them in which conventions had been called, except North Carolina.

§ 12. The constitution was to go into effect if ratified by

---

§ 9. How was this difficulty sought to be remedied? § 10. What was the result of the meeting at Annapolis? § 11. In what did the recommending of a convention result? How was the constitution ratified in the states? § 12. To give it effect, how many states must ratify? When were ratifications received from Rhode Island and North Carolina?

nine states. The ninth state, New Hampshire, sent its ratification to congress in July, 1788 ; and measures were taken by congress to put the new constitution into operation. Ratifications were received from North Carolina and Rhode Island the year after the organization of the new government.

CHAPTER XXVIII.

Nature of the Union under the Constitution.

§ 1. Having given, in the preceding chapter, a sketch of the union under the confederation, we shall next show the nature of the union under the present constitution, commencing with a brief comparison of the leading features of the two systems of government.

§ 2. The former union was a mere confederacy. A *confederacy* is a league, a federal compact. The word *federal* is from the Latin *fœdus*, a league, or alliance. Hence a confederacy is a combination or union of two or more parties, whether persons or states, for their mutual benefit and assistance. And let it be here particularly noted, that this union was a union of states, *as states.* The articles of confederation were framed by congress, whose members were appointed by the state legislatures, and, when framed, were submitted to the state legislatures for ratification.

§ 3. On the other hand, the union under the constitution is a union, not of the states, as such, but of the *people of the states.* Thus it is expressed in the preamble to the constitution : "We, the people of the United States, in order to form a more perfect union, ... do ordain and establish this constitution for the United States of America." And the constitution was submitted for ratification, not to the state legislatures, but to conventions whose members were elected by the people for that purpose.

§ 4. The states under the confederation were independent,

Chap. XXVIII. § 2. What is a confederacy ? Was the confederation a union of people ? or a union of states ? From what does this appear ? § 3. What is the union under the constitution ? Where is this declared ?

not only of each other, but of the general government. True, they agreed, for their common defense and mutual welfare, to do certain things; and certain other things they agreed not to do, but delegated to congress the power to do them; but, as we have seen, congress had not the power to compel the states to obey its requisitions. By the constitution, the states have given up a greater portion of their sovereignty to the general government, which has power, in certain cases, to control the state governments, and to enforce its laws upon them and upon individuals.

§ 5. Again, under the confederation, as in confederacies generally, the states were equal. They were entitled to an equal number of delegates in the congress, in which they voted by states, each state having one vote; that is, if a majority of the delegates of a state voted in favor of or against a proposed measure, the vote of the state was so counted; and a proposition having in its favor a majority of the states, was carried. Every state was entitled to seven delegates; but there must be at least two delegates present and voting, in order to give a state vote; and if an equal number of the delegates of a state voted for and against a proposition, the state was said to be divided, and to have no vote.

§6. Under the constitution there are two branches of congress, in one of which the number of representatives of each state is in proportion to its population; in the other, (the senate,) the states are equally represented, on the principle of the confederation, though by two senators only. But the vote in both is taken, not by states as under the confederation, but *per capita*, that is, by the head or poll, the vote of each member counting one.

§ 7. The articles of confederation were framed by congress, the members of which were appointed by the state legislatures; and the articles, when framed, were submitted for ratification to the state legislatures. The constitution was framed by a convention of delegates from the

---

§ 4. What is said of the former independence of the states? What power has the general government acquired by the constitution? § 5. How did the equality of the states in the old congress appear? To how many delegates were they entitled? How did they vote? § 6. How are the states now represented? **How** do representatives vote? § 7. State the difference between the bodies **that framed and ratified the two instruments respectively.**

states appointed for that purpose ; and was ratified, not by the state legislatures, but by state conventions whose members were elected by the people of the several states.

§ 8. The former union, as has been remarked, was a mere confederacy, composed of independent states, and united simply for purposes of defense and their mutual safety. In most respects they had no more political connection than so many different nations. The people of a state were not, properly speaking, citizens of the United States, but only citizens of the state in which they lived. But by the constitution, the people of the states were incorporated into a nation ; and a citizen of a state is also a citizen of the United States. The government of the confederation, although sometimes called the national government, was not really such, nor was it generally so regarded, as appears from the proceedings of the convention that framed the constitution.

§ 9. Among the earliest proceedings of the convention was the offering of a resolution, declaring that " a national government ought to be formed, consisting of legislative, judiciary, and executive." This resolution was strongly opposed by a large portion of the delegates, because it proposed to establish a *national* government. They were in favor of continuing the confederation with a slight enlargement of the powers of congress, so as to give that body the power to lay and collect taxes, and to regulate commerce. But the friends of a national government prevailed ; and we have now a complete government, consisting of the three departments, legislative, executive, and judicial.

§ 10. Under the confederation, there was no executive to execute the ordinances of congress ; nor a national judiciary, the state courts being used for all judicial purposes. There was only a legislature ; and that consisted of a single body, called the congress, appointed by the state legislatures, and having scarcely power enough to entitle it to the name of legislature.

§ 11. But, although the present government, with these three departments of power, and controlling, in matters of

---

§ 8. Was the government under the confederation properly *national?* How does it appear that it was not? What change did the constitution effect? § 9. What early act of the constitutional convention shows the present government to be national? § 10. What departments of power were wanting under the confederation? § 11. Is the present government wholly national? Why not?

general concern, the action of the state governments and of individuals, is properly a national government; yet it is not wholly such, but partly national and partly federal; some of the federal features of the confederation having been retained in the constitution, as will appear on a further examination of this instrument. Hence the union is still called, with propriety, the *federal union*, and the government the *federal government*

CHAPTER XXIX.

Legislative Department. House of Representatives.

§ 1. The first article of the constitution describes the manner in which the legislature is formed, and prescribes its principal powers. It declares, "All legislative powers herein granted shall be vested in a congress of the United States, which shall consist of a senate and house of representatives." Members of the old congress were appointed by the state legislatures for one year, and might be recalled by them at any time. Representatives are now chosen for two years. It was thought that a single session was too short a term for men in general to acquire the knowledge and experience necessary to a right performance of the responsible duties of a representative. Besides, measures are often left unfinished at the close of a session; and those who have once examined their merits and demerits, can dispose of them more promptly than new members.

§ 2. The same clause declares that "the electors in each state shall have the qualifications requisite for electors of the most numerous branch of the state legislature." The qualifications of electors were various in the different states. (Chap. VI, § 8.) In some of them, owners of property, or tax-payers, in others, freeholders only, were voters. In some, only the latter voted for the higher officers; in a

---

Chap. XXIX. § 1. Of what does congress consist? For what term were members of the old congress appointed? Why has the term of a representative been extended to two years? § 2. What qualifications are required for voting for representatives? What reasons were there for this rule?

few, suffrage was almost universal. It was presumed that no state would object to its own rule for electing the popular branch of its legislature. It is proper that a representative should be chosen directly by those whose wants he is to make known, and whose rights he is to guard.

§ 3. A representative must, at the time of his election, "have attained the age of twenty-five years; and have been seven years a citizen of the United States;" and he must "be an inhabitant of the state in which he is chosen." Few young men, on attaining the age of majority, have the knowledge, or experience, or wisdom, which is requisite to qualify them for the responsible duties of a representative. Nor is it to be presumed that an alien, at the earliest period at which he may become a naturalized citizen, would be sufficiently familiar with our institutions and the wants of our people to be a competent representative.

§ 4. The next clause prescribes the rule of apportionment. "Representatives and direct taxes shall be apportioned among the several states, according to their respective numbers, which shall be determined by adding to the whole number of free persons, including those bound to service for a term of years, and excluding Indians not taxed, three-fifths of all other persons." To the younger class of readers, this part of the clause needs explanation.

§ 5. The convention found it very difficult to agree upon a rule of apportionment. In the first place, the states, as will be recollected, were entitled to an equal number of delegates in the old congress; and each state had one vote. But as each member of the house of representatives was to have a vote, the small states opposed a representation according to numbers, while the large states as strenuously insisted upon it.

§ 6. In the next place, the slaveholding states claimed a representation according to numbers including slaves; the non-slaveholding states insisted on a representation according to the number of free persons. It may here be observed, that slavery then existed in all the states except Massachusetts; but as the slaves were so few in the north-

---

§ 3. What are the qualifications of a representative? Give the reasons for these qualifications. § 4. Give the rule of apportioning representatives and direct taxes. § 5, 6. What made it difficult to agree upon a rule of apportionment? In what states did slavery then exist? Name the present slaveholding states.

ern states, in which slavery has been since abolished, the latter are generally spoken of as if they were at that time non-slaveholding states. The controversy on this point rose so high, and the parties were for a long time so unyielding, that fears were entertained of a sudden dissolution of the convention.

§ 7. It became evident that the question could be settled only by compromise. The northern states consented that in ascertaining the number of persons to be taken as the basis of apportionment, three-fifths of the slaves should be added to the number of free persons. And as these states had opposed the computation of any slaves in fixing a rule of apportionment, on the ground that slaves are property, and that no property in these states entitled its owners to representation, the southern states consented, on their part, that *direct taxes* should be apportioned on the same basis as representatives.

§ 8. To illustrate this rule by an example: Suppose a state to contain 600,000 free persons, and 500,000 slaves. Adding three-fifths of the number of slaves, (300,000) to the number of free persons, gives 900,000 as the number of the representative population: and the state would be entitled to *three* representatives for every *two* that a state would have which contained 600,000 free inhabitants and no slaves. So in apportioning taxes according to population, the state in the case we have supposed, would have to raise *three* dollars for every *two* that it would raise if no slaves were counted.

§ 9. But the advantages of this arrangement are more unequal than may at first sight appear, or than was anticipated by the framers of the constitution. The benefits are chiefly on the side of the slaveholding states. In the first place, two-fifths of a large class of property in these states is exempt from taxation, while *all* the property in the free states is liable to taxation. Of this the framers were aware. But they did not foresee the fact, that the laying of direct taxes would be unnecessary, and that the slave states would consequently escape taxation for their slaves. Only three direct taxes have been laid; and it is not probable

---

§ 7. Upon what terms was the question of apportionment settled? § 8. Illustrate the rule by an example. § 9. How are the slave states benefited by this arrangement as to taxes?

that another will become necessary; the treasury being supplied from other sources, chiefly by duties on imports.

§ 10. Now, although nothing is gained by the slave states, nor is anything lost by the free states, by the exemption of the two-fifths of the slaves from taxation, since direct taxes are unnecessary; there is a great gain to the slave states, which have between thirty and forty representatives for what their laws hold to be "property to all intents and purposes whatsoever," for which the free states have nothing in return.

§ 11. The constitution does not limit the house to any definite number of representatives; it only declares that the number shall not exceed one for every 30,000 inhabitants. It requires an enumeration of the inhabitants every ten years; and the next congress thereafter determines the ratio of representation and the number of representatives, and apportions them among the states. The word *ratio* signifies rate, or proportion. It here means the number or portion of the inhabitants entitled to a representative.

§ 12. But as a representative for every 30,000 inhabitants, after the population became very numerous, would have made the house too large to transact business with due dispatch, and would have unnecessarily increased the public expense, the ratio of representation has from time to time been increased. But to whatever number the ratio may be raised, the constitution expressly declares, that "each state shall have at least one representative." Neither Delaware nor Florida had, in 1850, a population equal to the present ratio; and without the above constitutional provision, these states would have been deprived of a representation in the house, unless congress had adopted a smaller ratio.

§ 13. It will be seen by reference to the constitution, that the number of representatives was for the time fixed at sixty-five. After the first census, taken in 1790, the ratio was fixed at 33,000, which gave the house 106 mem-

---

§ 10. What do they gain as to representation? § 11. How is the number of representatives limited? How often is the ratio of representation fixed? § 12. Why has the ratio been from time to time increased? How is a representation secured to the smallest states? § 13. **State the ratio and the number of representatives after each census.**

bers. After the census of 1800, the same ratio was adopted, and the number of members was 142.

After 1810, the ratio was 35,000 ; number of members 182.
After 1820, the ratio was 40,000 ; number of members 213.
After 1830, the ratio was 47,700 ; number of members 240.
After 1840, the ratio was 70,680 ; number of members 233.

After 1850, the ratio was 93,000 and a fraction, making the number of members 233, of which California had one ; but in view of her rapid increase in population, she was allowed an additional member, making, in all, 234. Minnesota has since been admitted into the Union (1858) with two members, and Oregon (1859) with one member.

§ 14. Representatives are chosen by districts. Each state is divided by the legislature into as many districts as there are representatives to be elected in the state ; and one representative is chosen in each district. In most of the states, representatives are chosen at the general state election ; in the others, there are special elections for choosing representatives.

§ 15. By an act of congress, every territory belonging to the United States in which a government has been established, is entitled to send a delegate to congress, who has a right to take a part in the debates of the house, but not the right of voting.

CHAPTER XXX.

The Senate.

§ 1. "The senate of the United States shall be composed of two senators from each state; chosen by the legislature thereof, for six years ; and each senator shall have one vote." (Art. 1, sec. 3.) The convention readily agreed upon dividing congress into two branches ; but, as has been observed, it was difficult to settle the mode of repre-

---

§ 14. How is a state districted for choosing representatives ? When are they chosen ? § 15. How are territories represented ? Chap. XXX. § 1. How is the senate constituted ? Upon what points did the convention differ ? How was the matter settled ?

sentation. The delegates from the large states insisted upon a representation in proportion to numbers, in the senate as well as in the house; and the small states contended for equality in both branches. The debate was long and animated; and it became apparent that, as in the case of slave representation in the house, there must be a compromise. This was at length effected; the small states consenting to a proportional representation in the house, and the large states to an equal representation in the senate.

§ 2. It has been remarked, that the federative principle of the old system has been to some extent retained in the constitution. Both the equality of representation in the senate, and the election of senators by the state legislatures, are in strict conformity with the plan of the confederation, and of simple confederacies generally. Different modes of electing senators were proposed; but the one adopted by the convention seems preferable to any other.

§ 3. There is, however, in one particular, a material difference between the plan of the old congress and that of the senate. It is in the manner of voting. In the former, the vote was taken by states, each state having but one vote; (Chap. XXVIII, § 5,) in the latter, the senators vote separately, the vote of each senator counting one, as in the house; and a question is decided by the united votes of a majority of the members, and not by the vote of a majority of the states. Nor is the vote of a state lost if but one of its senators is present, as formerly. If, however, the two senators vote on different sides of a question, the effect is the same as when, in the old congress, the members from a state were equally divided.

§ 4. There were also various opinions as to the proper term of office of senators. Terms were proposed differing in length from three to nine years; and a proposition was even made by one distinguished member to make the term continue during good behavior, which is practically for life. There appear to be sound objections both to long and short terms. It is urged by those in favor of the latter, that an officer elected for a short term, especially if he de-

---

§ 2. In what provision does the federative principle appear? § 3. In what is there a difference between the old congress and the senate?

sires a reëlection, will have a strong inducement to please and faithfully serve those who are to elect or appoint him.

§ 5. Others, however, while they admit that short terms tend to insure responsibility on the part of a representative, consider this argument more than counterbalanced by the objections to which a short term is liable. Looking to a reëlection, he may act with a view to his popularity rather than to the public good. Again, the oftener a legislature is changed, the more changeable and uncertain will be the laws. Men having invested their capital in a business enterprise, and made a successful beginning under existing laws, may be ruined by a sudden and unexpected change of governmental policy.

§ 6. In view of these objections to both long and short terms, a medium term of six years was adopted. This was believed to be short enough to keep up in a senator a feeling of responsibility, and yet long enough to insure his acting independently and with a regard to the general interests of the nation Although a bad senator may occasionally be kept too long in office by a six years' term, cases also occur in which the act of a senator, especially in time of public excitement, is strongly condemned, but upon calm and mature reflection meets the public approbation.

§ 7. The next clause of the third section provides for the gradual change of the senate. One-third of the senators go out of office every two years. In favor of this arrangement are two important considerations. First, it secures to the public at all times the benefit of the experience of at least two-thirds of the body. Whereas, if the terms of all the senators expired at once, their places might be supplied mainly by new members without the requisite knowledge and experience. Secondly, while a long term is intended to guard against the too frequent changes in the laws, it may also prevent, for too long a time, the amendment or the repeal of bad laws. Such amendment or repeal may be hastened by the election of new members in the place of the one-third who retire every two years.

§ 8. Vacancies which happen in the representation of

---

§ 4, 5. What reasons are offered in favor of a short term of office? What in favor of a long term? § 6. What is said in favor of the present term? § 7 Why were not the terms of all the senators made to expire at once?

any state in the senate during the recess of its legislature, may be filled by the governor until the next meeting of the legislature. Without this provision, either the legislature must be assembled immediately to fill the vacancy, or the state must remain in part, or perhaps wholly unrepresented in the senate, until the next regular session of the legislature.

§ 9. But an appointment may not be made by an executive before the vacancy actually happens. In 1825, the term of a senator was about to expire during the recess of the legislature of his state, which had failed at its previous session to appoint a successor. As a special session of the senate was to be held immediately after the expiration of the senator's term, the governor, a few days before the term expired, in anticipation of the vacancy, reäppointed the senator. But the senate decided that, as the appointment had been made *before the vacancy happened*, the senator was not entitled to a seat.

§ 10. The next clause prescribes the qualifications of senators. A senator must have attained the age of thirty years, and been nine years a citizen of the United States; and he must, when elected, be an inhabitant of the state for which he is chosen. As many of the duties of a senator require more knowledge, experience, and stability of character than those of a representative, greater age and longer citizenship are required. The nature of these duties will be noticed in subsequent chapters.

§ 11. The seventh section of the first article provides for the passage of bills negatived, or vetoed, by the president. Bills returned by him with his objections, become laws when passed by majorities of two-thirds of both houses; that is, by two-thirds of the members present. They also become laws if not returned by him within ten days (Sundays excepted) after they have been presented to him, unless their return is prevented by the adjournment of congress.

§ 12. We have passed over several sections and clauses

---

§ 8. How are vacancies in the office of senator filled? § 9. Can an appointment be made before a vacancy actually happens? State a case. § 10. What reasons are there for the required qualifications of senators as to age, citizenship, and residence in the state? § 11. How do bills become laws after they have been vetoed by the president?

of this article without remark. Most of them are similar to some in the state constitutions, which we have noticed; and the propriety of others is so readily perceived, that any comment upon them is deemed unnecessary.

CHAPTER XXXI.

Power of Congress to lay Taxes, Duties, &c.; Power to Borrow Money.

§ 1. HAVING shown how the legislative department of the general government is constituted, we proceed to consider its powers. It is thought proper, however, first to notice one important characteristic of the general government, in which it differs from the state governments, and the knowledge of which is necessary to a right understanding of the powers of the state and national governments respectively.

§ 2. The general government is a government of *delegated* powers; that is, powers which have been intrusted or *delegated* to it by the states, or the people of the states. Having derived its powers from the states, or the people, it has such powers only as have been conferred by the constitution. Hence it is called a government of *limited* powers. The states, on the other hand, existing before the general government, and possessing entire sovereignty or supreme power, may exercise all powers which they have not surrendered to the general government. In other words, their powers are *unlimited*, except so far as they have parted with any of their original powers.

§ 3. Most of the powers of congress are enumerated in the eighth section of the first article of the constitution. The first in the list is in these words: "Congress shall have power to lay and collect taxes, duties, imposts, and excises, to pay the debts and provide for the common defense and general welfare of the United States; but all duties, imposts, and excises shall be uniform throughout the U. States."

CHAP. XXXI.—§ 2. What difference is here noticed between the general and state governments in respect to their powers? § 3. What is the first in the list of powers given to congress?

§ 4. We have already noticed the want of such a power in the old congress. The debt which had been contracted to carry on the war remained unpaid ; and congress, as we have seen, had no power to raise money either to pay debts or to defray the current expenses of the government. (Chap. XXVII : § 4, 6.) It could neither raise money by *direct* taxation ; that is, by taxing the persons and property of the citizens, nor by *indirect* taxation, which is by duties.

§ 5. *Duties, or customs*, are taxes on goods imported from, or exported to, a foreign country. *Imposts* are taxes on imported goods only. Duties on exports, however, being deemed inexpedient, are not laid by our government. An *excise* is a tax neither on imports nor exports, but on articles produced and consumed in the country, and on licenses to deal in certain commodities. The money paid for license to sell spirituous liquors is an *excise* tax.

§ 6. Duties are *specific* and *ad valorem.* A *specific* duty is a specified sum of money charged upon every yard, pound, or gallon of any commodity. Thus, a duty of ten cents on a pound of tea, or of one dollar on a yard of cloth, or of fifty cents on a gallon of wine, is a specific duty. *Ad valorem* is a Latin phrase, signifying *according to the value.* An *ad valorem* duty is a certain *per centage* on the value or price. Thus, thirty per cent. on a yard of cloth costing two dollars, is sixty cents ; on a yard costing three dollars, ninety cents ; the sum charged being varied by the difference in the price or value.

§ 7. The power to lay duties is very properly qualified by the provision that "all duties shall be uniform throughout the United States." This was intended to prevent the giving of unjust preference to any one or more states over others. Without this restriction upon the exercise of this power, the representatives of a part of the states might combine, and by laying higher duties upon goods imported into other states, than upon those imported into their own, might turn the trade chiefly into the latter. Or they might in laying duties on exports, impose high duties upon the productions of other states, and low duties, or none at all, upon the products of their own.

---

§ 4. For what purpose was this power necessary? What is *direct* and what *indirect* taxation? § 5. Define duties, customs, imposts, and excises. § 6. Define *specific* and *ad valorem* duties. § 7. Why are duties required to be uniform throughout the United States?

§ 8. Although Congress has power to lay direct taxes, it has seldom been exercised. The duties on foreign goods and on the vessels in which they were imported, have been found sufficient for the payment of the public debt, and for other government purposes. The national debt in 1791 was about $75,000,000, and, in 1804, had risen to $86,000,000; yet chiefly by duties was this debt reduced nearly one-half by the year 1812. By the war which commenced that year, the debt was again increased, being in 1816, $127,000,000. In 1835, this large debt had been, in the manner stated, entirely extinguished.

§ 9. The next power mentioned is the "power to borrow money on the credit of the United States." Although Congress may, under the power to lay taxes and duties, raise money to any extent, a large amount may sometimes be wanted before it can be raised from the regular income or revenue of the nation, or even before it could be raised by a direct tax, which would be burdensome to the people. Hence the utility of the power to borrow money until it can be reïmbursed from the national revenues

---

CHAPTER XXXII.

Power of Congress to Regulate Commerce. Commerce with Foreign Nations.

§ 1. Next in the list of powers is "the power to regulate commerce with foreign nations, and among the several states, and with the Indian tribes." The need of no power under the confederation was more deeply felt than the power to regulate foreign trade. It was the want of this power, as we have seen, which was the more immediate cause of calling the convention that framed the constitution. (Chap. XXVII: § 7–11.) The necessity of this power arose mainly from the policy of Great Britain, by which she had secured to herself undue advantages in her foreign commerce, especially in her trade with this country.

---

§ 8. By what means was the old national debt paid? How large was it at different periods? § 9. Why is the power to borrow money necessary? Chap. XXXII. § 1. From what arose the necessity of the power to regulate foreign commerce? What was the British policy?

§ 2. During the war of the revolution, the direct trade with Great Britain was interrupted. But when peace was restored, our markets were again open to British goods and vessels, while upon American produce and American vessels entering British ports, heavy duties were levied. To enable some young readers more clearly to understand the objects and the unequal operation of the policy of the British government, the subject may need some further illustration.

§ 3. One object was, to secure a market at home for the products of agricultural labor. How this is done by taxing foreign products, will appear from the following example: Suppose the market value of a bushel of wheat in Great Britain to be one dollar a bushel, and the cost of raising the article here and carrying it to that market to be the same. If now a duty of 40 cents a bushel is laid upon wheat from abroad, the English consumer, instead of buying it with this duty added, will buy of the English producer. But more wheat is produced here than there is a market for; and the American farmer must find a market abroad. But in order to sell it in the English market, he must pay 40 cents on every bushel to the British government; or, which is the same thing in effect, he must sell it for 40 cents a bushel less than its value to the British purchaser, who pays the duty to that government.

§ 4. Now, as much less American wheat will be sent to Great Britain than if it were free from duty, a better market is secured to the English farmer. Besides this, of the value of every bushel which Great Britain may please to admit, or which the people of other countries may be obliged to sell to her, 40 per cent. is paid into her treasury. Thus by one operation, are two benefits secured, namely, the reward of agricultural labor at home, and the raising of revenue. So by the duties imposed upon foreign vessels entering her ports, the national revenue was to some extent increased, and great advantages were secured to her citizens engaged in the carrying trade.

§ 5. The people of this country being nearly all employed in agriculture, and consequently dependent upon foreign

---

§ 2. In what consisted the inequality of trade between the two countries? § 3. Show, by example, how Great Britain secured a home market for her agricultural products. § 4. What other benefits did she derive from her policy?

markets for the sale of the surplus products of their labor, they were obliged to submit to the payment of these duties. And not possessing at that time the means of manufacturing to any considerable extent for themselves, goods in large quantities came in from Great Britain, for which they must pay in produce heavily burdened with duties, or with money obtained for the produce subject to these heavy duties.

§ 6. To remove the inequality in the trade between the two countries, it was thought necessary to retaliate upon Great Britain by subjecting her goods and vessels coming into our ports to the payment of duties similar to those imposed on our produce and vessels in her ports. But the power to lay duties was with the states; and, as we have seen, the states could not agree upon any effectual system; for, in order to make any system effectual, the duties must be uniform throughout the United States.

§ 7. It was intended, in regulating trade, to render our own country less dependent upon foreign nations for manufactured goods, by encouraging domestic or home manufactures by duties on goods imported. Duties laid for this purpose are called *protective* duties, being designed to *protect* our manufacturers against loss from the competition of foreigners. The nature and operation of a protective duty may be thus illustrated:

§ 8. Suppose foreign broadcloth of a certain quality is sold in this country for $2.50 a yard, and cloth of the same quality manufactured here can not be afforded for less than $3 a yard. There would now be no encouragement to any one to engage in the manufacture of such cloth; because in order to sell it, he must reduce the price to that of the foreign article, which would subject him to a loss of fifty cents a yard. Let now a duty of $1 a yard be laid upon the foreign cloth, and the price would be $3.50, and preference would be given to the domestic article, unless the importer should reduce the price of his foreign cloth to $3; in which case, it is to be presumed, about an equal quanti-

---

§ 5. Why were we obliged to submit to the payment of these duties? Why not manufacture for ourselves? § 6. Why did not our government retaliate by imposing like duties upon British goods and vessels? § 7. What are duties designed to encourage home manufactures called? § 8. Show, by example, the operation and effect of a protective duty.

ty of each would be consumed, and the duty of $1 a yard on the foreign cloth would go into the United States' treasury.

§ 9. The same objects may, to some extent, be effected by the first mentioned power, "to lay taxes, duties," &c. In laying duties for revenue, that is, raising money to pay the debts and other expenses of the government, congress may lay the duties upon those kinds of goods which it wishes to protect; and thus *indirectly* both encourage domestic industry and regulate commerce. From this it appears that the three objects mentioned may be accomplished under the grant of either one of the two general powers, to lay duties, and to regulate commerce.

§ 10. Why, then, it may be asked, were both these powers inserted in the constitution? The first *expressly* authorizes the laying of duties only to raise money for paying debts and government expenses; and protection and the regulation of commerce can only be effected *indirectly*. Hence, if our arrangements with foreign nations should be such as to render it unnecessary to lay duties to regulate commerce, or encourage domestic industry, money could not be raised without the *express* power to lay taxes, duties, &c. And such might be the state of things, that rates of duties sufficient for revenue would be insufficient for the purposes of protection and regulating trade. Therefore, both powers are properly granted to congress.

§ 11. Again, it may be asked, if foreign goods without duty can be had at lower prices than domestic, why is it not better for us to buy them than to force the manufacture and sale of our own at higher prices? and, if there is no other way of raising money, why not do it by direct taxation? Suppose, for example, as in a preceding section, (§ 8,) the price of foreign cloth to be $2.50 a yard, for which the farmer has to pay in wheat, or in cash received for it. But as the wheat has to be shipped to a foreign market, the merchant who takes it in exchange for the cloth, or the cash purchaser, deducts from the foreign market price the cost of transportation and the foreign duty, which, together, let us suppose to be fifty cents a bushel,

---

§ 9 By what other power may this object be partially effected? Show how.
§ 10 Why, then, was not one of these powers sufficient?

or one-half of the foreign market price. A yard of cloth would then cost five bushels of wheat.

§ 12 Let us now suppose a domestic article at $3 a yard to take the place of the foreign. A large portion of the laborers formerly employed in agriculture, are now engaged in building factories and in manufacturing. These, instead of being producers, have become only consumers of the wheat of the farmers, who now have a market at home, thus saving the duties and the cost of transportation. As there are now fewer producers, the price of wheat would probably be not less than $1 a bushel. Therefore a yard of domestic cloth would cost only *three* bushels of wheat, instead of *five* paid for the foreign cloth. And as there would be a corresponding rise in the price of labor, more cloth at $3 a yard could be bought for the avails of a day's labor than formerly.

§ 13. The protection of domestic industry received the early attention of congress. The second law passed by the first congress under the constitution, authorized "duties to be laid on goods, wares, and merchandises imported;" and among the objects of the law expressed in a preamble one was "the encouragement and protection of domestic manufactures." For a long time, however, little was done in the way of protection. The principal nations of Europe, England included, became involved in war. A large portion of their laboring population having been called from agricultural pursuits into the armies, a foreign demand was created for American produce; and we were enabled to supply ourselves at less disadvantage with foreign manufactures.

§ 14. But after peace had been restored in Europe, and people had returned to their usual employments, the foreign demand for our breadstuffs nearly ceased; and large quantities of foreign goods were again imported, for which our people were unable to pay. Congress now found it necessary to exercise, to a greater extent, its power to regulate trade, by discouraging importations, and encouraging domestic manufactures, and, in 1816, commenced an effective

---

§ 11, 12. Show, by example, why the free importation of foreign goods and direct taxation are not deemed the better policy. § 13. How early, and how, was domestic industry encouraged? What rendered high duties for a time unnecessary?

system of protection. Laws have from time to time been passed to favor manufactures from cotton, wool, iron, and other materials; and manufacturing is now carried on extensively in this country. By thus drawing a large portion of the people into manufacturing and mechanical employments, a market has been created at home for more grain, meat, and other agricultural products, than is required to supply all foreign demand.

§ 15. The laws relating to foreign commerce prescribe the manner of collecting the revenue. There is in every port of entry a *collector* of *customs*, who superintends the collection of duties. When a vessel arrives it is submitted, with the cargo and all papers and invoices, to the inspection of the proper officers; and the goods subject to duty are weighed and measured, and the duties estimated according to law.

CHAPTER XXXIII.

Power to regulate Commerce, continued. Navigation; Commerce among the States, and with the Indian Tribes.

§ 1. In regulating foreign commerce, congress has also passed navigation laws. *Navigation* is the art of conducting ships and other vessels. It has reference also to the rules to be observed by owners and masters engaged in the shipping trade. We have noticed the navigation acts of Great Britain by which she built up her shipping interest; (Chap. XXVII, § 7,) and we have stated that one object of the power to regulate commerce was to countervail the effects of those acts upon our shipping.

§ 2. To encourage and promote domestic navigation, an act was passed by the first congress conferring special privileges upon vessels built and owned by citizens of the

---

§ 14. What afterwards made it necessary for congress to exercise more extensively its powers to regulate trade? When did the system of protection properly commence? Where has since been the principal market for agricultural products? § 15. Where, and by whom, are the duties or customs collected? Chap. XXXIII. § 1. What is *navigation?*

United States. This was done by laying *duties on tunnage.* *Tunnage* means the content of a ship, or the burden that it will carry, which is ascertained by measurement, 42 cubic feet being allowed to a tun. This act imposed a duty of fifty cents a tun on foreign vessels, and upon our own a duty of only six cents a tun. As such a law discriminates, or makes a distinction or difference between domestic and foreign vessels, these duties are also called *discriminating* duties.

§ 3. By the aid of these protective duties, slightly changed from time to time, our shipping interest acquired great strength. But the necessity of discriminating duties no longer exists. By the stipulations of existing treaties between the principal commercial nations, each is to admit into her ports the vessels of the others on equal terms with her own. Our government having become a party to this agreement, discriminating tunnage duties have been abolished.

§ 4. The registry, however, of vessels of the United States, and other regulations concerning them, are for the most part continued. A vessel is measured by a surveyor to ascertain her tunnage, and the collector records or registers in a book her name, the port to which she belongs, her burden or tunnage, and the name of the place in which she was built, and gives to the owner or commander a certificate of such registry.

§ 5. The master of a vessel departing from the United States, bound to a foreign port, must deliver to the collector of the district, a *manifest*, which is an invoice, or account of the particulars of a cargo of goods, and of their prices or value. This statement is subscribed by the master, and sworn by him to be true. The collector then grants a *clearance* for the vessel, which is a certificate stating that the commander has cleared his vessel according to law.

§ 6. Vessels of the United States going to foreign countries, are, at the request of the masters, furnished with passports. A *passport* is a writing from the proper authority of a state or kingdom, granting permission to pass

---

§ 2. What is *tunnage?* *Tunnage duties?* For what purpose were these duties laid? Why were they called *discriminating* duties? § What has been their effect? What has caused their discontinuance? § 4. How are vessels registered? § 5. What is a *manifest?* A *clearance?*

from place to place, or to navigate some sea without hinderance or molestation. It contains the name of the vessel and that of her master, her tunnage, and the number of her crew, certifying that she belongs to the subjects of a particular state, and requiring all persons at peace with that state, to suffer her to proceed on her voyage without interruption. In this country the form of a passport is prepared by the secretary of state, and approved by the president.

§ 7. The navigation laws also provide for the safety of passengers and the crews of vessels, limiting the number of passengers on passenger vessels, and prescribing the quantity of water and certain kinds of provisions which merchant vessels are required to have for each person on board. They also declare what persons may be employed on board, and how funds shall be provided for sick and disabled seamen.

§ 8. Under the power to regulate commerce, congress has also passed laws relating to quarantines. The word *quarantine*, from the Latin *quarantina*, signifies the space of forty days. Originally vessels suspected of having contagious sickness on board, or of being infected with malignant, contagious disease, were forbidden, for forty days, to have intercourse with the place or port at which they arrived. The period for which ships are now detained is not defined, but is fixed by the proper officers at their discretion, according to circumstances. Quarantines are required by the health laws of the states ; and by the laws of congress, vessels are to be subject to the health laws of the state at whose ports they arrive.

§ 9. In connection with the power to regulate foreign commerce, power is given to regulate "commerce among the several states," or *internal* commerce. We have noticed the difficulties which attended the different commercial regulations of the states, and the necessity of a uniform system, which could be had only by giving congress alone the power to regulate commerce. (Chap. XXXI., § 7.)

§ 6. At whose request are passports furnished to vessels ? What is a *passport ?* By whom given ? § 7. How is the safety of passengers and crew provided for ? § 8. Define *quarantine.* What has congress enacted in relation to quarantines ? § 9. Why was power given to congress to regulate *internal* commerce, or commerce among the states ?

Without the power to regulate *internal* commerce, congress could not give effect to the power to regulate foreign commerce. One state might impose unjust and oppressive duties upon goods imported or exported through it by another state. But in the hands of congress, the power to regulate internal as well as foreign commerce, secures to all the states the benefits of a free and uninterrupted trade.

§ 10. In granting to congress the power to regulate commerce "with the Indian tribes," it was intended to lessen the dangers of war. Murders and war had been provoked by the improper conduct of some of the states It was believed, that, by a uniform policy, difficulties would be more likely to be prevented; and that if they should occur, they would be more likely to be amicably settled by the general government than by a state, which, being an interested party, would be more liable to misjudge the matter in dispute, and more rigid in demanding satisfaction for injuries, as well as more severe in redressing them.

CHAPTER XXXIV.

Powers of Congress in relation to Naturalization; Bankruptcy; Coining Money; Weights and Measures; Punishment of Counterfeiting.

§ 1. The next clause grants to congress the power "to establish a uniform rule of naturalization, and uniform laws on the subject of bankruptcies throughout the United States." We have already noticed some of the disqualifications of aliens. (Chap. VI., § 5.) By the common law of England and this country, aliens were not only politically disqualified, but they could not in their own name lawfully hold and sell real estate. To admit aliens to all the rights and privileges of citizens immediately on their arrival in this country, and before they shall have acquired a knowledge of our government and laws, and of the duties of citizens, would be expedient. Educated under monarchical

---

§ 10. Why the power to regulate commerce with the Indian tribes? CHAP. XXXIV. § 1. What were the disqualifications of aliens by the common law? Why are these disqualifications deemed proper?

governments, many of them, it is to be presumed, have little respect for our republican institutions, or at most but an imperfect knowledge of them.

§ 2. But to deny foreigners the rights of citizens after they shall have acquired a fixed residence here, and a knowledge of their civil and political duties, would be illiberal and unjust. Provision has therefore been made for removing their disqualifications, or for *naturalizing* them; that is, for investing them with the rights and privileges of *natural* born citizens. But if different rules were established by the different states, a person, having become naturalized in one state, would, on removing into another state, be deprived of the rights of citizenship, until he should have been naturalized by the laws of such state. Besides, by the constitution, a person, on becoming a citizen of any state, is a citizen of the United States, and entitled to the privileges of a citizen in any other state. (Art. IV., § 2.) As, therefore, there should be one uniform rule, the power of naturalization is properly given to congress.

§ 3. An alien, to become a citizen, must declare on oath before a state court or a circuit court of the United States, or before a clerk of either of said courts, after having resided three years in the United States, that it is his intention to become a citizen, and to renounce his allegiance to all foreign governments, and particularly that under which he formerly lived, and that he will support the constitution of the United States. Then after two years, the court, if satisfied that he has resided five years in the United States, and one year in the state in which the court is held, and that during that time he has behaved as a man of good moral character, and is attached to the principles of the constitution, may admit him as a citizen.

§ 4. An alien minor who has resided in the United States at least three years before he was twenty-one years of age, may, at any time after that age and five years' residence in the United States, be admitted as a citizen, without having previously declared his intention to become a citizen. Also the minor children of a naturalized citizen, if dwelling

---

§ 2. When ought they to be removed? Why should the rule of naturalization be uniform? § 3. Describe the manner in which an alien is naturalized? § 4. How do alien minors become citizens?

in the United States at the time of his naturalization, become citizens.

§ 5. A *bankrupt* is an insolvent debtor; that is, a person who is unable to pay all his just debts. A *bankrupt law* is a law which, upon an insolvent's giving up all his property to his creditors, discharges him from the payment of his debts. Such laws are designed for the benefit of honest and unfortunate debtors, who, by having the enjoyment of their future earnings secured to them, are encouraged to engage anew in industrial pursuits. But these laws, intended for the benefit of the unfortunate poor, have enabled dishonest and fraudulent debtors to procure a release from their debts.

§ 6. Experience had shown the propriety of intrusting to congress the power to make these laws. The dissimilar and conflicting laws of the different states, and the entire want of them in others, had caused great inconvenience. A debtor, though discharged from debt by the laws of one state, was liable to be prosecuted on removing into another state. Important as such laws were deemed, there is no existing law on the subject. A bankrupt law was passed in April, 1800, and repealed in December, 1803. Another was passed in 1841, which was of still shorter duration.

§ 7. The next power mentioned is the power "to coin money and regulate the value thereof." As a consequence of giving this power to Congress, we have a uniform currency throughout the union. We have also, instead of the awkward system of reckoning by pounds, shillings, and pence, the more convenient decimal mode of calculation by dollars and cents. The old system was rendered the more inconvenient by the difference in the value of a pound, shilling, and penny in the different states. A merchant in a New England state, buying goods in New York or Philadelphia, must, in order to put prices upon them, reduce the currency of the state in which he bought them to New England currency. Thus, the cost of an article being in New York two shillings and four pence a pound, would be in Connecticut one shilling and nine pence. One shilling and

---

§ 5. What is a *bankrupt?* A bankrupt law? What is the object of such laws? § 6. Why is the power to pass them given to congress? Why should they be uniform? § 7. Why is the power to coin money and regulate its value given to congress? What change in the system of reckoning has been effected?

six pence in New York would be in any New England state one shilling and a penny and a half.

§ 8. The place where money is coined is called *mint*. The principal mint in the United States, and the first that was established in this country, is at Philadelphia. The business of coining is under the superintendence of a director. Under him are a treasurer, an assayer, a chief coiner, an engraver, and a melter and refiner. The gold and silver, before it is coined, is called *bullion*. There is a branch mint in New Orleans, one at Charlotte, in North Carolina, one at Dahlonega, in Georgia, one in California, and one in the city of New York. At the place last mentioned, gold is assayed, but not coined.

§ 9. The clause containing the power last quoted, gives power also to "fix the standard of weights and measures." For the convenience of trade between the states, the standard of weights and measures should be the same in all the states. Without such uniformity, commerce among the states would meet with embarrassments scarcely less than those experienced from the want of a uniform currency. To effect the desired object, this power was given to congress.

§ 10. The next power in the list is the power "to provide for the punishment of counterfeiting the securities and current coin of the United States." By securities here are meant bonds and other evidences of debt. As the general government has the power to borrow money and to coin money, it is proper that it should also have the power to provide for punishing those who forge its written obligations for the payment of the money borrowed, and who counterfeit its coin. These offenses are tried in the courts of the United States.

---

§ 8. At what places is money coined? What is *bullion?* § 9. Why is the power to fix the standard of weights and measures vested in congress? § 10. Why has congress the power to provide for punishing the counterfeiting of the securities and coin of the United States?

CHAPTER XXXV.

Powers of Congress in relation to Post-Offices, Copy-Rights, and Patents, and Inferior Courts.

§ 1. Congress has power "to establish post-offices and post-roads." The post-office department, from the facilities which it affords for the circulation of intelligence and the transaction of business, is an institution of incalculable value to the union. It is impossible to conceive all the difficulties which would attend the exercise of this power by the different states. A uniform system of regulations is indispensable to the efficiency of this department, and could be secured only by placing this power in the hands of congress.

§ 2. Congress has power "to promote the progress of science and the useful arts, by securing, for limited times, to authors and inventors, the exclusive right to their respective writings and discoveries." Useful sciences and arts are promoted by new books and new inventions. But if every man had the right to print and sell every book or writing, without compensation to the author, there would be little to encourage men of ability to spend, as is often done, years of labor in preparing new and useful works. Nor would men of genius be likely to spend their time and money in inventing and constructing expensive machinery, if others had an equal right to make and sell the same. In pursuance of the power here given, congress has enacted laws for the benefit of authors and inventors.

§ 3. The exclusive right of an author to the benefits of the sale of his books or writings, is called *copy-right*, and is obtained thus: The author sends a printed copy of the title of his book to the clerk of the district court of the United States of the district in which the author resides. The clerk records the title in a book, for which he receives fifty cents, and gives the author, under the seal of the court, a copy of the record, for which also he receives fifty cents.

Chap. XXXV. § 1. Why is the power to establish post-offices given to congress? § 2. How are useful arts and sciences promoted? § 3. How does an author of a work proceed in procuring a copy-right? By whom, and where, is the title recorded?

§ 4. The author must also, within three months after the first publication of the work, deliver a copy of the same to the clerk of the district court. And he must cause to be printed on the title page or page immediately following, of every copy of the book, words showing that the law has been complied with. This secures to the author the sole right to print and sell his work for twenty-eight years, at the expiration of which time, he may have his right continued for fourteen years longer, by again complying with the requirements of the law as before, provided it be done within six months before the expiration of the first term, and a copy of the record published in a newspaper for the space of four weeks.

§ 5. *Patents* for new inventions are obtained at the patent office at the seat of government. This office is connected with the department of the interior. (Chap. XLI, § 7.) The commissioner of patents superintends the granting of patents under the direction of the secretary of the interior. To secure an exclusive right to an invention, the inventor must deliver to the commissioner of patents, a written description of his invention, and specify the improvement which he claims as his own discovery ; and he must make oath that he believes he is the discoverer thereof.

§ 6. Before the petition of an inventor is considered, he must pay the sum of thirty dollars. If the commissioner, upon examination, does not find that the invention had been before discovered, he issues a patent therefor. Patents are granted for the term of fourteen years, and may be renewed for a further term of seven years, if the inventor has not been able to obtain a reasonable profit from his invention.

§ 7. Congress has power "to constitute tribunals inferior to the supreme court." As the first section of the third article of the constitution, in providing for a national judiciary, authorizes congress to ordain and establish such inferior courts, the insertion of the power in this place seems to have been unnecessary. (Chap. XLII, § 1.)

---

§ 4. What else must the author do ? For how many years is the right obtained ? For what term, and how, may the right be continued ? § 5. Where are patents for inventions obtained ? How does the inventor proceed ? § 6. How much must he pay before his petition is considered ? For what term are patents granted ? For what term may they be renewed ?

CHAPTER XXXVI.

Powers of Congress in relation to Piracy and Offenses against the Law of Nations; War; Marque and Reprisal, Public Defense, District of Columbia; Implied Powers.

§ 1. The next clause grants to congress the power "to define and punish piracies and felonies committed on the high seas, and offenses against the law of nations." *Piracy* is commonly defined to be forcible robbery or depredation upon the high seas. But the term *felony* was not exactly defined by the laws of England, whence the common law of this country was derived; consequently its meaning was not the same in all the states. It was sometimes applied to capital offenses only; at other times, to all crimes above misdemeanors. For the sake of uniformity, the power to define these offenses is given to congress: and as the states have no jurisdiction beyond their own limits, it is proper that congress should have the power to punish as well as define crimes committed on the high seas.

§ 2. Nor were offenses against the law of nations more clearly defined: therefore the power to define these are with equal propriety given to congress. As our citizens are regarded by foreign nations as citizens of the United States and not as citizens of their respective states; and as the general government alone is responsible to foreign nations for injuries committed on the high seas by citizens of the United States, this power is vested in congress.

§ 3. Congress is also properly intrusted with the power "to declare war; grant letters of marque and reprisal; and make rules concerning captures on land and water." It is very evident that a single state ought not to be allowed to make war. As the people of all the states become involved in the evils of war, the power to declare it is justly given to the representatives of the whole nation. In monarchical governments this power is exercised by the king, or supreme ruler. But so important a power should

---

Chap. XXXVI. § 1. Define *piracy* and *felony*. Why is the power to define and punish these crimes given to congress? § 2. Why also the power to define and punish offenses against the law of nations? § 3. Why the power to declare war? Who exercises this power in monarchies?

not be intrusted to a single individual. The framers of the constitution have wisely intrusted it to the representatives of those who have to bear the burdens of the war.

§ 4. *Marque* means passing the frontier or limits of a country; *reprisal*, taking in return. *Letters of marque and reprisal* authorize persons injured by citizens or subjects of another nation to seize the bodies or goods of any of the citizens of such nation, and detain them until satisfaction shall be made. To permit an individual to act as judge in his own case in redressing his private wrongs would increase the dangers of war.

§ 5. Nor should a state be permitted to authorize its citizens to make reprisals; for, although such authority is designed to enable the citizens of one country to obtain redress for injuries committed by those of another, without a resort to war, the tendency of reprisals is to provoke rather than to prevent war; and as the whole nation becomes involved in a war, the power to authorize reprisals properly belongs to the general government. Indeed it is not clear that such license ought ever to be given. It does not appear strictly just to capture the bodies or goods of unoffending persons, especially before war has been declared between the two countries. But if the power to grant such license is ever to be exercised, it ought to be vested in congress.

§ 6. As congress has the power to declare war, it ought to have power to make rules concerning the property captured in time of war. The general practice is to distribute the proceeds of the property among the captors as a reward for bravery and a stimulus to exertion. But proof must be made in a court of the United States that the property was taken from the enemy, before it is condemned by the court as a prize.

§ 7. The next five clauses provide for the security and defense of the nation. The power to declare war would be of little use in the hands of congress, without power over the army, navy and militia. This had been proved by ex-

---

§ 4. What are letters of marque and reprisal? Why should not an individual redress his private wrongs? § 5. Why should not the states authorize reprisals? § 6. Why has congress the power to make rules concerning captures? How is captured property distributed? § 7. Why is the general power to provide for the national defense intrusted to congress?

perience Congress had power under the confederation to declare war; but, as we have seen, it could not raise troops, nor compel the states to raise them. To guard against similar difficulties in future, power to control the public forces was placed where it can be promptly and effectively exercised.

§ 8. The next power of congress is, "to exercise exclusive legislation over such district, not exceeding ten miles square, as may, by cession of particular states, and the acceptance of congress, become the seat of government of the United States." If the seat of the general government were within the jurisdiction of a state, congress and other public officers would be dependent on the state authority for protection in the discharge of their duties. To guard the public business more effectually against the danger of interruption, complete and exclusive power at the seat of government is given to congress. The old congress had once, near the close of the Revolution, been treated with insult and abuse while sitting at Philadelphia; and the executive authority of Pennsylvania having failed to afford protection, congress adjourned to Princeton in the State of New Jersey.

§ 9. It appears that the cession of this territory to the general government had not yet been made; but it was in contemplation by the states of Virginia and Maryland to cede it. It is called the *District of Columbia.* Its inhabitants are subject to the laws of congress. That part of the district which was ceded by Virginia, was in 1846, retroceded by congress to that state. To congress is given, with equal propriety, exclusive authority over all places purchased "for the erection of forts, magazines, arsenals, dock-yards, and other needful buildings."

§ 10. The last power granted in this section, is the power "to make all laws which shall be necessary and proper for carrying into execution the foregoing powers, and all other powers vested by this constitution in the government of the United States, or in any department or officer there-

---

§ 8. Why was given to congress entire control over the district containing the seat of government? § 9. What district is here referred to? Over what other places has congress exclusive authority? § 10. What is the last power granted in the list here enumerated? Why is this general grant of power to make laws deemed necessary?

of." As it was impossible to enumerate in the constitution every particular act which congress might find it necessary to perform, certain powers were expressly granted ; and to these powers was added this general grant of power to pass laws for carrying them into effect.

§ 11. It is the opinion of eminent statesmen that this clause confers no additional power. They hold that the power therein granted is necessarily *implied* or included in the foregoing powers. For example : The power " to regulate commerce " includes the power to cause the construction of break-waters and light-houses, the removal of obstructions from navigable rivers, and the improvement of harbors ; for in regulating and facilitating commerce, these works and improvements are absolutely necessary. So the power " to establish post-offices " implies the power to punish persons for robbing the mail. The doctrine is, " that wherever a general power to do a thing is given, every particular power for doing it is included." Hence it is inferred that congress would have had the power to pass the laws here authorized, though no express power for that purpose had been given.

§ 12. Besides the long list of powers contained in the eighth section of the first article of the constitution, and considered in preceding chapters, there are sundry other powers of congress in subsequent articles, which will be noticed in their order.

CHAPTER XXXVII.

Prohibitions on Congress.

§ 1. While the constitution confers on congress all the powers deemed necessary to be exercised for the general welfare, it imposes on congress certain restrictions, the most of which are contained in the next section. (Art. I, sec. 9.) The first prohibition is in these words : " The mi-

---

§ 11. What opinion is held by some in regard to this power ? On what reasons is this opinion founded ? Chap. XXXVII. § 1. What is the first prohibition on congress ?

gration or importation of such persons as any of the states, now existing, shall think proper to admit, shall not be prohibited by the congress prior to the year one thousand eight hundred and eight; but a tax or duty may be imposed on such importation, not exceeding ten dollars for each person."

§ 2. It is generally known that, from an early period, slaves had been imported into the colonies from Africa. At the time when the constitution was formed, laws prohibiting the foreign slave trade had been passed in all the states except North Carolina, South Carolinia, and Georgia. The delegates from these states in the convention insisted on having the privilege of importing slaves secured, by withholding from congress the power to prohibit the importation. A majority of the convention were in favor of leaving congress free to prohibit the trade at any time. But as it was doubtful whether these states would in such case accede to the constitution; and as it was desirable to bring as many states as possible into the union; it was at length agreed that the trade should be left open, and free to all the states choosing to continue it, until 1808, (twenty years;) congress being allowed, however, to lay a duty or tax of ten dollars on every slave imported.

§ 3. It has ever been a cause of wonder and regret to many, that the traffic in human beings should have been permitted by the constitution, even for the most limited period. It is, however, a gratifying fact, that congress exercised its power for terminating the foreign slave trade, at the earliest possible period. A law was passed in 1807, to go into effect in January, 1808, making it unlawful, under severe penalties, to import slaves into the United States; and in 1820, the African slave trade was by law declared *piracy*, and made punishable by death.

§ 4. The next clause is, "The privilege of the writ of *habeas corpus* shall not be suspended, unless when, in cases of rebellion or invasion, the public safety may require it." *Habeas corpus*, (Latin,) signifies, *have the body*. A person deprived of his liberty, may, before the final judgment of a

---

§ 2. To what has this reference? For what reasons was this prohibition assented to? § 3. Have men a natural right to buy and sell each other? When was the foreign slave trade prohibited? How is it now punishable? § 4. Define *habeas corpus*. What is the privilege of this writ?

court is pronounced against him, petition a court or judge, who issues a writ commanding the party imprisoning or detaining him, to produce his body and the cause of his detention before the judge or court. If the imprisonment or detention is found to be illegal, or without sufficient cause, the prisoner is set at liberty.

§ 5. The next clause declares, "No bill of attainder or *ex post facto* law shall be passed." A *bill of attainder* is an act of the legislature by which the punishment of death is inflicted upon a person for some crime, without any trial. If it inflicts a milder punishment, it is usually called a bill of pains and penalties. Such laws are inconsistent with the principles of republican government, and are therefore properly prohibited.

§ 6. An *ex post facto* law is literally a law made after an act is done, or which has effect upon an act after it is done. But it here means a law that makes punishable as a *crime*, an act which was not criminal when done. A law is also an *ex post facto* law that increases the punishment of a crime after it has been committed. If, for example, a law should be passed by which a person, having previously killed another in lawfully defending his own life, should be made to suffer death, it would be an *ex post facto* law, because killing in self-defense, before the passage of the law, was not punishable as a crime. Such also would be a law that should require all persons now charged with stealing, to be imprisoned for life, if found guilty; because the crime, when committed, was punishable by a shorter imprisonment.

§ 7. The next prohibition is, "No capitation or other direct tax shall be laid, unless in proportion to the census or enumeration herein before directed to be taken." The words *capitation* and *capital* are from the Latin *caput*, the head, or poll. Hence a *capitation-tax* or a *poll-tax*, is a tax upon each head or person. (Chap. VII. § 4.) The above clause means, that poll-taxes, if laid, must be laid in conformity to article 1st, section 2d, clause 3d, of the constitution, which requires three-fifths of the slaves to be counted in apportioning taxes among the states according to population.

---

§ 5. What is a bill of attainder? When is it a bill of pains and penalties? § 6. What is an *ex post facto* law? Give examples of ex post facto laws. § 7. What is a capitation tax? To what provision of the constitution does this prohibition refer? What does it mean?

§ 8. The next prohibition is, "No tax or duty shall be laid on articles exported from any state." Probably no law for taxing exports could be devised which would operate equally upon the interests of the different states. Of some states the principal product is cotton, rice, or tobacco; of others, grain; and of others, manufactures; and some of these products might not bear the same rates of duties as others. But though it were possible to devise a plan which would be equal in its operation, a majority of the representatives might be opposed to it. The representatives of the grain producing, and those of the planting states, might combine in imposing excessive taxes upon the productions of the manufacturing states. Or the manufacturing and the grain producing states might, with the same intent, combine against the planting states.

§ 9. As it was the purpose of the framers of the constitution to make taxation, as nearly as possible, equal in the different states, by uniform duties; and as every necessary object of indirect taxation may be attained by duties on imports; duties on exports are properly prohibited. And to secure to all the states freedom and equality in trade, it is expressly provided in the same clause, that "no preference shall be given, by any regulation of commerce or revenue, to the ports of one state over those of another; nor shall vessels bound to or from one state be obliged to enter, clear, or pay duties in another."

§ 10. The next clause provides that "no money shall be drawn from the treasury, but in consequence of appropriations made by law." This places the public money beyond the reach or control of the executive or any other officer, and secures it in the hands of the representatives of the people. In pursuance of this provision, congress, at every session, passes laws specifying the objects for which money is to be appropriated. The latter part of the clause requires, that "a regular statement and account of the receipts and expenditures of all public money shall be published from time to time." And it is by law made the duty of the sec-

---

§ 8. Why are duties on exports forbidden? How might the interests of the different states be injuriously affected by taxing exports? § 9. What further reasons are given for this prohibition? How is freedom and equality in trade secured to the states? § 10. By what provision is the proper disposal of the public moneys secured?

retary of the treasury to make to congress annually such statement, which is published by order of congress; so that the people may know for what purposes the public money is expended.

§ 11. It is next declared, that "no title of nobility shall be granted by the United States." Although the bare titles of lord, duke, &c., which are conferred upon citizens in monarchical governments, could not add to the political power of any person under our constitution; yet, as it is desirable that there should be equality of rank as well as of political rights, it is proper that congress should be prohibited from creating titles of nobility. And to guard public officers against being corrupted by foreign influence, they are forbidden to "accept of any present, emolument, office, or title of any kind whatever, from any king, prince, or foreign state."

CHAPTER XXXVIII.

Prohibitions on the States.

§ 1. The next section contains restrictions on the powers of the states. "No state shall enter into any treaty, alliance, or confederation." [For the definition of *treaty* and the manner in which a treaty is made, see Chapter XL: § 3–5.] An *alliance* is a union between two or more nations, by a treaty, or contract, for their mutual benefit. *Confederation* and *alliance* have nearly the same meaning. If the states, separately, were allowed to make treaties or form alliances with foreign powers, the rights and interests of one state might be injured by the treaties made by another state. As the states united constitute but one nation, it is obvious that the power to treat with other nations properly belongs to the general government. If the states also

---

§11. Why is the granting of titles of nobility forbidden? How are public officers guarded against corruption from foreign influence? Chap. XXXVIII. § 1. What is a treaty? An alliance? A confederation? Why are states forbidden to enter into them?

had the power, they might counteract the policy of the national government.

§ 2. Nor may a state "grant letters of marque and reprisal." If, as has been shown, this power is properly given to congress, it could not be safely intrusted to the states. (Chap. XXXVI, § 5.)

§ 3. The power to "coin money" is also prohibited to the states. It was given to the general government to secure a uniform currency. (Chap. XXXIV, § 7.) But this object would not be likely to be attained, if the power to coin money were exercised by the states.

§ 4. A state may not "emit bills of credit." *Bills of credit*, to a vast amount, were issued by the states during the war, and for some time thereafter. They were in the nature of promissory notes, issued by the authority of the state, and on the credit of the state, and put in circulation by the continental congress and the states as money. This paper money, having no funds set apart to redeem it, became almost worthless. Bank bills issued upon the credit of private individuals, do not come under the prohibition. It is also held that the prohibition does not apply to the notes or bills of a *state* bank, drawn on the credit of a particular fund set apart for that purpose.

§ 5. No state shall "make any thing but gold and silver coin a tender in payment of debts." *Tender* signifies an offer, or to offer. In law, it is an offer of something in payment of a debt, or the thing itself which is offered in payment. Some of the states had declared their irredeemable paper money a lawful tender. But paper money and property of all kinds are continually liable to fluctuation in value, and might subject those who should be compelled to receive it to great inconvenience and loss. But although no person is obliged to take in payment any thing but coin, bank bills are by common consent taken in the course of business and in payment of debts, because they may be converted into specie by presenting them at the bank by which they are issued.

---

§ 2. Why should not states issue letters of marque and reprisal? § 3. Why should they not coin money? § 4. Why were they forbidden to emit bills of credit? Does the prohibition extend to bank bills? § 5. What is meant by *tender*, usually termed *lawful* or *legal tender?* Why should coin only be made tender in payment of debts?

§ 6. Nor may a state "pass any bill of attainder, ex post facto law, or law impairing the obligation of contracts." Bills of attainder and ex post laws have been defined and considered. (Chap. XXXVII, § 5.) If these laws are in their nature wrong, the states as well as congress should be prohibited from passing them. Not less unjust are laws impairing the obligation of contracts. Laws that should weaken the force of contracts, or that would release men from their obligations, would be contrary to the principles of justice, and destroy all security to the rights of property.

§ 7. As bankrupt laws release debtors from the payment of their debts, and consequently impair the obligation of contracts, the question has arisen whether the states have power to pass insolvent or bankrupt laws. From decisions of the supreme court of the United States, which is the highest judioial authority, it appears, that a state may not pass a bankrupt law discharging a debtor from the obligation of a contract made before such law was passed. But it was not to be considered a law impairing the obligation of a contract, if it existed before the contract was made; because the parties, who are presumed to know that such law exists, may guard themselves against loss.

§ 8. The last thing prohibited in this clause, is, "to grant any title of nobility." This is forbidden to the states for the same reason as it is prohibited to congress. (Chap. XXXVII, § 11.)

§ 9. The first prohibition to the states in the next clause is to "lay any imposts or duties on imports or exports, except what may be absolutely necessary for executing their inspection laws." The objections to the power of the states to lay duties have been considered. They are founded upon the same reasons as have been given for intrusting congress with this power; one of which is to secure uniformity throughout the United States. (Chap. XXXII, § 6.) And as congress is properly prohibited from laying duties on exports, (Chap. XXXVI, § 8, 9,)

---

§ 6. Why is the passing of bills of attainder and ex post facto laws by states forbidden? Why are laws impairing the force of contracts prohibited? § 7. Do insolvent or bankrupt laws impair the obligation of contracts? States have passed such laws; were they constitutional? How has the question been decided? § 8. Why is the granting of titles forbidden to the states? § 9. What objections to the general power of the states to tax exports or imports? What exception is made to the prohibition?

there can be no good reason for allowing it to be done by the states.

§ 10. The exception allowing a state to lay duties necessary to execute its inspection laws was deemed proper. Laws are passed by the states for the inspection or examination of flour and meat in barrels, leather, and sundry other commodities in commercial cities, to ascertain their quality and quantity, and to be marked accordingly. By this means the states are enabled to improve the quality of articles produced by the labor of the country, and the articles are better fitted for sale, as the purchaser is thereby guarded against deception. A small tax is laid upon the goods inspected, to pay for their inspection. But, lest the states should carry this power so far as to injure other states, these "laws are to be subject to the revision and control of congress."

§ 11. The last restrictions upon the power of the states contained in this section, are: "No state shall, without the consent of congress, lay any duty of tunnage; keep troops or ships of war in time of peace; enter into any agreement or compact with any other state, or with a foreign power; or engage in war, unless actually invaded, or in such imminent danger as will not admit of delay." Some of the prohibitions here enumerated have been noticed in this and preceding chapters; and the reasons of the others are so obvious as to render any remarks upon them unnecessary.

CHAPTER XXXIX.

Executive Department. President and Vice-President; their Election, Qualifications, &c.

§ 1. The second article of the constitution relates to the executive department. Of the necessity of a separate and distinct power to execute the laws, we have already spoken. (Chap. VIII, § 7.) Under the confederation, as will be

---

§ 10 What is the object of this exception? § 11. What other restrictions are there upon the power of the states?

recollected, there was no national executive. This defect has been supplied by the constitution. "The executive power shall be vested in a president of the United States of America. He shall hold his office during the term of four years, and, together with the vice-president, chosen for the same term, be elected as follows." (Art. 2, § 1.)

§ 2. In regard to the organization and powers of the executive department, there was a great diversity of opinion. Ought the chief executive power to be vested in one person, or a number of persons? Laws should be executed with promptness and energy. This is more likely to be done by one man than by a number. If several were associated in the exercise of this power, disagreement and discord would be likely to happen, and to cause frequent and injurious delays. Unity being deemed favorable to energetic and prompt action, the chief executive power of the nation was given to a single person.

§ 3. Secondly, as to the duration of the office. Much of what has been said in relation to the term of office of senators, will apply to that of president. (Chap. XXX, § 4–6.) His term of office should not be so short as to induce him to act more with a view to his re-election than to the public good; yet it should be short enough to make him feel his responsibility. And it should be long enough to insure a due degree of independence, and to enable him to carry out his system of public policy. The term of four years was accordingly adopted.

§ 4. Thirdly, the mode of election. Among the various modes proposed, the one adopted was that of electing the president by electors chosen in the several states for that purpose; the number of the electors chosen in each state to be equal to the number of its senators and representatives in congress. A material alteration in the mode of election has been made since the adoption of the constitution, as will be seen by examining the two modes. (Art. 2, § 1; and Art. 12 of Amendments.) This amendment does not change the manner of choosing the electors, but the manner of choosing the president by the electors.

Chap. XXXIX. § 1. In whom is the executive power of the nation vested? § 2. For what reasons was this power given to one person only? § 3. Why were four years agreed on as the official term? § 4. By whom is the president elected? Has the mode of election ever been altered?

§ 5. The constitution does not prescribe the manner in which the electors shall be appointed or chosen ; it only declares that each state shall appoint them " in such manner as the legislature thereof shall direct." No uniform mode was adopted by the different states. In some states the electors were appointed by the legislature ; in others, by the people. At present the latter mode prevails in all the states except South Carolina, where presidential electors are still chosen by the legislature.

§ 6. The electors are, by the laws of the several states, chosen by *general ticket.* The names of two men, corresponding to the number of senators to which a state is entitled in congress, together with the names of as many others as there are representatives of the state in the lower house of congress, one to reside in each congressional district, are all placed on the same ballot ; so that every voter votes for the whole number of presidential electors to be chosen in the state. And, by a law of congress, the electors are required to be chosen in all the states on the same day, which is the Tuesday next after the first Monday of November.

§ 7. The electors so chosen are required by a law of congress, to meet in their respective states on the first Wednesday of December, and vote for president and vice-president ; and to make and sign three certificates of all the votes given by them, and seal up the same. One of these is to be sent by a person duly appointed by them, to the president of the senate at the seat of government, before the first of January next ensuing ; another is to be forwarded by mail, also directed to the president of the senate ; and the third is to be delivered to the United States judge of the district in which the electors are assembled.

§ 8. On the second Wednesday of February, the president of the senate, in presence of all the senators and representatives, opens the certificates from all the states, and the votes are counted. The person having a majority of all the electoral votes for president is elected. If no person

---

§ 5. By what authority is the manner of choosing the electors prescribed ? By whom are they chosen at present ? § 6. In what manner are they chosen ? Describe particularly the election by general ticket. When are electors chosen ? § 7. Where and when do the electors vote for president ? How, when, and to whom, are certificates of their votes sent ?

has a majority of all the electoral votes, the house of representatives must choose the president from those candidates, not exceeding three, who had the highest numbers of the electoral votes. But in so doing, the members do not all vote together ; but those of each state vote by themselves ; and the candidate who receives the votes of a majority of the representatives of a state, has but one presidential vote for such majority ; and the person who receives the votes of a majority of the states, is elected. Thus in the election of president by the house of representatives, voting is done *by states*, as was done in passing laws by the old congress. (Chap. XXVIII, § 5.)

§ 9. There have been two elections by the house of representatives. The second was 1825. The votes of the electoral colleges (assemblies) had in December, 1824, been divided upon four candidates. Andrew Jackson had received 99 electoral votes ; John Quincy Adams, 84 ; William H. Crawford, 41 ; and Henry Clay, 37. Neither having received a majority of all the electoral votes, the election devolved upon the house of representatives. Of the three candidates who had received the highest numbers of the electoral votes, Mr. Adams received in the house of representatives the votes of thirteen states ; Gen. Jackson, the votes of seven states ; and Mr. Crawford, the votes of four states. Mr. Adams having received the votes of a majority of all the states, he was elected.

§ 10. By the 12th article of amendments, if there is no election of vice-president by a majority of the electors, then, from the two highest numbers on the list, the senate shall choose the vice-president. Two-thirds of the whole number of senators shall constitute a quorum for such election ; and a majority of the whole number shall be necessary to a choice.

§ 11. To be eligible to the office of president or vice-president, a person must be a natural born citizen of the United States, thirty-five years of age, and must have been

---

§ 8. When, where, and by whom are the votes counted? How is the election determined? If no person has a majority of all the votes, by whom is the election made? How do the members vote? § 9. Describe the election of president by the house in 1825. § 10. How is the vice-president elected if there is no choice by the electors? § 11. What are the qualifications of the president and vice-president?

fourteen years a resident within the United States. The reasons for requiring long terms of citizenship and residence, and mature age and experience, in the case of senators, apply with equal force in the case of president.

§ 12. In case of a vacancy in the office of president, the vice-president becomes the president. The power of making further provision for supplying vacancies is, by the constitution, given to congress. (Art. 2, § 1.) Congress has accordingly enacted, that, when there is neither president nor vice-president, the president *pro tempore* shall act as president; and if there should be none, the speaker of the house of representatives would assume the duties of the office.

§ 13. The same section declares that the salary of the president shall neither be increased nor diminished during the time for which he shall have been elected. It would be improper to allow congress to reduce his salary at pleasure. This would make the executive dependent upon the legislature for his support. On the other hand, if his compensation could be increased during his official term, he might be tempted to use undue influence to procure a needless increase of his salary.

§ 14. The presidential term commences the 4th of March next after the election, and ends the 3d day of March four years thereafter. Each successive congress also commences and ends its term every two years, on the same days of that month; and it is called a new congress, although only one-third of the senators go out of office when a congress is said to expire, and are succeeded by new ones when the next congress is said to commence its official term.

---

§ 12. How is a vacancy in the office of president supplied? What further provision is made for supplying vacancies? § 13. Why may not the salary of a president be increased or diminished? § 14. When does the presidential term commence and expire?

CHAPTER XL.

Powers and Duties of the President; Treaties; Public Ministers; Appointments and Removals.

§ 1. The powers and duties of the president are next given. "The president shall be commander-in-chief of the army and navy of the United States, and of the militia of the several states when called into the actual service of the United States." (Art. 2, § 2.) Some of the reasons for giving to the executive the command of the public forces, have been given. (Chap. XXV, § 2, 5.) It has also been observed, that a prompt and effectual execution of the laws is best secured by intrusting this power to a single individual. (Chap. XXXVIII, § 2.) The constitution, (Art. 1, § 8, clauses 12–16,) give congress power over the army, navy, and militia, and "to provide for calling forth the militia to execute the laws of the union, suppress insurrections, and repel invasions." As this power is to be exercised upon sudden emergencies, congress has by law authorized the president to call out the militia for these purposes. And as the direction of the public forces is a power of an executive nature, it is intrusted to the executive.

§ 2. The president has also "power to grant reprieves and pardons for offenses against the United States, except in cases of impeachment." The same power is exercised by the governors of the several states. (Chap. XII, § 4.) Through partial or false testimony, or the mistakes of judges or juries, an innocent person may be convicted of crime; or facts may subsequently come to light showing the offense to be one of less aggravation than appeared on the trial. There should therefore be somewhere a power to remit the punishment, or to mitigate the sentence, or postpone its execution, as the case may seem to require; and by no other person or persons, it is presumed, would this power be more judiciously exercised than by the executive.

Chap. XL. § 1. What high military office has the president? Why is the command of the public forces intrusted to him? § 2. For what reasons the power to grant reprieves and pardons?

§ 3. The president has "power, by and with the advice and consent of the senate, to make treaties, to appoint embassadors, other public ministers and consuls, judges of the supreme court," and other officers, "provided two-thirds of the senators concur." A *treaty* is an agreement or contract between two or more nations, for regulating trade, or for restoring or preserving peace. This power ought therefore to be in the national government. In monarchical governments it belongs to the king. To confide so important a trust to the president alone, would be imprudent. To associate the house of representatives with the president and senate, as in making laws, would render it impossible to act with the decision, secrecy, and dispatch, which are sometimes necessary in making treaties.

§ 4. As the treaty-making power appears to be in its nature neither wholly executive nor wholly legislative, but to partake of the nature of both, a *part* of the legislature is properly associated with the president. As the senate, being less numerous than the house, is capable of acting more promptly as well as more easily convened and at less expense, that body is more properly united with the executive in the exercise of this power. And it is equally proper that the power to appoint embassadors and others by whom treaties are negotiated, should be placed in the same hands.

§ 5. Treaties are negotiated; that is, the provisions or terms are arranged and agreed upon, by the agents of the two governments; and a copy of the articles of agreement is sent to each government to be approved and confirmed, or, as it is usually expressed, to be *ratified*. Both governments must ratify, or the treaty fails. Treaties are ratified, on the part of our government, by the president and senate. This is what is meant by their making treaties. The persons by whom treaties are negotiated are sometimes appointed by their governments for that special purpose; but the business is perhaps more frequently done by the permanent representatives or ministers of the respective governments.

---

§ 3. What other powers has the president? For what purposes are treaties made? Who exercises this power in monarchies? Why is not the house associated with the president and senate? § 4. For what reasons is the senate preferred? Who appoint embassadors? § 5. By whom and how are treaties negotiated? By whom ratified?

§ 6. Each of the principal civilized nations has some officer at home who acts as agent in negotiating treaties and transacting business with foreign governments, and has also a representative at the seat of each foreign government for this purpose, and for keeping his government apprised of what is done abroad. Our government has a minister in Great Britain, one in Russia, one in France, one in Spain, and one in each of the other principal commercial nations; and each of these nations has a minister residing at the city of Washington, the seat of government of the United States. The officer of our government who corresponds with foreign ministers here, and with our ministers abroad, is the secretary of state. The negotiation of treaties at home with the ministers of foreign governments residing here, is done by him.

§ 7. Representatives at foreign courts have different names or titles: embassadors, envoys, ministers, and chargès des affaires. An embassador who is intrusted with the ordinary business of a minister at a foreign court, is called an *embassador in ordinary*. An *embassador extraordinary* is a person sent on a particular occasion, who returns as soon as the business on which he was sent is done. He is sometimes called *envoy;* and when he has power to act as he may deem expedient, he is called *envoy plenipotentiary;* the latter word signifying full power. An ordinary embassador or minister resides abroad, and acts in obedience to instructions sent him from time to time.

§ 8. Agents or representatives sent by our government to reside at foreign courts, are called *ministers*. Formerly those sent to the less important countries, were called *chargès des affaires*, who are ministers of a lower grade. The name, usually written chargès d'affaires, is French, and is pronounced *shar-zha-daf-fair*, accented on the first and last syllables. It means a person having charge of the affairs of his nation. It is not at present applied to any of our representatives abroad, all being called by the common name of minister.

---

§ 6. What is here mentioned as the practice of civilized nations? What are the duties of the secretary of state in our intercourse with foreign nations? § 7. What titles have representatives at foreign courts? Who are embassadors *in ordinary* and *extraordinary?* Envoys? Envoys *plenipotentiary?* § 8. What are our representatives abroad called? What are *charges des affaires?*

§ 9. *Consuls* are agents of inferior grade. They reside in foreign seaports. Their business is to aid their respective governments in their commercial transactions with the countries in which they reside, and to protect the rights, commerce, merchants, and seamen of their own nation. Hence much of their business is with masters of vessels, and with merchants. They also dispose of the personal estate of citizens of their own nation who die within their consulates, leaving no representative or partner in trade to take care of their effects.

§ 10. The appointment of judges of the supreme court by the president and senate, seems to be proper. Their election by the people, most of whom could have little or no knowledge of the persons who should be chosen, would be injudicious. Besides, the mass of the voters are not so competent to judge of the qualifications necessary for so important a judicial office, as those to whom the constitution has given the power of appointment.

§ 11. The power of appointing the head officers of the several executive departments, is with equal propriety given to the president and senate. As the president is in a measure responsible for the acts of his subordinates who conduct the business of these departments, and as, without their coöperation, he could scarcely carry out his own measures, it is proper that he should have the right of selecting them ; and by being required to submit his choice to the body of senators for their approval, a sufficient safeguard is provided against the appointment of unworthy or incompetent men.

§ 12. "The president shall have power to fill up all vacancies that may happen during the recess of the senate, by granting commissions which shall expire at the end of the next session." (Art. 2, sec. 2, clause 3.) Without such a power somewhere, the public interests would often suffer serious injury before the senate should again be in session to act upon a nomination by the president. As it is his duty to see that the business of the executive offices is

---

§ 9 What is the business of consuls ? § 10. Why is the appointment of judges of the supreme court given to the president and senate ? § 11. For what reason should the president have the right to select the heads of the departments ? § 12. What power has the president alone in filling vacancies ? Why is such a power necessary ?

faithfully done, he seems to be the proper person to make such temporary appointment.

§ 13. The powers and duties of the president enumerated in the next section of the constitution, are all necessary to insure a successful administration of the government; and they are so clearly of an executive nature, that they could not with any degree of propriety have been devolved upon any other officer or department of the government.

§ 14. The last section of this article of the constitution enumerates the persons liable to be removed from office by impeachment, and the offenses for which they are thus removable. As in the state governments, so in the general government, impeachments are made by the house of representatives, and tried by the senate. (Chap. XX, § 6–8; Cons. U. S., art. I, § 2, 3.)

CHAPTER XLI.

Auxiliary Executive Departments. Departments of State, of the Treasury, of the Interior, of War, of the Navy, of the Post-Office; Attorney-General.

§ 1. The great amount and variety of the executive business of the nation, requires the division of this department into several subordinate departments, and the distribution among them of the different kinds of public business. At the head of each of these departments is a chief officer. These chief officers, sometimes called *heads of departments*, with the attorney general, being private advisors or counselors of the president, are called the *cabinet*. They are appointed by the president and senate.

§ 2. By the first congress under the constitution, were established the state, treasury, and war departments, whose head officers, called secretaries, and the attorney-general,

---

§ 13. What other powers and duties of the president are mentioned in the constitution? § 14. What officers are removable by impeachment? and for what offenses? Chap. XLI. § 1. Among what departments is the executive business of the nation distributed? By what names are the head officers called? How appointed? § 2. What departments did the first congress establish? What officers constituted the first cabinet? When were the heads of the navy, post-office, and interior departments respectively added?

constituted the first cabinet. In 1798, the navy department was established. During president Jackson's term of office, the postmaster-general was made a cabinet officer. And the establishment, in 1849, of the department of the interior, added to the cabinet the seventh member.

§ 3. The *secretary of state* performs such duties as are committed to him by the president relating to foreign intercourse. Some of these duties have been mentioned. (Chap. XXXIX, § 6.) He conducts all our diplomatic correspondence, being the official organ of communication with the ministers of foreign governments sent to this country, and with our ministers abroad. *Diplomacy* signifies the rules and customs which govern the intercourse of nations through their ministers or agents; also the management of the business of a nation by its minister at a foreign court. And such minister, especially if he manages with ability and skill, is called a *diplomatist.*

§ 4. The secretary of state keeps the seal of the United States; and he makes out, records, and seals all civil commissions to officers appointed by the president and senate, or by the president. His duties in relation to the publishing and distributing the laws, and certain other matters, are similar to the duties of a secretary of state of a state government.

§ 5. The *secretary of the treasury* has charge of the finances of the nation. He superintends the collection of the revenue, and performs certain other duties of the nature of the controller or auditor of a state. (Chap. XIII, § 3.) He lays before congress annually a report of the finances, containing a statement of the public revenue and expenditure during the past year, the value of the imports and exports, and estimates of the revenue and expenditures for succeeding years, and plans for improving the revenues. He also makes annually a statement of appropriations of money, and of sums remaining in the treasury.

§ 6. The vast amount of business in this department requires a great number of assistants; among whom are several controllers and auditors of accounts; a treasurer,

---

§ 3. What are the duties of the secretary of state relating to foreign affairs? Define diplomacy and diplomatist. § 4. What are the duties of the secretary in relation to home affairs? § 5. What are the duties of the secretary of the treasury? § 6. What are his principal assistants?

a register, who keeps the accounts of goods imported and exported, and of the shipping employed in our foreign trade; a solicitor; a recorder; and numerous clerks.

§ 7. The *secretary of the interior* superintends the business relating to the public lands, public buildings, the lead mines and other mines of the United States, Indian affairs, patents, and pensions. A *pension* is a yearly allowance to a person by the government for past services. In this country pensions are granted for services in war. They were at first allowed only to such as had been disabled in the war of the revolution and in the war of 1812; and subsequently to all who had served at least six months in the revolutionary war, and to their widows during their lives. Those disabled in the late war with Mexico have also been added to the pension list. And by recent acts of congress, bounties of lands were to be allowed to all the surviving soldiers of the war of 1812, who had served one month therein.

§ 8. The *secretary of war* performs duties relating to military commissions, or to the land forces and warlike stores of the United States. The standing army of the nation consists at present of about 15,000 men, who are distributed among the several military stations, armed and ready for service. He reports annually a statement of the expenditure and application of moneys drawn from the treasury for his department, and makes such suggestions relative to its condition as he thinks proper. He is assisted by subordinate officers and clerks.

§ 9. The *secretary of the navy* executes the orders of the president for procuring naval stores and materials, and for equipping and employing vessels of war, and performs such other duties pertaining to the naval establishment as are required of him. Three officers are appointed by the president and senate, who constitute a board of *commissioners for the navy*, and discharge the ministerial duties of the office of the secretary, and furnish estimates of the expenditures of the department.

§ 10. The *postmaster-general* establishes post-offices, ap-

---

§ 7. What are the duties of the secretary of the interior? What is a *pension?* To what classes of persons are pensions allowed? To whom are bounties of lands allowed? § 8. To what do the duties of the secretary of war relate? § 9. What is the business of the secretary of the navy? and of the navy commissioners?

points postmasters and other persons employed in the general post-office, and provides for carrying the mails. He is assisted by three assistant post-masters-general, an auditor of the post-office treasury, to audit and settle the accounts of the department, and to superintend the collection of the debts due the department. The business of this department requires a large number of clerks. He reports annually all contracts made for the transportation of the mail, and a statement of the receipts and expenditures of the department.

§ 11. Postmasters keep an account of all letters sent from and received at their respective offices, stating the names of the offices from which letters are received, and of those to which letters are sent, and whether they are post paid or sent free. Postmasters, at stated periods, (in most places quarterly,) advertise all letters remaining in their offices ; and they send quarterly to the general post-office accounts of letters sent and received, and of moneys received for postage, and of those paid out on orders of the department. Letters also which have lain in their offices during the time for which they were required to be advertised, are sent as *dead* letters to the general post-office, where they are opened ; and such as contain money or other valuable matter are returned by mail to the writers.

§ 12. Postmasters are allowed for their services a commission on the amount of postage received by them *quarterly*. Those at whose offices the sums received are small, are allowed a greater per centage than those where the receipts are large. Thus, the commission at present (1859) is, on the first $100 received, sixty per cent. ; on the next $300, fifty per cent. ; on the next $2,000, forty per cent. ; on all over 2,400, fifteen per cent. Stamped letters are considered as paid in cash. On newspaper postages, fifty per cent. on all sums, large or small. If a postmaster's commission exceeds $2,000 a year, besides the expenses of the office, the excess is paid to the general post office.

---

§ 10. What are the principal duties of the postmaster general ? Who are his principal assistants ? § 11. What is the business of postmasters in relation to keeping accounts of letters, advertising letters, and making returns to the general post-office ? What are *dead* letters ? § 12. How are postmasters paid for their services ? State the rates of commission. To what amount of compensation are postmasters limited ? What postmasters are appointed by the president and senate ?

Postmasters may also receive for pigeon-holes or boxes, not exceeding $2,000, the excess, if any, to be paid to the general post-office. Postmasters whose compensation amounts to $1,000 or more in a year, are appointed by the president and senate.

§ 13. Postmasters whose commission on postages has been less than $200 during the preceding year, may receive and send, free of postage, letters on their own private business, weighing not more than half an ounce. And members of congress, during their term of office, and until the first of December after its expiration, may send and receive letters and packages weighing not more than two ounces, and all public documents free. A person to be entitled to send matter free, must write on the outside his name and the title of his office. This is called *franking*. Civil officers at the seat of government also may frank matter relating to the business of their offices, by marking it outside, "official business."

§ 14. The *attorney-general* attends to all suits in the supreme court of the United States in which the United States is a party or is concerned, and gives his opinions on questions of law when requested by the president or heads of departments.

CHAPTER XLII

Judicial Department.

§ 1. WE come now to the third article of the constitution. The first two sections provide for the organization, and prescribe the powers, of the courts of the United States. The want of a national judiciary was a material defect of the confederation. Dependence upon the state courts to enforce the laws of the union, subjected the government to great inconvenience and embarrassment. A government that

---

§ 13. Who are entitled to the franking privilege? and to what extent? How is franking done? What government officers frank matter on official business?
§ 14. What are the duties of the attorney-general?

has a legislature and an executive, should also have a judiciary to judge of and interpret the laws. The constitution declares that "the judicial power of the United States shall be vested in one supreme court, and in such inferior courts as the congress may ordain and establish." Under the authority here given, congress passed the judiciary act of 1789, by which the several courts of the United States were established.

§ 2. The same section declares, "The judges of both the supreme and inferior courts shall hold their offices during good behavior." In no other department of the general government are offices held for so long a term, which is virtually for life, unless removed on impeachment, or for inability. To insure a correct and impartial administration of justice, the judges should be independent. If they could be displaced at the pleasure of the appointing power, or by frequent elections, they might be tempted to conform their opinions and decisions to the wishes of those on whom they were dependent for continuance in office. The object of the framers was to remove them as far as possible from party influence.

§ 3. It is further provided, with a view to the independence of the judges, that their "compensation shall not be diminished during their continuance in office." Salaries are fixed by congress. To give congress power over the purse of an officer, is to give it power over his will. Dependence upon the legislature would be as great an evil as dependence upon the appointing power. Besides, men generally selected for high judicial offices are eminent lawyers, pursuing a lucrative professional business; and, without a liberal salary, men of the greatest ability would not accept these offices; or if in office, an essential reduction of their compensation might induce them to resign their offices.

§ 4. The next section enumerates the cases to be tried in these courts. It is evident from their nature that state courts are not the proper tribunals to try them. Also all violations of the laws of the United States are tried in the

---

CHAP. XLII. § 1. Was there a national judiciary under the confederation? In what courts is the judicial power of the U. S. vested? § 2. By whom, and for what term, are the judges appointed? Why is the term made so long? § 3. How is the independence of the judges further secured? Why should congress not have power to reduce their salaries? § 4. Cases of what nature are tried in the national courts?

national courts. Thus, the counterfeiting of United States coin, murder and other crimes committed on the sea, beyond the jurisdiction of a state, smuggling goods, that is, secretly importing dutiable goods without paying the duties, infringements of patent rights, &c., are prosecuted in courts of the United States.

§ 5. The third clause of this section declares, that "the trial of all crimes, except in cases of impeachment, shall be by jury ; and such trial shall be held in the same state where the said crimes shall have been committed." This is intended to secure the trial of the accused among his friends and acquaintances, and near the residence of his witnesses, whose attendance in a distant state could not be had without great inconvenience and expense, which might deprive him of the benefit of an important witness.

§ 6. There are three kinds of national courts : the supreme court, circuit courts, and district courts. Every state constitutes at least one district. The larger states are divided into two or more districts. In each district is a *district judge*, who holds a court four times a year. There are also in each district, a *district attorney*, to conduct suits on the part of the United States, and a *marshal*, whose business is similar to that of a sheriff. This court tries the more common civil cases, arising under the laws of the United States, and the lower crimes against the laws of the United States, committed on land and sea. This court has in some cases a jury.

§ 7. There are nine *circuits*, each embracing several states. In each circuit is a justice or a judge, who holds a court in his circuit twice a year. The district judge of the district in which a circuit court is held, sits with the circuit judge in holding a circuit court. This court tries causes between citizens of different states, between aliens and citizens, and those in which the United States are a party. It also tries some cases in appeal from the district courts. It tries matters relating to affairs on the high seas, and all felonies punishable with death. It has a grand and a petit jury.

§ 8. The *supreme court* is composed of the nine judges of

---

§ 5. Why is the trial of crimes to be held in the state where committed? § 6. Which are the lowest national courts? How is a district court constituted? What cases does it try? § 7. How many circuits are there? How is a circuit court constituted? What cases does it try?

the circuit courts, one of whom is chief-justice, the others are called associate justices. It holds one session annually at the seat of government, commencing in January or February, and continuing about two months. It will be seen from this section of the constitution, that this court has *original* jurisdiction in but few cases. Its principal business is to rejudge cases brought up from the circuit courts.

§ 9. An important object of a supreme court of the United States, is to secure a correct and uniform interpretation of the constitution and laws of the United States. State laws and decisions of state courts, are sometimes made which are supposed to be repugnant to the constitution and laws of the United States. What may be pronounced constitutional in one state, may be declared unconstitutional in another. Therefore it is provided that when an act or judgment in a case tried in the highest or last court in a state is deemed inconsistent with the constitution or laws of the United States, such case may be removed to the supreme court of the United States, whose decision governs the judgment of all inferior courts throughout the union.

CHAPTER XLIII.

Treason defined; its Punishment.

§ 1. The constitution defines treason, as follows: "Treason against the United States shall consist only in levying war against them, or in adhering to their enemies, giving them aid and comfort." Art. 3, sec. 3. A proneness to construe less aggravated crimes into acts of treason, made it proper that the constitution should define the crime. The term *levying war* has the sense here which it was understood to have in the English statute, from which it was

---

§ 8. How is the supreme court constituted? Where, and when, does it hold sessions? What is its principal business? § 9. What important object is secured by the supreme court? How are state laws and the decisions of state courts affected by the decisions of the supreme court of the United States?

adopted. An assemblage of men for a treasonable purpose, such as war against the government, or a revolution of any of its territories, and in a condition to make such war, constitutes a levying of war.

§ 2. War can be levied only by the employment of force; troops must be embodied; men must be openly raised; but there may be treason without arms, or without the application of force to the object. When war is levied, all who perform a part, however remote from the scene of action, being leagued in the conspiracy, commit treason. But a mere conspiracy to levy war is not treason. A secret, unarmed meeting of conspirators, not in force, nor in warlike form, though met for a treasonable purpose, is not treason; but these offenses are high misdemeanors.

§ 3. The constitution also prescribes the proof necessary for the conviction of treason. "No person shall be convicted of treason, unless on the testimony of two witnesses to the same overt act, or on confession in open court." No evidence less than this should be considered sufficient to convict a person of a crime for which he is to suffer death.

§ 4. "Congress shall have power to declare the punishment of treason." Art. 3, sec. 3. By the common law, the punishment of treason was of a savage and disgraceful nature. The offender was drawn to the gallows on a hurdle; hanged by the neck and cut down alive; his entrails taken out and burned while he was yet alive; his head cut off; and his body quartered. Congress, in pursuance of the power here granted, has very properly abolished this barbarous practice, and confined the punishment to simple death by hanging.

§ 5. But the same clause provides, that "no attainder of treason shall work corruption of blood, or forfeiture, except during the life of the person attainted." *Attainder* literally signifies a staining, or rendering impure; but it here means a conviction and judgment in court against the offender. By the common law, the sentence of death for treason was made to affect the *blood* of the traitor; so that

---

CHAP. XLIII. § 1. Why was the definition of treason put into the constitution? What is levying war? § 2. State more particularly what does and what does not constitute levying war and treason? § 3. What proof is required to convict of treason? § 4. How was treason punished by the common law? How has congress made it punishable?

he could neither inherit property nor transmit it to heirs ; but his estate was forfeited. This practice, so unjust to the innocent relatives of an offender, is properly abolished by the constitution ; and congress has declared that "no conviction or judgment shall work corruption of blood, or any forfeiture of estate." So that while this law continues, there is no forfeiture, even during the life of the person attainted.

CHAPTER XLIV.

State Records; Privilege of Citizens ; Fugitives ; Admission of New States; Power over Territory ; Guaranty of Republican Government.

§ 1. "Full faith and credit shall be given in each state to the public acts, records, and judicial proceedings of every other state. And the congress may, by general laws, prescribe the manner in which such acts, records, and proceedings shall be proved and the effect thereof." Art. 4, sec. 1. Without this provision, a person against whom a judgment has been obtained, might remove with his property into another state, where the property could not be taken on execution without a new trial and judgment ; which, at so great a distance from the residence of the creditor and his witnesses, would be very difficult and expensive, and perhaps impossible. Now, the proceedings of the court in which a judgment is obtained, if sent to the place where the debtor resides, have the same effect as in the state in which such proceedings were taken.

§ 2. There are several other cases which this provision is intended to meet. But, as is seen, the effect of these acts, records, and judicial proceedings, and the manner of proving them are to be prescribed by congress. In pursuance of the power here granted, congress has enacted, that a certificate under seal of the clerk of a court of record,

---

§ 5. What is attainder? Its meaning here? By the common law, how did the sentence of death for treason affect the traitor? What has congress declared concerning conviction for treason? Chap. XLIV. § 1. What is the object of the provision concerning state records?

transmitted to any state of the union, shall there be deemed evidence of the facts therein stated. But if the thing certified is a judicial proceeding, such sealed certificate must be accompanied by the certificate of the presiding judge or justice, that the attestation of the clerk is in due form. Acts of a state legislature, to be entitled to credit in another state, must have the seal of the state affixed to them.

§ 3. The next section of this article provides, that "the citizens of each state shall be entitled to all the immunities and privileges of citizens in the several states." This means that the citizens of any state going into other states, shall not, by the laws of those states, be deprived of any of the privileges of citizens; but shall be entitled to the privileges which are enjoyed by persons of the same description in the states to which they remove. Without such a provision, any state might deny to citizens coming into it from other states, the right to buy and hold real estate, or to become voters, or to enjoy equal privileges in trade or business. A state may, however, prescribe a certain term of residence therein as a qualification for voting at elections.

§ 4. The next clause of this section provides for apprehending "a person charged with crime, who shall flee from justice and be found in another state." The governor of the state from which such person has fled, sends a requisition to the governor of the state in which he is found, demanding his delivery to the proper officers, to be conveyed back for trial. Without such authority to apprehend criminals, they might escape justice by taking shelter in another state.

§ 5. In the same section it is provided, that "no person held to service or labor in one state, under the laws thereof, escaping into another, shall, in consequence of any law or regulation therein, be discharged from such service or labor, but shall be delivered up on claim of the party to whom such service or labor may be due." This clause was in-

---

§ 2. In giving effect to this provision, what has congress enacted? In case of a judicial proceeding, what is required? What in case of an act of a state legislature? § 3. What is meant by the clause concerning the privileges of citizens in the several states? Without such provision, what might a state do? § 4. How is a fugitive from justice arrested and returned for trial? § 5. Who are meant by "persons held to service or labor, escaping into another state?" What provision of the common law induced the adoption of this clause?

tended for the benefit of the slaveholding states. By the common law, a slave escaping into a non-slaveholding state became free. As it was presumed that other northern states would follow Massachusetts in abolishing slavery, the southern states wanted some provision to enable them to reclaim their fugitive slaves.

§ 6. The manner in which slaves are to be reclaimed, is prescribed by an act of congress. The owner of a runaway slave, finding him in a free state, arrests him and brings him before a magistrate ; and if he proves his title to the slave to the satisfaction of the magistrate, the slave is delivered to the owner or claimant. Free colored persons have sometimes been arrested, and, on false testimony, delivered to claimants, taken to slave states and held as slaves. Hence the opinion prevails extensively that a person claimed as a slave should be entitled to trial by a jury ; and that the fact of his being a slave should be proved to the satisfaction of a jury before his delivery to a claimant. Many persons, believing freedom to be the natural right of all men, hold that all laws for returning fugitive slaves are wrong, and ought not to be obeyed.

§ 7. The first clause of the next section provides, that "new states may be admitted into this union," and requires the consent of congress and of the states concerned, to the formation of new states from old ones. A provision of this kind was deemed necessary in view of the large extent of vacant lands within the United States, and of the inconvenient size of some of the states then existing. The territory north-west of the Ohio river had been ceded to the general government by the states claiming the same ; and a territorial government had already been established therein by the celebrated ordinance of 1787. From this territory have since been formed and admitted, the states of Ohio, Indiana, Illinois, Michigan and Wisconsin.

§ 8. South of the Ohio river also was a large tract, principally unsettled, within the chartered limits of Virginia, North Carolina and Georgia, extending west to the Missis-

---

§ 6. How are fugitives from slavery apprehended and returned? Is the law requiring the capture and return of fugitive slaves, in your opinion, morally binding? § 7. What induced the provision for admitting new states? What states have been formed from the north-western territory?

sippi river, from which, it was presumed, new states would be formed. Justice, however, to these states, as well as to others in all future time, required the general provision above mentioned, that " no state should be divided without the consent of its legislature and of congress."

§ 9. The next clause authorizes congress " to dispose of and make all needful rules and regulations respecting the territory and other property of the United States." If the general government has power to acquire territory, it must have the right to exercise authority over it. This express grant establishes beyond doubt a power which had been questioned under the confederation. In pursuance of the power here granted, congress has made rules and regulations for governing the people of different portions of such territory previously to their admission as states into the union.

§ 10. The next section declares, that " the United States shall guaranty to every state in this union a republican form of government; and shall protect each of them against invasion, and on the application of the legislature, or of the executive (when the legislature cannot be convened,) against domestic violence." Art. 4, sec. 4. The propriety of a power to prevent a state from changing its government to any other than a republican form, is evident. It is equally proper that a state, when invaded by a foreign enemy, or in case of an insurrection within its own borders, should have protection and aid from the general government; especially as the states have surrendered to it the right to keep troops or ships of war in time of peace. (Art. 1, sec. 10.)

---

§ 8. What unsettled tract was south of the Ohio? Whose consent to the division of a state does the constitution require? § 9. In the right to acquire territory, what other right is implied? Had the old congress this power? What has congress done under the power here granted? § 10. How is a republican form of government secured to the states? How are they to be protected against invasion and domestic violence? What is meant by domestic violence?

CHAPTER XLV.

Provision for Amendments; Assumption of Public Debts; Supremacy of the Constitution, &c.; Oaths and Tests; Ratification of the Constitution.

§ 1. THE 5th article provides for amending the constitution. It prescribes two different modes for proposing amendments, and two modes of ratifying them. Amendments may be proposed by two-thirds of both houses of congress; or, on the application or request of two-thirds of the states, congress shall call a convention for proposing amendments. Proposed in either of these modes, amendments, to become valid as parts of the constitution, must be ratified by the legislatures of three-fourths of the states, or by conventions in three-fourths of them; the mode of ratification, whether by the legislatures or by conventions, to be proposed by congress.

§ 2. As the best human government is imperfect, and as all the future wants and necessities of a people can not be foreseen and provided for, it is obvious that every constitution should contain some provision for its amendment. But if amendments could be made whenever desired by a bare majority of the states, the strength and efficiency of the constitution might be greatly impaired by frequent alterations. It is therefore wisely provided, that a mere proposition to amend cannot be made but by a majority of at least two-thirds of congress, or of the legislatures of at least of two-thirds of the states; and that such proposition must be ratified by a still larger majority (three-fourths) of the states. It was thought better to submit occasionally to some temporary inconvenience, than to indulge in frequent amendments of the constitution.

§ 3. The 6th article acknowledges the obligation of the general government to pay "all debts contracted before the adoption of the constitution." As has been observed, congress had borrowed money for the payment of which it

---

CHAP. XLV. § 1. How are constitutional amendments proposed? How ratified? § 2. What good is supposed to have resulted from so difficult a mode of amendment? § 3. For what reasons was the new government made to assume the debts of the old?

was unable to provide ; and one object of a change of government was to make provision for fulfilling the engagements of the nation. This clause, it is said, was also intended to allay the fears of public creditors, who apprehended that a change in the government would release the nation from its obligations.

§ 4. The next clause declares, "This constitution, and the laws made in pursuance thereof, and all treaties made under the authority of the United States, shall be the supreme law of the land, and the judges in every state shall be bound thereby, any thing in the constitution or laws of any state to the contrary notwithstanding." If all state authorities were not bound by the constitution and laws of the United States, nothing would have been gained by the union. If the laws and treaties made by the general government could be disregarded or nullified by any power in a state, why was power to make them given to the general government?

§ 5. The last clause of the 4th article requires certain officers, both of the United States and of the several states to be "bound by oath or affirmation to support this constitution." Binding the conscience of public officers by oath or solemn affirmation, has ever been considered necessary to secure a faithful performance of their duties. They are generally required to swear not only to support the constitution, but also to discharge the duties of their offices to the best of their ability.

§ 6. The same clause declares that "no religious test shall ever be required as a qualification to any office or public trust under the United States." *Test* here means an oath or a declaration in favor of or against certain religious opinions, as a qualification for office. In England, all officers, civil and military, were formerly obliged to make a declaration against transubstantiation, and to assent to the doctrines and conform to the rules of the established church. Desirous of securing to every citizen the full enjoyment of religious liberty, the introduction of tests was prohibited by the constitution.

---

§ 4. Why is the constitution of the United States, and the laws and treaties made under it, made binding above all state authority ? § 5. Why are public officers bound by oath to support the constitution, and to discharge their duties faithfully ? § 6. What is a religious *test ?* What was it in England ? Why was it forbidden by the constitution ?

§ 7. The 7th and last article declares: "The ratification of the conventions of nine states shall be sufficient for the establishment of this constitution between the states so ratifying the same." The immediate ratification of the constitution by all the states was hardly to be expected; a unanimous ratification, therefore, was not required. But a union of less than nine states was deemed inexpedient. The framers concluded their labors on the 17th of September, 1787; and in July, 1788, the ratification of New Hampshire, the ninth state, was received by congress.

§ 8. The dates of the ratifications of the several states are as follows: Delaware, December 7, 1787; Pennsylvania, December, 12, 1787; New Jersey, December 18, 1787; Georgia, January 2, 1788; Connecticut, January 9, 1788; Massachusetts, February 6, 1788; Maryland, April 28, 1788; South Carolina, May 23, 1788; New Hampshire, June 21, 1788; Virginia, June 26, 1788; New York, July 26, 1788; North Carolina, November 21, 1789; Rhode Island, May 29, 1790. The two last named states did not accede to the constitution until after proceedings under it had commenced. The ratification of North Carolina was received by congress in January, 1790; that of Rhode Island in June following.

§ 9. The first Wednesday of January, 1789, was appointed by congress for choosing electors of president in the several states, and the first Wednesday of February for the electors to meet in their respective states to elect the president. Gen. Washington was unanimously elected, and on the 30th of April was inaugurated president. Proceedings under the constitution, however, had commenced on the 4th of March preceding.

---

§ 7. What does the last article declare? Why was not the ratification of all the states required? Why was the ratification of so many as nine required? § 8. When did this state ratify? When did North Carolina and Rhode Island come into the union? § 9. When were electors of president chosen? When was the president elected, and when inaugurated? When did proceedings under the constitution commence?

CHAPTER XLVI.

Amendments to the Constitution.

§ 1. It is remarkable that, during a period of seventy years, the constitution has received so few alterations. Although twelve articles of amendment, so called, have been adopted, only two, (the 11th and 12th,) have in any manner or degree changed any of its original provisions. Most of them, it will be seen, are merely declaratory and restrictive. As the principles which they declare were so generally acknowledged, and as the general government was a government of limited powers, having such only as were expressly authorized by the constitution, the framers deemed these declarations and restrictions unnecessary. But as several of the state conventions had, at the time of adopting the constitution, expressed a desire that declarations and guaranties of certain rights should be added, in order to prevent misconstruction and abuse, the first congress, at its first session, proposed twelve amendments, ten of which were ratified by the requisite number of states. Virginia, the last state necessary to make up such number, ratified December 15, 1791.

§ 2. Freedom in matters of religion, freedom of speech and of the press, and the right to petition the government for the redress of grievances, guarantied in the first article, are rights so essential to civil liberty, and so evidently just, that it can hardly be presumed that congress would ever have passed laws directly violating these rights, even though such laws had not been prohibited.

§ 3. The second article guaranties "the right of people to bear arms." Without this right, ambitious men might, by the aid of the regular army, overthrow the liberties of the people, and usurp the powers of government.

§ 4. The third article declares, that "no soldier shall, in

Chap. XLVI. § 1. How many articles of amendment are there? What is the nature of most of them? Why then were they added? When were the first ten proposed and ratified? § 2. What is forbidden by the first amendment? § 3. What right is guarantied by the second amendment? Why is this right necessary?

time of peace, be quartered in any house without the consent of the owner, nor in time of war, but in a manner to be prescribed by law." It is a principle of the common law, that "a man's house is his own castle." Among the grievances enumerated in the Declaration of Independence, was one "for quartering large bodies of armed troops" among the people of the colonies. To secure the people against intrusions of this kind, is the object of this prohibition.

§ 5. The fourth article guaranties "the right of the people to be secure in their persons, houses, papers, and effects, against unreasonable searches and seizures." But there could be no such security, if every man could, on mere pretense or suspicion of injury, obtain a warrant for arresting his neighbor or searching his premises and seizing his property. Innocent men would often be subjected to much trouble and perplexity; and unjust suspicions would be thrown upon their characters. It is proper, therefore, that a magistrate shall not issue a warrant, unless it shall be made to appear, by the oath of the applicant or of some other person that there is probable cause.

§ 6. The rights guarantied by the fifth article are common law rights, and founded upon just principles. We have elsewhere stated the object of grand juries, and noticed the opinion of some, that this object is sufficiently secured by the examination before the magistrate; and, consequently, that grand juries are unnecessary. (See Chap. XIX, § 8–10.) But while this article continues to be a part of the constitution, grand juries in courts of the United States can not be dispensed with. It is quite proper, as is provided in this article, that, after a fair and impartial trial and an acquittal, a person should not be tried a second time. The provisions of the next article (6th) are also necessary to secure the same object—the rights of liberty and life to every citizen.

§ 7. The seventh article of amendment secures, in courts of the United States, "in suits at common law, where the

---

§ 4. What does the third amendment declare? What probably suggested it? § 5. What right is guarantied by the fourth article? What evil is it intended to prevent? § 6. What rights does the fifth article guaranty? Can you give any reason why a person fairly tried and acquitted should not be tried again? What does the sixth article require?

value in controversy shall exceed twenty dollars, the right of trial by jury." By suits at common law are meant those tried in the ordinary courts, as distinguished from those tried in courts of equity and courts of admiralty. This article further declares, that "no fact tried by a jury shall be otherwise reëxamined in any court of the United States, than according to the rules of the common law." That is, if a fact tried by a jury in a lower court, is carried up to a higher court for reëxamination, such reëxamination or new trial shall also be by jury.

§ 8. "Excessive bail shall not be required, nor excessive fines imposed, nor unusual punishments inflicted." Amend. art. 8. The object of bail and the manner in which it is given, have been stated. (Chap. XVIII.) Without the above restriction, the sum might be fixed so high as to prevent persons accused of crime from procuring the necessary sureties; whereby innocent persons might be subjected to long imprisonment before the time of trial. It is therefore properly left to the court to fix the sum, which should correspond to the aggravation of the offense. Courts have the same discretion as to the measure of punishment to be inflicted in each particular case of crime.

§ 9. The ninth amendment is, "The enumeration in the constitution of certain rights, shall not be construed to deny or disparage others retained by the people." There were persons who feared that, because the constitution mentioned certain rights as belonging to the people, those not mentioned might be considered as having been surrendered to the general government. This article was therefore inserted to prevent such a misconstruction of the constitution.

§ 10. The tenth amendment is similar to the preceding. "The powers not delegated to the United States by the constitution, nor prohibited by it to the states, are reserved to the states respectively, or to the people." In other words the powers which the constitution has not given to the general government, nor prohibited the states from exercising,

---

§ 7. What is secured by the seventh amendment? What is meant by suits at common law? What are courts of admiralty? How is the latter part of this article explained? § 8. What does the eighth article forbid? What evils was it designed to prevent? § 9. What is the ninth article? What evil was it designed to prevent? § 10. What does the tenth amendment declare? Explain it.

the states or the people have reserved to themselves. So clear is it, that they retain all power which they have not in words parted with, that it seems strange to many that the insertion of such a provision should ever have been thought necessary.

§ 11. The eleventh amendment was proposed at the first session of the third congress, March 5, 1794, and its ratification by the constitutional number of states was announced to congress by the president in a message dated January 8, 1798. This article prohibits a court of the United States from trying "any suit in law or equity commenced or prosecuted against one of the states by citizens of another state, or by citizens or subjects of any foreign state." This is intended to prevent a state from being sued in an original suit, by a private person, the citizen of another state.

§ 12. The twelfth and last amendment effects a change in the mode of electing the president and vice-president, and has been considered. (Chap. XXXIX, § 4.) This amendment was proposed at the first session of the eighth congress, December 12, 1803, and was adopted by the requisite number of states in 1804, according to a public notice by the secretary of state, dated the 25th of September of the same year.

COMMON AND STATUTORY LAW.

CHAPTER XLVII.

Rights of Persons. Personal Security; Personal Liberty; **Religious Liberty;** Liberty of Speech, and of the Press; Right of Property.

§ 1. Having taken a general view of the state governments and the government of the United States, and seen how wisely they are adapted to promote the general wel-

---

§ 11. When was the eleventh article proposed and ratified? What is it? What was it intended to prevent? § 12. What does the twelfth amendment effect? When was it proposed and ratified?

fare and secure the blessings of liberty ; we proceed to give a digest of the laws which more particularly define the rights and prescribe the duties of citizens, or by which their social and civil intercourse is to be regulated. These laws, it will be recollected, we have elsewhere called the *municipal* or *civil* laws, as distinguished from the *political* or *fundamental* law of the state. (Chap. III, § 6.)

§ 2. These laws are of two kinds, the written or statute law, and the unwritten or common law. *Statute laws* are those which are enacted by the legislature, and recorded in writing, and are usually collected and published in books. The word *statute* is from the Latin *statuo*, to set, fix, or establish.

§ 3. The *common law* is not a code of written laws enacted by a legislature, but consists of rules of action which have become binding from long usage and established custom. It is said to be founded in reason and the principles of justice. The common law of England was brought over by our ancestors, and established here before the revolution. Some of the states, in their constitutions, adopted after the revolution, declared it to be the law of their respective states ; and it has continued to be law in all the states, and is still so considered, except such parts as have been altered or repealed by constitutional or legislative enactments, or by usage.

§ 4. The most valuable rights protected by law are the rights of personal security and personal liberty. The right of *personal security* is the right to be secure from injury to our persons or good names. By *personal liberty* is meant the freedom of our bodies or persons from restraint or confinement. Provisions guarantying these rights have been incorporated into our national constitution, and the constitutions of the several states.

§. 5. The right of personal security is also protected by the law, by which a man, on showing reasonable cause of danger of personal injury, may require his adversary to be bound with sureties to keep the peace. And for violence

CHAP. XLVII. § 1. How are the municipal or civil laws distinguished from the fundamental or political law? § 2. What are statute laws? § 3. What is the common law? Is it law in this country? § 4. What are the rights of person? Personal security? Personal liberty? How are they guarantied? § 5. How may a man protect himself when in danger of personal injury? What remedy for violence committed?

committed, the offender may be prosecuted in behalf of the state and punished, and is liable also to the party aggrieved in a civil suit for damages.

§ 6. This right is further protected by the law which permits a man to exercise the natural right of self-defense. In defending his person in case of a felonious assault, he may lawfally take the life of his assailant. This is by law pronounced justifiable homicide, and is allowed also in defense of one's property against felonious and violent injury. But homicide (man-killing) is not justifiable in case of a private injury, nor upon the pretense of necessity when the party is not free from fault in bringing that necessity upon himself.

§ 7. The right to be secure in our good names, which is included in the right of personal security, is protected by the law against slander and libel. A *slander* is a false and malicious report or statement tending to injure another in his reputation or business, and which, if true, would render him unworthy of confidence or employment; or it is the maliciously charging of another with anything by which he sustains special injury. The slander of a person by words spoken, is a civil injury, that is, an injury for which redress is to be obtained in a civil suit for damages.

§ 8. A slander written or printed, is called *libel.* A libel is a malicious publication in print or writing, signs or pictures, tending to expose a person to public hatred, contempt, or ridicule. And it is considered in law a publication of such defamatory writing, though communicated to a single person. A slander written or printed is likely to have a wider circulation, to make a deeper impression, and to become more injurious. A person may therefore be liable in damages for words in print or writing, for which he would not be liable if merely spoken. In case of libel, a person is not only liable to a private suit for damages, but may be indicted and tried as for other public offenses.

§ 9. It is a principle of English common law, that in a criminal action for libel it is immaterial whether the matter of it is true or false; and a person prosecuted for libel is

---

§ 6. How far may a man go in defending himself or his property? What is such killing called? § 7. How are we protected in our good names? What is slander? § 8. What is libel? Which is considered the greater injury? For which is a person liable in both a civil and criminal suit?

not allowed, in justification, to prove to the jury the truth of his statement, since the provocation, not the falsity, is to be punished. And, whether true or false, the libelous publication is equally dangerous to the public peace, and is presumed to have been made with malicious intent.

§ 10. It is held—and perhaps it is the prevailing opinion—that in a civil action for damages, a libel must be false as well as scandalous, and, consequently, that the truth may be pleaded in justification. This point, however, is not fully settled. The reason for this distinction between cases of public and private prosecution, it is not easy to perceive. If it is just to inquire into the good or bad intentions of the publisher in one case, it would seem to be equally so in the other.

§ 11. But the common law has been materially modified and relaxed in this country. In most of the states it is provided by their constitutions or by law, that the truth may be given in evidence, and if it shall appear to the jury "that the matter charged as libelous is true, and was published with good motives and for justifiable ends, the party shall be acquitted." As it may sometimes be proper to speak or publish an unfavorable truth concerning others, the principle of the above provision would seem to be founded in justice. In the state of Vermont, and perhaps in a few other states, if the party prosecuted proves the truth of his statement in any case, he is acquitted.

§ 12. The right of *personal liberty* is secured by express provision of the national constitution, which guaranties to every citizen "the privilege of the writ of *habeas corpus*." (Cons. U. S. art. 1, sec. 9.) The nature of this writ has been explained. (Chap. XXXVI, § 4.) The same provision has been inserted in the state constitutions. This was a common law privilege, independently of any constitutional enactment. The principal object of the provision seems to be to take from congress and the state legislatures the power to abolish this privilege, or even to suspend it for any time, or in any case, except the particular cases mentioned.

---

§ 9. What is the rule of the common law in the case of a criminal action for libel? What is the reason for this principle? § 10. What distinction do some make between cases of public and private prosecution for libel? § 11. Does the common law still prevail in this country? How has it been modified? § 12. How is personal liberty secured? What is the nature of the writ of *habeas corpus*?

§ 13. Freedom of religious opinion and worship, or liberty of conscience, is a valuable personal right, included in the term, personal liberty, and is effectually secured in this country. In England, the country of our ancestors, there is a church established and supported by the government. This is sometimes called "union of church and state." The American people, from their love of religious freedom, have, in their constitutions, expressly prohibited congress from making laws "respecting the establishment of religion, or prohibiting the free exercise thereof." (Amend. art. 1. And the state constitutions have adopted similar provisions.

§ 14. Another important personal right comprehended in the term personal liberty, and guarantied in the same article of the national constitution, and in the state constitutions, is the liberty of speech and of the press. Some of the monarchical governments of Europe prohibited the people from speaking against the sovereign or his government. Books and papers could not be published until they had been examined and approved. The persons authorized to examine the manuscripts, were called *censors.* Hence the expression sometimes heard, "censorship of the press." To secure the liberty of speaking and publishing their sentiments freely upon all subjects, the people of this country have made express provision in their constitutions; which, however, while they properly guaranty this right, leave men "responsible for its abuse," and liable to prosecution for slander or libel. (§ 7, 8.)

§ 15. The *right of property* is the right to acquire property, and to be free in the use and enjoyment of it. To protect men in the enjoyment of this right, is one of the principal objects of constitutions and laws. The rights of property will constitute the subject matter of several subsequent chapters of this digest of "common and statutory law." (Chap. L, and onward.)

---

§ 13. What is liberty of conscience? How is it secured? § 14. Is this right secured to the same extent in England? § 15. What is meant by the right of property? By what is it protected?

CHAPTER XLVIII.

Domestic Relations. Husband and Wife.

§ 1. To render a marriage contract lawful, the parties must be of sufficient age, called the age of consent; which, by the common law of the land, is fourteen years in males, and twelve in females. In some states the age of consent has been altered by statute. In Ohio, Indiana, and Michigan, it has been raised to eighteen years in males, and fourteen in females; in Illinois to seventeen and fourteen; in Wisconsin, to eighteen and fifteen.

§ 2. The parties must also have sufficient understanding to transact the ordinary business of life. Idiots and lunatics cannot legally contract marriage. Persons must also act freely. If the consent of either party has been obtained by force or fraud, the marriage may be declared void. The parties must not be nearly related. The degrees of relationship at which they are forbidden to marry are in some states fixed by law; but the laws of these states on the subject are not uniform. Some states have forbidden marriages which come within what is called the Levitical degrees; but these degrees have received different interpretations. According to the interpretation of some, the relation of uncle and niece and aunt and nephew, come within this rule.

§ 3. No person can lawfully remarry who has a wife or husband living. Such second marriage is, by the common law, null and void. In some of the states, perhaps in most of them, it is declared *polygamy*, and a state prison offense, except in certain cases; as when the husband or wife of the party who remarries has been long absent, and the party re-marrying does not know the other to have been living within the time; or when the former husband or wife of the party remarrying has been sentenced to imprisonment for life; or when the former marriage has been

---

CHAP. XLVIII. § 1. What is meant by the age of consent? At what periods of life is it fixed? At what in this state? § 2. What three requisites to a lawful marriage are next mentioned? § 3. May a person remarry who has a wife or husband living? What is the crime called? What cases are excepted?

lawfully annulled or dissolved. If, however, a marriage has been annulled or dissolved for the cause of adultery, the criminal party is, in some states at least, not allowed to remarry.

§ 4. In some of the cases excepted in the preceding section, the second marriage is merely excusable. Although the party to such marriage is exempt from the *penalty*, yet if the former wife or husband is living, though the fact is unknown, and no divorce has been duly announced, or the first marriage has not been duly annulled; the second marriage is void. Where there is no statute regulation, the common law governs, which is, that nothing but death, or a decree of a competent court, can dissolve the marriage tie.

§ 5. The manner in which marriages are to be solemnized, and by whom, and the manner in which marriage licenses are to be obtained, or notices of marriage published, (which are required in some states,) are prescribed by the laws of the states in which such regulations exist. Marriages may usually be solemnized by ministers of the gospel, judges, justices of the peace, and certain other officers. But by the common law, a marriage is rendered valid by a simple consent of the parties declared before witnesses, or subsequently acknowledged; or such consent may be inferred from continual cohabitation and reputation as husband and wife.

§ 6. In law, the husband and wife are regarded as one person. By the common law, the husband, by marriage, acquires a right to the property of the wife which she had before marriage, and which she may acquire after marriage. To her personal property, including debts due her by bond, note, or otherwise, he has an absolute right, and may use and dispose of the same as he pleases. Her chattels real, however, which are leases of land for years, though personal property, he can not dispose of by will; and if he makes no disposition of them during his life time, and she outlives him, she takes them in her own right. If he survives his wife, he acquires an absolute right to them.

---

§ 4. Are the marriages in these excepted cases binding? What is the common law on the subject? § 5. How, and by whom are marriages solemnized? What regulations exist in some states? Is a license or a notice required in this state? § 6. By common law, what right to the personal property does the husband acquire by marriage?

§ 7. But to the real estate of the wife, the husband does not acquire an absolute right. He has only a right to the use, rents, and profits thereof during his life, if he shall die before his wife ; and in that event she takes the estate again in her own right. If the wife dies first, and there are no children, her heirs immediately take the estate. If there are children living, the husband holds the estate for life, and on his death it goes to the wife or her heirs.

§ 8. But this rule of the common law which gives to the husband the possession and disposal of the property of the wife, has been repealed by special enactments in most of the states. By these state laws, the real and personal property of the wife owned by her before marriage, or conveyed to her by any other person than her husband after marriage, with the rents and profits of such property, is declared to be her own, and at her disposal, and not liable for the debts of her husband, except in a few cases specified in the law of each state. In some of these states, although the property of the wife is not liable for the husband's debts, he has the control and management, and the rents and profits of it.

§ 9. As the husband, by common law, acquires, by marriage, an interest in the property of his wife, he becomes liable for her debts contracted before marriage ; but if they are not recovered of him during coverture, he is discharged. *Coverture*, in law, is the state of a married woman, considered as under *cover*, or under the power of her husband. Some of the states which have abolished the common law right of the husband to the property of the wife acquired before marriage, have also abolished the common law obligation of the husband to pay the debts of the wife contracted before marriage ; her property alone being liable for such debts.

§ 10. The husband is bound to maintain his wife, and is liable for debts which she may contract for necessaries, but for nothing more. If he refuses to provide for her wants,

§ 7. Does he acquire an absolute right also to her real estate ? How is his right limited ? § 8. How h is this common law rule been changed ? Can you tell what the law is in this state ? § 9. By common law, what liability does a husband incur by marriage ? What is coverture ? Is this now the law in all the states ? Is it in this state ? § 10. How far is a husband bound for the maintenance of his wife ?

or if, through other ill treatment or fault on his part, they become separate, he is liable to fulfill her contracts for necessaries, even though he has forbidden persons to trust her. If they part by consent, and he secures to her a separate maintenance, and pays it according to agreement, he is not liable, even for necessaries.

§ 11. The husband and wife can not be witnesses for or against each other; but any declarations made by a wife when acting as agent for her husband, may be admitted in evidence against him. In a few states, laws have been proposed, and, it is believed, in some they have been passed, removing, to some extent, this restriction upon the right of a husband or wife to the testimony of the other.

CHAPTER XLIX.

Domestic Relations, continued. Parent and Child; Guardian and Ward; Minors; Masters, Apprentices, and Servants.

§ 1. Parents, as the natural guardians of their children, are obliged to provide for their support and education during their minority, or while they are under twenty-one years of age. At twenty-one they attain the age of majority, when they are said to be *of age.* Under this age they are, in law, *infants,* or *minors.* The father, if he is able, is bound to support his minor children, even if they have property of their own; but in such case the mother is not so bound. But a husband is not obliged to maintain the child of his wife by a former husband. If, however, he takes the child into his family, he is responsible for its maintenance and education while it lives with him.

§ 2. A father may be liable for necessaries sold to a child. But to be so liable, it must be proved that the contract for the articles was made by his actual authority, or the circumstances must be sufficient to imply authority; or that neglect to provide for the child, or some other fault

---

§ 11. May they be witnesses for each other? Chap. XLIX. § 1. What are the obligations of parents? What is the age of majority? In law, who are infants, or minors?

on the part of the father, rendered assistance to the child necessary. Being bound to provide for his children, the father has a right to their labor or service; and he may recover their wages from any person employing them without his consent.

§ 3. In general, a minor cannot bind himself by contract. If he lives with his father or guardian, by whom he is properly supplied, he can not bind himself even for necessaries. But if, on contracting a debt, he agrees to pay it after he shall have become of age, he will then become liable. If a minor has no father or other guardian, his contracts for necessaries are binding upon him.

§ 4. If a minor takes an estate and agrees to pay rent, he will be liable for its payment after he shall have become of age. If he receives rents, he can not demand them again when of age. If he pays money on a contract, and enjoys the benefit of the contract and then avoids it when he comes of age, he can not recover back the consideration paid. And if he avoids an executed contract when he comes of age, on the grounds of infancy, he must restore the consideration.

§ 5. Minors are answerable for crimes, and may be indicted and tried, and, on conviction, be fined and imprisoned. They are responsible also for acts of fraud. Their age and the peculiar circumstances in which they were placed, might be such as to exempt them from liability; but in cases of gross and palpable fraud committed by minors who have arrived at the age of discretion, they would be bound by a contract.

§ 6. In general, male infants and unmarried females under eighteen years, may, of their own free will, bind themselves, in writing, to serve as *apprentices* and servants, in any trade or employment; males until the age of twenty-one, and females until the age of eighteen years, or for a shorter time. But the minor must have the consent of the father; or if the father is dead, or disqualified by law, or

---

§ 2. How far, or in what cases, is a father liable for the contracts of a child? § 3. Can a minor bind himself by contract? In what cases is he bound? § 4. How in cases of rent? How in cases of contracts which he avoids when he comes of age? § 5. Are minors answerable for crimes? How in cases of fraud? § 6. What right have they to bind themselves as apprentices and servants? By whose consent?

neglects to provide for his family, consent must be had of the mother; or, if the mother is dead or disqualified, then of the guardian.

§ 7. Pauper children may be bound out by the officers having charge of the poor. And the laws of many of the states, perhaps of most or all of them, very properly require, that a person, to whom a poor child is bound, shall agree to cause such child to be taught to read and write, and, if a male, to be also instructed in the general rules of arithmetic.

§ 8. Masters have a right to correct their apprentices with moderation for negligence and misbehavior; and they may recover damage at law of their apprentices for willful absence. On the other hand, a master may be prosecuted for ill usage to his apprentice, and for a breach of his covenant. A master is liable to pay for necessaries for his apprentice, and for medical attendance, but he is not so liable in the case of a hired servant.

§ 9. When an apprentice becomes immoral and disobedient, an investigation of the matter may be had by the proper authorities; and for good cause the indenture may be annulled, and the parties discharged from their obligations. Upon the death of a master, an apprenticeship is dissolved.

§ 10. There is, it is believed, no statute law in any state, particularly defining the rights and obligations of *hired servants* and the persons employing them. Both are obliged to fulfill their agreement. If a hired servant leaves the service of his employer, without good cause, before he has worked out the time for which he was hired, he cannot recover his wages. And for immoral conduct, willful disobedience, or habitual neglect, he may be dismissed. On the other hand, ill usage, or any failure on the part of the employer to fulfill his engagement, releases the laborer from his service.

§ 11. How far a master is answerable for the acts of his hired servant, is not clear. As a general rule, the master

---

§ 7. Who may bind pauper children? What provision is made for their education? § 8. What are the rights of the master and apprentice respectively? § 9. When may apprenticeships be dissolved? § 10. How may a hired servant forfeit his wages? For what may he be dismissed? For what cause released from his service?

is bound for contracts made, and liable for injuries done, by a servant actually engaged in the business of his master, whether the injury proceeds from negligence or from want of skill. But for an injury done by a willful act of the servant, it is considered that the master is not liable. If the servant employs another to do his business, the master is liable for the injury done by the person so employed. But a servant is accountable to his master for a breach of trust, or for negligence in business, or for injuring another person in his master's business.

CHAPTER L

Right of Property. How Title to property is acquired; Wills and Testaments Title to Property by Descent.

§ 1. Every citizen of the United States is capable of holding lands, or real estate, and of taking them by devise, descent, or purchase, and of selling and conveying away such estate. Aliens, by common law, have not this power. In many of the states, however, this disability has been removed by statute. On declaring their intention to become citizens, and complying with certain regulations, aliens acquire the right to take and hold real estate to themselves and their heirs. But they may hold and dispose of personal property without any special enactment.

§ 2. To *devise* property is to give or bequeath it by will. A *will* is a written instrument in which a person declares his will concerning the disposal of his property after his death. It is also called *testament.* This word is from the Latin *testis,* meaning witness. Hence the word has come to be applied to this instrument, which is the witness or proof of a person's will. A person making a will is called *testator;* one who dies without making a will or testament, is called *intestate.*

---

§ 11. What are the mutual liabilities of master and servant? Chap. L. § 1. By whom, and in what ways, may real estate be taken, held, and conveyed? Have aliens this right? § 2. What is it to *devise* property? What is a will, or testament? Define testator, and intestate.

§ 3. All persons of full age and sound mind, except married women, may give and bequeath real and personal estate by a last will and testament. In many of the states, personal estate may be willed at an earlier age. In a few states, females at eighteen may make a will of real and personal estate. In a few states, personal estate may be willed verbally, if the will is within a specified time reduced to writing, and subscribed by disinterested witnesses. In Ohio such will must be written within ten days after the speaking of the testamentary words. A will of this kind is called a *nuncupative* will.

§ 4. In most of the states, laws have been enacted, allowing married women to hold, in their own exclusive right, all the property, real and personal, which they owned at the time of marriage, and which they may acquire after marriage. (Chap. XLVIII, § 8.) With the right of possession is also given, it is presumed, the power of disposing of the property by will.

§ 5. A will devising real estate must be subscribed by at least two, in some states three, attending witnesses, in whose presence the testator must subscribe the will, or acknowledge that he subscribed it, and declare it to be his last will and testament. If the testator is unable to sign his will, another person may write the testator's name by his direction ; but he should sign his own name as witness to the will.

§ 6. A testator may revoke or alter his will by a later will or writing, executed in the same manner. But the second will, to revoke the former, must contain words expressly revoking it, or directing a different disposal of the property. A will may also be revoked by a sale of the property. And any alteration of the estate or interest of the testator in lands devised, is held to be an implied revocation of the will. Lands purchased after a will has been made, are not conveyed by it. As a general rule, a will is also revoked by the subsequent marriage of the testator and birth of a child, unless the wife and child have been otherwise provided for. The will of an unmarried woman is revoked by her marriage.

---

§ 3. Who may bequeath property ? What special rights to bequeath property are given in some states ? What is a nuncupative will ? § 4. How has the right of married women to bequeath property been extended ? § 5. How is a will executed ? § 6. In what different ways may a will be revoked ?

§ 7. By the statutes of some states, a child born after the death of the testator, or born in his lifetime and after the making of the will, inherits a share of the estate, as if the father had died intestate. In some other states, the statute goes further, and gives the same relief to all the children who are not provided for in the will, and who have not had their portion in the parent's lifetime.

§ 8. A *codicil* is an addition or a supplement to a will, and must be executed with the same solemnity. It is no revocation of a will, except in the precise degree in which it is inconsistent with it.

§ 9. After the death of a testator, the will is brought before the court of probate to be proved. (Chap. XX, § 5.) When a will has been duly proved and allowed, the court issues letters testamentary to the executor. An *executor* is a person named in the will of a testator to carry the will into effect. *Letters testamentary* give him the power to act in settling the estate of the deceased. If he refuses to act, or is not lawfully qualified, the court appoints a person, who, in that case, is called *administrator;* and the court issues *letters of administration* with the will annexed. Letters of administration are also issued in case of a person dying intestate. They give to the administrator the requisite authority to settle the estate.

§ 10. Taking property by *descent*, is the receiving of it from an ancestor or other relative dying intestate. If a person dies without making a will, his property falls, or *descends* to his lawful heirs. The order or rule of descent is not uniform in this country, being determined, to a great extent, by the laws of the states. In general, however, the real estate of an intestate descends, first to his lineal descendants, that is, persons descending in a direct line, as from parents to children, and from children to grandchildren. The lineal descendants most nearly related to the intestate, however distant the relation may be, takes the estate.

§ 11. If any children of an intestate are dead, and any

§ 7. What is the effect of the subsequent birth of a child? What else have some states provided? § 8. What is a codicil? Its effect? § 9. How is a will proved? What are letters testamentary, and letters of administration? § 10 What is meant by the *descent* of property? Is the rule of descent uniform in the states? To whom, generally, does it descend first?

are living, the inheritance descends to the children living, and to the descendants of the children dead, so that each child living shall receive such share as he would receive if all were living, and the children of those who are dead such share as the parents would receive if living. Thus, suppose an intestate had three sons, one of whom is dead, but has left children. In this case, each of the sons living would share one-third of the property, and the children of the deceased son the remaining third.

§ 12. But if the children are all dead, and there are grand-children living, the grand-children share equally, though not an equal number are children of each parent. If, for example, an intestate dies leaving no children, but having had two sons, one of whom had left three children, and the other two, the five share equally in the estate. The laws of Rhode Island, New Jersey, North Carolina, South Carolina, Tennessee, Louisiana, and Alabama, unless recently altered, are exceptions to this rule. In these states, and perhaps in a few others, though the children of the intestate are all dead, the grand-children do not share equally, but those of each stock, or family, take the portion which their parent would have taken if living.

§ 13. The order of descent is so different in the states, especially when there are no lineal descendants of an intestate, that it can be ascertained only by reference to the laws of each state. As a general rule, real estate passes, (1.) to the lineal descendants ; (2.) to the father ; (3.) to the mother ; (4.) to the collateral or *side* relatives, as brothers, sisters, nephews, nieces, &c. But even to this general rule there are exceptions in the laws of some states.

§ 14. The rule of descent given in the preceding sections, it will be seen, relates to *real*, and not to personal estate. The rule in regard to real estate, and that relating to personal estate, are generally somewhat different in the same state.

---

§ 11. If any children of the intestate are dead, how does it descend ? Give an example. § 12. If all the children are dead, how do the grand-children share ? Is this state an exception to the rule ? § 13. Do real and personal estate generally come under the same rule ?

CHAPTER LI

Deeds and Mortgages.

§ 1. In whatever manner a person acquires possession of real estate, whether by devise, descent, purchase, or gift, evidence of possession consists, usually, in a *deed*, which is a written instrument conveying real estate to an heir, a purchaser, or a donee. A deed of land sold, contains the names of the seller and the purchaser, the consideration, or sum paid for it, and a description of it ; and in express words grants and conveys all the interest of the seller or grantor to the purchaser and his heirs forever : and the seller affixes his name and seal to the instrument, usually in the presence of one or more subscribing witnesses.

§ 2. But a deed thus executed does not give to the purchaser sure possession of the land, until it has been duly recorded in the office of the proper recording officer of the county in which the land lies ; or in the office of the town clerk, in those states in which conveyances are required to be there recorded. If the land should be conveyed by the seller to a subsequent purchaser who should get his deed first on record, such purchaser would hold the land, unless, before purchasing, he had had notice of a sale and deed to a prior purchaser.

§ 3. In some states, a reasonable time is allowed a purchaser to get his deed recorded before he loses his right of possession by the earlier recording of another's deed. In some other states, the time is fixed by law, and varies in these different states from fifteen days to two years. But a deed, though not recorded in season to secure the title against a second purchaser, or though not recorded at all, is good against the sellor or grantor ; and the dispossessed purchaser has a lawful claim against him for the value of the land.

Chap. LI. § 1. What is the benefit of a deed of real estate? What is expressed in a deed? How is it executed? § 2. What is necessary to secure possession to the purchaser? Where are conveyances recorded in this state? § 3. How long, in some states, are first purchasers secure before recording? What is the law in this state? What claim does a purchaser thus disposssessed still retain? Can you tell why conveyances are required to be recorded at all?

§ 4. A recorder or register may not record a conveyance of land without proof that it was executed by the person named in it as the maker or grantor. This proof consists, usually, in a certificate of a proper officer, on the back or margin of the deed, stating that the person so named appeared before him, and, being duly sworn, acknowledged that he was the person who had executed the deed. In every state, judges of courts and justices of the peace, mayors of cities and aldermen, notaries public, or some of these officers, and commissioners of deeds appointed for that special purpose may take acknowledgments. In New York and a few other states, the acknowledgment may be dispensed with, and the execution of the deed may be proved by the subscribing witnesses. Deeds duly acknowledged, are, with the acknowledgments, copied by the recorder, word for word, in books provided for that purpose.

§ 5. As a person can not give a good title unless he has one himself, the seller or grantor covenants and agrees that he is seized of the premises in *fee-simple,* (meaning that he is the absolute owner,) and that he will *warrant and defend* the premises in the quiet and peaceable possession of the purchaser and his heirs forever. Hence such deed is called a *warranty deed.* [For definition of *fee* and *fee-simple,* see Chap. LIII, § 1.] A *quit-claim* deed merely conveys the interest or claim of the grantor. It contains no warranty of title against any other claimant.

§ 6. A *mortgage* is a grant of land as security for the payment of money, on condition that, if the money shall be paid according to contract, the grant shall be void. When only a part of the purchase money is paid on receiving a deed, the purchaser usually executes a mortgage to the seller, pledging the land as security for the remainder of the purchase money. And if the money shall not be paid as agreed, the land may be sold; but if sold for more than the amount due, the overplus is to be paid to the mortgager.

§ 7. To effect a full conveyance of real estate, a wife

---

§ 4. How are deeds proved? Before whom are they acknowledged? How are they recorded? § 5. What is meant by *fee-simple?* What does the grantor in a warranty deed bind himself to do? In what does such deed differ from a quit-claim deed? § 6. What is a mortgage? How is the balance of the purchase money usually secured? How is the money raised?

must join with her husband by signing the deed with him; or, in case of the husband's death in her lifetime, she would be entitled, for life, to the use of one-third of the estate. This interest of a widow in the estate of a deceased husband, is called *dower*. It is necessary also for the wife to acknowledge, before the officer taking the acknowledgment, and apart from her husband, that she signed the deed freely, and without compulsion of her husband. In some states, the acknowledgment of the wife out of the presence of her husband is not required.

CHAPTER LII.

Incorporeal Hereditaments. Right of Way; Aquatic Rights, &c.

§ 1. The term *incorporeal hereditaments* may, to some readers, need explanation. A *hereditament* is a thing capable of being inherited. Land, and all things attached to it by the course of nature or the hands of men, as trees, herbage, water, buildings, &c., which are comprehended in the term real estate, are *corporeal* hereditaments. *Incorporeal* hereditaments are inheritable rights which grow out of corporeal inheritances, or which consist in their enjoyment; as the right of pasturing a common; a right of passage over the land of another; a right to the use of waters, sometimes called *aquatic rights*, &c.

§ 2. A *right of way* is a right of private passage over another man's ground. This right is sometimes granted by the owner of the soil; and to make it a freehold right, it must be created by deed, though it be only an easement upon the land of another, and not an interest in the land itself. An *easement* is, in general, an accommodation. In law, it is any privilege or convenience which one has of

---

§ 7. Why does a wife join with her husband in a conveyance? What is the interest thus retained by a widow called? In what else must a wife join? Does a wife acknowledge apart from her husband in this state? Chap. LII. § 1. Define corporeal and incorporeal hereditaments. What are aquatic rights? § 2. What is a right of way? How is this right obtained? What is an easement?

another, by grant or otherwise, as a right of way, &c. By the grant of an easement, the grantee acquires no other right than what is necessary to the fair enjoyment of the privilege.

§ 3. If it is a mere personal right, it can be enjoyed only by the owner of the right, and when he dies, the right dies with him. But a right of way belonging to an estate may be conveyed when the land is sold. Thus, if a man owns lot A and lot B, and he used a way from lot A, over lot B, to a mill, or to a river ; and if he sells lot A with all ways and easements, the grantee will have the same privilege of passing over lot B as the grantor had.

§ 4. A right of way may arise from necessity. If a man sells a part of his land, and there is no other way to the remaining part, he is entitled to a right of way to it over the land sold. And if a man sells land wholly surrounded by his own land, the purchaser is entitled to a right of way to it over the other's ground, even though no such right is reserved. The right of way passes to the purchaser, as necessarily incident to the grant, or included in it.

§ 5. A man having license to conduct lead pipes through the land of another, may enter on the land, and dig therein, to mend the pipes. The general rule is, that when the use of a thing is granted, every thing is granted which is necessary to the enjoyment of its use.

§ 6. A person has a temporary right of way over land adjoining a public highway, if the highway is out of repair, or is obstructed by snow, a flood, or otherwise. But the right of going upon adjoining lands does not apply to private ways. A person having a right to a private way over another's land, has no right to go upon adjoining land, even though the private way is impassable.

§ 7. A right of way sometimes arises by *prescription;* which is the right or title to a thing derived from long use and enjoyment. Such is the right which, by common law, a man acquires to land which has been peaceably held by himself, or by himself and preceding owners, for twenty years. Although the first occupancy was obtained with-

§ 3. In what case does a right of way pass with the land ? Give an example. § 4. In what cases does this right arise from necessity ? § 5. When the use of a thing is granted, what is generally granted with it ? § 6. How is a temporary right of way acquired ? Does the obstruction of a private way give the same right ?

out grant, the long free use of the land is, in law, equivalent to a grant, and implies a valid title. In some states, shorter periods have been fixed by statute in which a right by prescription may be obtained. In Pennsylvania, and Ohio, the period is fixed at twenty-one years.

§ 8. The owners of land adjoining highways, have a right to the soil to the centre of the road: the public have only a right of passage while the road is continued. The owners of the soil may maintain a suit against any person who encroaches upon the road, or digs up the soil, or cuts down trees growing on the side of the road. They may carry water in pipes under it, and have every use of it that does not interfere with the rights of the public.

§ 9. Every proprietor of lands adjoining a stream, has naturally an equal right to the use of the water that flows in the stream adjacent to his lands, "as it was wont to run." Each may use the water while it runs upon his own land; but he can not unreasonably detain it, or give it another direction; and he must return it to its ordinary channel when it leaves his estate. He can not, by dams or any obstruction, cause the water injuriously to overflow the grounds of the neighbor above him, nor so use or apply it as materially to injure his neighbor below him.

§ 10. But this right to the use of waters, as an easement to the land, may be acquired and lost, or enlarged and abridged, by prescription. A man may diminish the quantity of the water, or corrupt its quality, by the exercise of certain trades; and by such use of the water for a sufficient length of time, he is in law *presumed* to have acquired it by grant: and this presumption is the foundation of his right by prescription. The time of such use and enjoyment of water necessary to establish such right is twenty years, except in states in which a different period is fixed by statute. (§ 7.)

§ 11. It is a general and established doctrine, that an

---

§ 7. What is a right by *prescription?* How many years' peaceable use gives a person such right? What change in this term has been made in some states? What is it in this state? § 8. What right have the public to the soil of a highway? Who own the soil? What right and power concerning it do they retain? § 9. What are the rights of the owners of lands adjoining a stream? How is the use of the water restricted? § 10. How may the right to the use of the water be affected by prescription?

exclusive and uninterrupted enjoyment of water, or of light, or of any other easement, in any particular way, for twenty years, or for any other period which in any particular state is the established period of limitation, is a sufficient enjoyment to raise a presumption of title as against the right of any other person. The enjoyment is deemed to have been uninterrupted, whether it has been continued from ancestor to heir, and from seller to buyer; or whether the use has been enjoyed during the entire period by one person.

§ 12. As a right may be acquired by use, so it may be lost by disuse; and as an enjoyment for twenty years, or such other period as is prescribed by statute, is necessary to establish a right; an absolute discontinuance of the use for such period will raise the presumption that the right has been released or extinguished. Thus a title to land may pass from its actual owner by non-occupancy for the period above stated; and a title to it may be acquired by an undisturbed occupant who shall hold it in peaceable and uninterrupted possession for the same period.

CHAPTER LIII.

Leases:—Estates for Life; Estates for Years; Estates at Will; Estates by Sufferance; Rent, &c.

§ 1. Real estate, the title to which is conveyed by deed, as distinguished from other estates in land, is called an *estate of inheritance*. An estate of inheritance, that is, an estate in lands that may be transmitted by the owner to his heirs, is a *fee*. No estate is deemed a fee unless it may continue forever. When it is a pure and absolute inheritance, clear of any qualification or condition, it is called a *fee-simple*.

---

§ 11, 12. What is the general and established doctrine on this subject? Must the use be enjoyed by one person during the whole period to give a prescriptive right? Chap. LIII. § 1. What is an estate of inheritance? A *fee?* A *fee-simple?*

§ 2. An interest in lands which is to continue for a limited period, is usually conveyed by a written instrument called lease. *To lease* means to let; but generally to grant the temporary possession of real estate to another for rent or reward. Sometimes the word *demise* is used for ease. The landlord, or person letting the estate, is called *lessor;* and the tenant, or person to whom the land is leased, is called *lessee.* Leases for a term longer than one year, are usually required to be sealed, and in some states, proved and recorded also, as deeds and mortgages.

§ 3. These limited interests in land are divided into estates for life, estates for years, estates at will, and estates by sufferance. An *estate for life* is an estate conveyed to a person for the term of his natural life. Life estates held by lease, however, are not common in this country. Another kind of life estate is that which is acquired, not by the acts of the parties, as by lease, but by the operation of law. Such is the right of a husband to the real estate of his wife acquired by her before or after marriage. Such also is the right of dower. (Chap. XLVIII, § 6, 7. Chap. LI, § 7.)

§ 4. An *estate for years* is a right to the possession and profits of land for a determinate period, for compensation, called rent; and it is deemed an estate for years, though the number of years should exceed the ordinary limit of human life. And if a lease should be for a less time than a year, the lessee would be ranked among tenants for years. Letting land upon shares for a single crop is not considered a lease; and possession remains in the owner.

§ 5. A lessee for years may assign over his whole interest to another, unless restrained by agreement not to assign without leave of the lessor. And he may underlet for any less number of years than he himself holds; but he is himself liable to the landlord.

§ 6. A tenant for years, whose lease expires after the land is sown or planted, and before harvest, is not entitled to the crop, if the lease is for a certain period; for, knowing that his lease would expire before harvest time, he

---

§ 2. What is the writing which conveys an interest in lands for a limited period called? What means to lease? Define lessor and lessee. What leases must be sealed? § 3. How are these limited interests in land divided? What is an estate for life? How, otherwise than by lease, are life estates acquired? § 4. What is an estate for years? § 5. May a lessee for years underlet without the lessor's leave? For how long a time?

might have avoided the loss of his labor. But if the lease for years depends upon an uncertain event, the occurring of which would terminate the lease before the expiration of the term, the tenant would be entitled to the crop, if there were time to reap what has been sown, in case he should live. It is believed that, in a few states, the tenant has a right to the crop from grain sown in the autumn before the expiration of the lease, and cut the next summer after its expiration.

§ 7. Where there is an express agreement to pay rent, the tenant can not avoid payment even if the premises are destroyed by fire or flood, or if he is in any other manner deprived of their enjoyment and use, even without any default on his part. Hence, if land should be leased with a flock of sheep, and the sheep should die, the full rent must be paid. But if the land should be recovered from the tenant by a person having a better title than that derived from his landlord, he is not liable for rent after his use of the land has ceased.

§ 8. A tenant can not make repairs at the expense of the landlord, or deduct the cost of them out of the rent, unless by special agreement. But if the premises, from want of repair, have become unsafe or useless, the tenant from year to year may quit without notice ; and he would not be liable for rent after the use had ceased to be beneficial.

§ 9. When rent is due, payment may be made or tendered upon the premises ; and if no place of payment has been agreed on, a personal tender off the land is also good. As to the time of payment, where there is no special agreement to the contrary, rent is due yearly, half-yearly, or quarterly, according to the usage of the country. Where there is no particular usage, the rent is due at the end of the year.

§ 10. An *estate at will* is where land is let to another, to hold at the will of the lessor. Tenancies at will, strictly such, are not common. Such estates, when no certain term is agreed on, are construed to be tenancies from year

---

§ 6. Who is entitled to the growing crop if the lease expires before harvest? In what case the tenant? § 7. Does the destruction of rented premises release the tenant from payment of rent? In what case would he not be liable? § 8. Can a tenant charge his landlord for repairs? What may he do when the premises have become unsafe or useless? § 9. Where and when must payment of rent be made or tendered?

to year, and each party is bound to give reasonable notice of an intention to terminate the lease. If the tenant holds over after the expiration of a lease for years, either by express consent, or under circumstances implying consent, it is held to be evidence of a new contract without any definite period, and is construed to be a tenancy from year to year: and in those states where the old English rule prevails, six months' notice must be given the tenant to quit.

§ 11. What turns leases for uncertain terms into leases from year to year, is the landlord's reserving annual rent. A tenant placed on land without any terms prescribed or rent reserved, is strictly a tenant at will; and it has been held that such tenant is not entitled to notice to quit; but the general rule now seems to be, that even in such case the six months' notice is necessary; or, as in some states, a reasonable notice.

§ 12. An *estate at sufferance* is that which is acquired by a tenant who has come into lawful possession of land, but who holds over by wrong after his interest has ceased. He is not entitled to notice to quit; and where there is no special statute, he is not liable for rent; and the landlord may enter, and remove the tenant and his goods with such gentle force as may be necessary. If undue force is used, the landlord would be liable to an action for forcible entry and detainer.

CHAPTER LIV

Contracts in General

§ 1. A *contract* is an agreement between two or more persons, by which the parties agree to do, or not to do, a particular thing. Contracts are *executory*, when the stipula-

§ 10. What is an estate at will? Are such estates common? In what case are they held to be tenancies from year to year? What if a tenant for years hold over after his lease? § 11. What turns leases from uncertain terms into leases from year to year? Who is strictly a tenant at will? Can he be dispossessed without previous notice to quit? § 12. What is an estate at sufferance? What are the rights of a landlord and a tenant by sufferance, respectively?

tions remain to be executed, or when one party agrees to sell and deliver, at a future time, for a stipulated price, and the other agrees to accept and pay. Contracts are *express*, when the parties contract in express words, or by writing; *implied*, when an act has been done which shows that the parties must have intended to contract; as, when a person employs another to do some service, it is presumed that the party employing intended to pay for the labor performed.

§ 2. Contracts are also distinguished as specialties and simple contracts. A *specialty* is a contract under seal; as a deed, or a bond. But we shall here consider chiefly that common class of contracts called *simple contracts*, or *contracts by parol*. *Parol* signifies by word of mouth. Applied to contracts, however, it not only means verbal contracts, but includes written contracts not under seal. Both are simple contracts; the distinction between them is in the mode of proof. The mutual understanding of the parties to a verbal contract may be proved by parol evidence. But as the real intention of parties is more likely to be expressed in a written contract, the rule of law is, that parol evidence may not be admitted to contradict or vary the terms of a written instrument. It may however be admitted to explain what is doubtful, or to supply some deficiency.

§ 3. To make a valid contract, *the parties must be capable of contracting*. They must be of sound mind. Hence idiots and lunatics are generally incompetent to make contracts. Contracts by lunatics and idiots are not necessarily void, but only *voidable;* the validity or invalidity depending upon facts to be proved. To avoid a contract on the ground of mental imbecility, it must be proved that the party contracting was at the time incompetent. But if a general derangement is once established or conceded, the person is presumed to be incompetent; and the party seeking to enforce the contract must prove the other to have been sane. The general rule in the case of idiots is, that if the party is incapable of acting in the ordinary affairs of life, or in the particular contract, his idiocy will annul the contract.

CHAP. LIV. § 1. Define contract. What is an executory contract? An express contract? An implied contract? § 2. What is a specialty? A simple or parol contract? Define *parol*. What effect has parol evidence upon written contracts? § 3. Who are deemed incapable of contracting? How are contracts made by such persons voided? How enforced? What is the general rule?

§ 4. Drunkards also are incompetent to contract while in a state of intoxication, provided the drunkenness is such as to deprive them of reason for a time, and create impotence of mind. But for absolute necessaries, if the drunkard consumes them during his drunkenness, or keeps them after becoming sober, he is liable. Intoxication only renders a contract voidable, not void, as the party intoxicated may adopt it on recovering his understanding.

§ 5. Another requisition to a valid contract, is the *mutual assent of the parties.* A mere offer by one party not assented to or accepted by the other, constitutes no contract. Assent must also be given freely. A contract entered into under duress, or compulsion, is not binding ; as where assent is extorted by threats of personal injury. Assent must also be given with a knowledge of facts. A contract made under an injurious mistake, or ignorance of a material fact, may be avoided, even though the fact is not fraudulently concealed. But a mistake made through ignorance of the law, will not render a contract void.

§ 6. A *valuable consideration* also is necessary to a valid contract. A *consideration* is what is given or done, or to be given or done, as the cause or reason for which a person enters into an agreement. Thus, the money given or offered, for which a man agrees to perform certain labor, is the consideration of the agreement. So the money or other thing for which a promissory note is given, is the consideration. A valuable consideration is any thing that is either a benefit to the party promising, or some trouble or injury to the party to whom the promise is made.

§ 7. Mutual promises are sufficient considerations to make a contract binding ; but they must be made at the same time. Such promises support each other. The promise of one party constitutes a sufficient consideration for a promise by the other party. In case the parties are distant from each other, if the proposition is made in writing and sent by mail, and a letter of acceptance is written and put in the mail, the contract is complete, unless, before

---

§ 4. What is the rule in regard to drunkards ? § 5. What is mentioned as the second requisition to a valid contract ? How must assent be given ? § 6. What is next mentioned as necessary to a valid contract ? What is a consideration ? § 7. What is the effect of mutual promises ? How must they be made ? How when the parties are distant ?

mailing the letter of acceptance, a second letter has been received containing a retraction of the proposal.

§ 8. Promises which are wholly gratuitous are void; because, being neither a benefit to the promiser, nor an injury to the promisee, they are not regarded in law as a valuable consideration. Hence, subscriptions to public works and charitable, literary, and religious institutions, if they are merely gratuitous, can not be collected, unless they have operated to induce others to advance money, make engagements, or do other acts to their own injury.

§ 9. As gratuitous promises are void for want of consideration, so merely gratuitous services, as voluntarily assisting to save property from fire, or securing beasts found straying, or paying another's debts without request, afford no consideration upon which payment for their value can be lawfully claimed; there being no promise of compensation. But if a person knowingly permits another to do certain work, as plowing his field, or hoeing his corn, although the work may have been commenced without his order or request, his consent will be regarded in law as an *implied promise* to pay for the value of the labor, unless the circumstances of the case are such as to forbid the presumption.

§ 10. A consideration must also be *possible*, and in accordance with law, sound policy, and good morals. A contract founded upon an impossible consideration is void. No man can be lawfully bound to do what is not in the power of man to do. But it is otherwise, if the thing to be done is only at the time impossible in fact, but not impossible in its nature. Hence, inability from sickness to fulfill an agreement, or the impossibility of procuring an article of a certain kind or quality which a person has agreed to deliver, would not exempt him from liability in damages for the non-performance of his contract.

§ 11. A contract, the consideration of which is *illegal* or *immoral*, may be avoided by either party. A man can not be held to an agreement to do acts forbidden by the law of God or by the laws of the state. But if an illegal contract

---

§ 8. Why are gratuitous promises void? In what case are subscriptions binding? § 9. Why can not payment be lawfully claimed for gratuitous services? In what cases is a person bound to pay for unasked labor? § 10. What else is mentioned as necessary to a valuable consideration? What kind of impossibility will not void a contract?

has been executed ; in other words, if the wrong has been done, the party in the wrong can not renounce the contract ; for the general rule is, that no man can take advantage of his own wrong ; and the innocent party alone has the privilege of avoiding the contract. If both parties are guilty, neither can, in ordinary cases, obtain relief on a contract that has been executed.

§ 12. The rule that a consideration is necessary to a valid contract applies to all contracts and engagements not under seal, except bills of exchange and negotiable notes after they have passed into the hands of an innocent indorsee. (See Promissory Notes.) In contracts under seal, a consideration is necessarily *implied* in the solemnity of the instrument.

§ 13. It is declared by the English statute of frauds, which prevails generally in the United States, that an agreement which is not to be performed within one year from the time of making it, shall not be valid, unless such agreement, or some memorandum or note thereof, is in writing, and signed by the party to be charged. The statutes of some of the states have adopted this provision of the English statute, and require further, that a special promise to answer for the debt, default, or misdoing of another person, and an agreement or promise upon consideration of marriage, (except mutual promises to marry,) shall likewise be void without such writing, in which the consideration shall be expressed.

CHAPTER LV.

Contracts of Sale.

§ 1. A SALE is a transfer of the title to property to another person for a certain price ; or the exchange of a commodity for its equivalent value in money. The exchange of

---

§ 11. What is said of illegal and immoral considerations ? § 12. To what kind of contracts does the rule that a consideration is necessary apply ? Why not to those under seal ? § 13. What is declared by the English statute of frauds ? What do some states further require ?

one commodity for another, is *barter*. Unless the absolute title is conveyed, the contract is merely a mortgage. The same general principles of law which apply to contracts in general, are applicable to contracts of sale, viz. : the competency of the parties to contract ; the sufficiency of the consideration ; its legality and morality ; the assent of the parties ; and the absence of fraud.

§ 2. To make a sale valid, the thing to be sold must have an *actual or a possible existence*, and be *capable of delivery*. Thus, if A sells a horse or certain goods to B ; and if, at the time of the sale, the horse is dead, or the goods are destroyed ; the sale is void. If the goods are partially destroyed, the buyer may either take them at a proportionate reduction of the price, or abandon the contract.

§ 3. But, although the thing to be sold has no actual and present existence ; yet if its future existence is possible, and if it is the product or increase of something to which the seller has a present right, it is the subject of sale. Thus, a man may sell the wool that may grow on his sheep, the fruit that may grow on his trees, or the future increase of his cattle. But he cannot sell the products of the sheep or cattle which he may hereafter buy. A man may, however, agree to procure goods which he has not, and to furnish at a future time, for a certain price ; and his contract will be good ; though this is not strictly a sale, but an agreement to sell.

§ 4. There can be no sale without a *price ;* and the price must be fixed and definite, or susceptible of being ascertained by reference to some criterion prescribed in the contract, so as to render any further negotiation of the parties unnecessary. Thus, a man may agree to pay what shall be the market price at a particular time, or a price to be fixed by a third person. The price must also be payable in money or its negotiable representative, as notes or bills. One article given for another is merely *barter*. The same principles of law, however, govern in both cases.

§ 5. There must be a *mutual consent of the parties*, and the contract is binding when a proposition made by one party

---

Chap. LV. § 1. What is a sale ? What general principles apply to contracts of sale ? § 2. What if a man contracts to sell what has no existence ? Give an example. § 3. Can he sell what may have a future existence ? Give examples. § 4. What is said about *price*, as essential to a sale ? § 5. What about the mutual consent of parties ?

is accepted by the other. The negotiation may be carried on by letter, as before stated. (Chap. LIV, § 7.)

§ 6. In contracts of sale which are not perfected at once by payment and delivery, certain formalities are to be observed. These forms generally are prescribed by what is called the English statute of frauds, which requires, (1.) that the buyer shall accept and receive part of the goods sold ; or (2.) give something in earnest to bind the bargain, or in part payment ; or (3.) that some note or memorandum in writing of the bargain shall be made and signed by the party to be charged, or by his authorized agent. These provisions, however, apply only to cases in which the price of the goods sold is ten pounds sterling, or more. The same rule prevails generally in this country, with slight variations in some states. The price of the goods sold, in cases to which the provisions of that statute apply, is fixed by law in many of the states, and varies from $30 to $200.

§ 7. To complete a contract of sale, and pass the title to the property to the buyer, there must be a *delivery of the goods sold.* When the goods are such as cannot be manually or immediately delivered, or are not in the actual custody of the seller, the law does not require an actual delivery. But they must be placed in the power of the purchaser ; or there must be such acts and declarations of the parties as imply a change of ownership. When the right of property has been transferred to the buyer, whether by an actual or only a constructive delivery, he immediately assumes the risk of the goods ; so that if they shall be afterward injured or destroyed, he must bear the loss.

§ 8. When nothing is said at the sale as to the time of delivery, or the time of payment, the buyer is entitled to the goods on payment or tender of the price, and not otherwise ; for, though he acquires the *right of property* by the contract of sale, he does not acquire the *right of possession,* until he pays or tenders the price. But if the seller delivers the goods absolutely, and without fraudulent con

---

§ 6. What is to be done if the goods are not immediately delivered? Below what price is this unnecessary? What is the sum fixed in this state? § 7. What is said about delivery to complete a contract? § When does the buyer acquire the right of property? When the right of possession?

trivance on the part of the buyer, the buyer will hold possession of them.

§ 9. But when goods are sold on credit, and nothing is said as to the time of delivery, the buyer is immediately entitled to the possession. If, however, it is ascertained, before the buyer obtains possession of the goods, that he is insolvent, or so embarrassed as to disable him from meeting the demands of his creditors, the seller may stop the goods as a security for the price. But if they are stopped without good cause, or through misinformation, the buyer is entitled to the goods, and to damages which he may have sustained in consequence of their stoppage.

§ 10. In the sale of a chattel, if the seller has possession of the article, and sells it as his own, he is understood to *warrant the title.* A fair price implies a warranty of title; and the purchaser may have satisfaction from the seller, if he sells goods as his own, and the title proves deficient. But if the possession is at the time in another, and there is no covenant or warranty of title, the party buys at his peril. It is thought, however, if the seller affirms that the property is his own, he warrants the title, though it is not in his possession.

§ 11. With regard to the *quality* of the thing, the seller is not bound to make good any deficiency, except under special circumstances, unless he expressly warranted the goods to be sound and good, or unless he made a fraudulent representation or concealment concerning them. The rule is, if there is no express warranty by the seller, nor fraud on his part, and if the article is equally open to the inspection of both parties, the buyer who examines the article for himself, must abide by all losses arising from latent defects equally unknown to both parties.

§ 12. But this rule does not reasonably apply to cases in which the purchaser has ordered goods of a certain character, or in which goods of a certain described quality are offered for sale, and, when delivered, they do not answer the description. There being no opportunity of examining them, there is an *implied* warranty of the quality. An in-

---

§ 9. In case the goods are sold on credit, when has the buyer a right to them? In what case has he not? § 10. What is said about the warranty of title? § 11. In regard to quality, what? § 12. To what cases does not this rule apply? Is a seller bound to disclose hidden defects?

tentional concealment or suppression of a material fact, when both parties have not equal access to means of information, is unfair dealing, and renders the contract void.

§ 13. As a general rule, each party is bound to communicate to the other his knowledge of material facts, provided he knows the other to be ignorant of them, and they are not open and naked, or equally within the reach of his observation. Surely the *moral law* and fair dealing require, in all cases, a full disclosure of all defects within the knowledge of the contracting parties.

CHAPTER LVI.

Fraudulent Sales; Assignments; Gifts, &c.

§ 1. The title to property is sometimes transferred with fraudulent intent. A debtor, to place his property beyond the reach of his creditors, sells or assigns it to others by way of mortgage, under the false pretense of securing the payment of a debt; the property to remain in the possession and use of the assignor.

§ 2. Any agreement which operates as a fraud upon third persons, is void. It is a rule of common law, that all deeds of gift, and all transfers of goods and chattels made by any person to secure them for his future use, shall be void as against creditors; and that if property assigned or sold remains with the seller or assignor, the transaction is to be presumed fraudulent. But whether such conveyance of goods is only *prima facie* (at first view) evidence of fraud, which the vendee or assignee may rebut by proving the sale or assignment to have been made honestly and in good faith; or whether the transaction is fraudulent in point of *law*, and void, is a question upon which the decisions of

---

§ 13. What is the general rule? Chap. LVI. § 1. For what purposes are fraudulent sales made? § 2. What is here stated to be a common law rule? Upon what question do the courts differ?

the courts in England as well as those in this country differ, and which, therefore, may be considered as not conclusively settled.

§ 3. Some have made a distinction between bills of sale and assignments that are absolute and those that are conditional. The supreme court of the United States has affirmed the doctrine that an absolute and *unconditional* bill of sale or conveyance, when the property is retained in possession, is of itself conclusive evidence of fraud; in other words, it is presumed to be fraud in point of law, whatever it may be in fact. It has been held by the same court, that a conveyance with a *condition* that the property is to remain with the vendor until the condition shall be performed, or a conveyance in the nature of a mortgage or security, expressing an agreement between the parties, that the mortgager shall retain possession, is valid.

§ 4. In some states, the doctrine established by the courts is, that a continuance of possession is only *prima facie* evidence of fraud; in which case the mortgagee or assignee is allowed to show by proof, that the conveyance was made in good faith and for a valuable consideration. In other states, the strict rule prevails, that, without a change of possession, the transaction is fraudulent *in law;* in which case the assignee, or person claiming the property under the assignment, is not permitted to show that, in point of *fact*, the transaction was *bona fide*, (in good faith.)

§ 5. The rule that holds every conveyance to be fraudulent unless the property immediately changes hands, often operates to inconvenience and even injury of honest debtors. A debtor may be obliged to part with property, however convenient or needful its present use may be to him, when, but for this stringent rule of law, he might borrow the money to pay a debt, or procure a postponement of payment, and retain the use of the property pledged.

§ 6. In many of the states, this perplexing question has been settled by statute. In the state of New-York, the law expressly declares, that a sale or an assignment without immediate delivery and a change of possession, shall be pre-

---

§ 3. What distinction has been made between conditional and unconditional bills of sale and assignments? § 4. In different states, what different rules prevail? § 5. How does the strict rule sometimes operate to the injury of honest debtors?

sumed to be fraudulent and void as against creditors, unless the party claiming the property under the assignment shall make it appear that the same was made in good faith, and without any attempt to defraud. Laws more or less similar to this, and securing to the assignor the use of the mortgaged property, are believed to exist in a majority of the states. The instruments conveying the property are usually called *chattel mortgages*, and are required to be recorded as deeds; in New-York, and perhaps a few other states, only filed in the town or county clerk's office.

§ 7. In the sale of personal property, though there should be a judgment against the vendor, and the purchaser should have notice of it, that fact would not of itself render the sale fraudulent. But if the purchaser, knowing of the judgment, purchases with the view or purpose to defeat the creditor's execution, the transaction is fraudulent. The question of fraud depends upon the motive.

§ 8. Assignments are sometimes made by debtors for the benefit of their creditors. A person deeply indebted, or in embarrassed circumstances, assigns his property, in trust, to one or more persons, who are to dispose of it, and to apply the avails to the payment of his creditors, or a part of them; for the law does not forbid a debtor's giving a preference to one or more creditors over others, provided the assignment is for a sufficient consideration. A debtor may directly assign or transfer all his property to a single creditor, and the assignment be valid; but if the value of the property is manifestly excessive, and disproportionate to the debt which it is intended to cover, the other creditors have a right to the surplus.

§ 9. When an embarrassed debtor agrees to pay his creditors a certain proportion of their claims in consideration of a discharge of their demands, if he privately agrees to give a better or further security to one than to others, the contract is void; because the condition upon which they agree to discharge the debtor is, that they shall share equally.

§ 10. A gift, or conveyance founded merely upon a con-

---

§ 6. How has this question been settled in some states? What are these instruments of conveyance called? Must they be recorded in this state? § 7. In what case, when there is a judgment against the seller, would a sale of personal property be fraudulent? § 8. How are assignments made for the benefit of creditors? May such assignor prefer any of his creditors? § 9. If he agrees to pay all a certain share, and then privately prefers some, what is the effect?

sideration of affection, or blood, or consanguinity, may be set aside by creditors, if the grantor was in embarrassed circumstances when he made it; for a man is bound, both legally and morally, to pay his debts before giving away his property. But if he is indebted to only a small amount in proportion to the value of his property, and wholly unembarrassed, the gift is not rendered voidable by his indebtedness, even though he should afterwards become insolvent.

CHAPTER LVII.

Bailment.

§ 1. The word *bailment* is from *bail*, French, to deliver. (Chap. XVIII, § 14.) Bailment, in law, is a delivery of goods, in trust, upon agreement that the trust shall be executed, and the goods restored by the bailee, when the purpose of the bailment shall have been answered.

§ 2. A person who receives goods to be kept and returned without reward, must keep them with reasonable care, or, if they receive injury, he will be liable for the damage: in other words, he is responsible only for gross neglect. Gross neglect is a want of that care which every man of common sense takes of his own property. A *depositary*, who is a person with whom goods are deposited, has no right to use the goods intrusted to him.

§ 3. A *mandatary*, or one who undertakes to do an act for another without recompense, in respect to the thing bailed to him, is responsible for gross neglect, if he undertakes and does the work amiss; but it is thought that for agreeing to do, and not undertaking or doing at all, he is not liable for damage.

§ 4. The borrower of an article, as a horse, carriage, or book, without reward, is liable for damage in case of

---

§ 10. In what cases are gifts valid against creditors? Chap. XVII. § 1. Define bailment. § 2. For what is a bailee without reward responsible? What is a depositary? § 3. A mandatary? For what is he responsible?

slight neglect. But if the article is applied only to the use for which it is borrowed, is used carefully by the borrower only, and returned within the time for which it was borrowed, he is not liable.

§ 5. Property taken in pledge as security for a debt or an engagement, must be kept with ordinary care; in other words, the pawnee is answerable only for ordinary neglect; and if the goods should then be lost or destroyed, the pawner is still liable for the debt. If the pawnee derives any profit from the use of the property, he must apply the profits, after deducting necessary expenses, toward the debt.

§ 6. Another kind of bailment is the hiring of property for a reward. If an article is injured or destroyed without any fault on the part of the hirer, the loss falls on the owner, for the risk is with him.

§ 7. If work or care is to be bestowed for a recompense on the thing delivered, the workman is liable for ordinary neglect; and the work must be performed with proper skill, or he is answerable for damage. If a tailor receives cloth to be made into a coat, he is bound to do it in a workmanlike manner.

§ 8. Innkeepers are in general responsible for all injuries to the goods and baggage of their guests, even for thefts. But for loss caused by unavoidable accident, or by superior force, as robbery, they are not liable.

§ 9. A person who carries goods for hire in a particular case, and not as a common carrier, is answerable only for ordinary neglect, unless he expressly takes the risk of a common carrier.

§ 10. A common carrier is one who carries goods for hire as a common business, whether by land or by water, and is responsible to the owner of the goods, even if robbed of them. He is in the nature of an insurer, and is answerable for all losses, except in cases of the act of God, as by lightning, storms, floods, &c., and public enemies, as in time of war.

---

§ 4 For what is a borrower liable? How is he restricted in the use of the article? § 5. In the case of property pledged as security for debt, what are the liabilities? § 6. What in case of a hired article? § 7. What if work or care is to be bestowed upon a thing delivered? § 8. The liability of innkeepers? § 9. Of persons carrying goods for hire in a particular case? § 10. What is a common carrier? To what extent is he liable?

§ 11. A common carrier is bound to receive from any person paying or tendering the freight charges, such goods as he is accustomed to carry, and as are offered for the place to which he carries. But he may refuse to receive them if he is full, or if they are dangerous to be carried, or for other good reasons. He may refuse to take them unless the charges are paid; but if he agrees to take payment at the end of the route, he may retain them there until the freight is paid. A carrier must deliver freight in a reasonable time; but he is not liable for loss by the freezing of a river or canal during his voyage, if he has used due diligence.

§ 12. Proprietors of a stage coach do not warrant the safety of passengers as common carriers; and they are not responsible for mere accidents to the persons of the passengers, but only for the want of due care. Slight fault, unskillfulness, or negligence, either as to the sufficiency of the carriage, or to the driving of it, may render the owner responsible in damages for injury to passengers. But as public carriers, they are answerable for the loss of a box or parcel of goods, though ignorant of its contents, unless the owner fraudulently conceals the value or nature of the article, or deludes the carrier by treating it as of little or no value. Public carriers are responsible for the baggage of their passengers, though they advertise it as being at the risk of the owners.

CHAPTER LVIII.

Principal and Agent, or Factor; Broker; Lien, &c.

§ 1. An *agent*, or factor, is a person intrusted with the management of the business of another, who is called *principal*. The words *agent* and *factor* both signify a deputy, a

---

§ 11. What are his rights and obligations as to receiving and carrying goods?
§ 12. What are the liabilities of proprietors of stage coaches as to passengers? What as to the carrying of goods and the baggage of passengers?

substitute, or a person acting for another ; but *agent* seems to be the more comprehensive term, being applied to one who is intrusted by another with any kind of business ; *factor* more properly denotes an agent employed by merchants residing in other places to buy and sell, and transact certain other business on their account. A factor, from his being commissioned or authorized to act for his principal, and especially if allowed a commission, or a certain rate per cent. of the value of the goods bought or sold, is called a *commission merchant.*

§ 2. If a factor advances money on property intrusted to him, he can hold it until the money shall be refunded, and all charges paid. If the actual owner of the property is unknown to the factor, the person in whose name the goods were shipped, is to be deemed the owner.

§ 3. The right of a factor to hold property against the owner in satisfaction of a demand, is called *lien ;* and the factor may sell the goods to satisfy his claim ; but he must pay the surplus, if any, to the principal or owner. A factor can not pledge goods intrusted to him for sale, as security for his own debts. If he disposes of merchandise intrusted or consigned to him, and applies the avails to his own use, with intent to defraud the owner, he may be punished by fine and imprisonment.

§ 4. How far, in ordinary business, a principal is bound by the acts of an agent, it is not easy to determine. As a general rule the acts of a general agent ; that is, one who either transacts all kinds of business for his employer, or who does all acts connected with a particular business or transaction, or which relate to some particular department of business, bind his principal, so long as he keeps within the general scope of his authority, though he may in some special cases act contrary to his private instructions. But an agent employed for a particular purpose, if he goes beyond the limits of his power, does not bind his principal.

§ 5. An agent is bound, in ordinary cases, to observe the instructions of his principal, even though an act contrary

---

CHAP. LVIII. § 1. Define agent, principal, factor. What is a factor sometimes called ? § 2. How is a factor secured for money advanced on property ? § 3. What is this right to hold property called ? How is he restricted ? § 4. How far is a principal bound by the acts of a general agent ? What is a general agent ?

to such instructions should be intended for the benefit of the principal. The agent must bear, personally, all losses growing out of a non-compliance with his orders; and the profit accruing therefrom goes to the benefit of the principal. An agent, however, is excused from a strict compliance with his orders, if, after receiving them, some sudden and unforeseen emergency has arisen, in consequence of which such compliance would operate as an injury to the principal, and frustrate his intention.

§ 6. When an agent receives no instructions, he must conform to the usage of trade, or to the custom applicable to the particular agency; and any deviation therefrom, unless justified by the necessity of the case, renders him solely liable for any loss or injury resulting from it.

§ 7. An agent is bound to exercise ordinary diligence and reasonable skill; and he is responsible only for the want thereof. Ordinary diligence is that which persons of common prudence use in conducting their own affairs. Reasonable skill is that usually possessed by persons of common capacity employed in the same business.

§ 8. If an agent exceed the limits of his authority, he becomes personally responsible to the person with whom he deals, if the limitations of his authority are unknown to such person. He is in like manner responsible, if he makes a contract in his own name; or if he does not disclose the name of the principal, so as to enable the party with whom he deals to have recourse to the principal in case the agent had authority to bind him. And if the agent even buys in his own name, but for the principal, and without disclosing his name, the principal also is bound, provided the goods come to his use. Also if the principal is under age, or a lunatic, or otherwise incompetent to contract, the agent is liable.

§ 9. A *broker* is an agent employed to negotiate sales between parties for a compensation in the form of a commission, which is commonly called *brokerage*. His business

---

§ 5. How far is an agent bound to his principal? In what case may he depart from his instructions? § 6. By what rule is he to be governed? § 7. What degree of diligence and skill must he exercise? What is ordinary diligence? Reasonabie skill? § 8. In what cases is an agent responsible to the person with whom he deals? In what case is a principal liable for goods bought by an agent in his own name?

consists chiefly in negotiating exchanges; or in buying and selling stocks, goods, ships, or cargoes; or in procuring insurances and settling losses; and as he confines himself to one or the other of these branches, he is called an exchange broker, stock broker, insurance broker, &c. A broker differs from a factor. He has not the custody of the goods of his principal. He is merely empowered to effect the contract of sale; and when this is done, his agency ends. If a broker executes his duties in such a manner that no benefit results from them, or is guilty of gross misconduct in selling goods, he is not entitled to a commission or compensation.

§ 10. A *lien*, as the claim of a factor upon goods intrusted to him for sale, has been noticed. (§ 3.) The right of lien extends to others than factors. It is intended also for the benefit of manufacturers, mechanics, and other persons carrying on business for the accommodation of the public. A tailor has a lien upon the garment made from another's cloth until he is paid for the making; a shoemaker upon the shoes made from another's leather; a blacksmith upon the horse he has shod; an innkeeper upon the horse or goods of his guest; and common carriers upon the goods they transport. But they cannot hold the property for any other debt; nor can they sell it to satisfy their claim. Whenever a person allows property to go out of his possession, he loses his lien.

CHAPTER LIX.

Partnership.

§ 1. A PARTNERSHIP is an association formed by contract between two or more persons, for joining their money, labor, or skill, in lawful business, the profits to be divided and the loss to be borne by the partners in certain proportions. It is a partnership if one furnishes the funds and

§ 9. What is a broker? His ordinary business? In what does he differ from a factor? § 10. What is a lien? For whose benefit is the right intended? How is their right restricted? CHAP. LIX. § 1. Define partnership?

the other performs the labor ; or if, when no money is necessary, each agrees to do his share of the labor. A partnership or association of this kind is denominated a *firm*, or *house.*

§ 2. The act of any one of the firm is considered the act of all, and binds all ; and either of them is liable for all the debts. But if a bill or note is drawn by one partner in his own name only, without appearing to be on partnership account, he alone is bound, though it were made for a partnership purpose. A partner buying goods on his own account for his individual use, is alone liable ; but if they afterward go to the use of the partnership, all become responsible.

§ 3. Sometimes a person agrees to receive, by way of rent, a portion of the profits of a farm, a tavern, or a manufactory ; or an agent or a clerk receives a share of the profits for his labor. But as there is in these cases no partnership, the persons who buy the stock and hire the labor are alone responsible.

§ 4. All the partners must unite in suing and being sued. One who should conceal his name so as not to be known when the debt is contracted, may be sued when discovered to be a partner, if he shares in the profits of the trade.

§ 5. A partner cannot sell his interest to another person, who is to take his place in the partnership, without the consent of all the partners : nor can a partner, without such consent, withdraw when he pleases, and dissolve the partnership, except in cases in which the partnership is without any definite term. A partnership is dissolved by the death, insanity, bankruptcy, or other inability of one of the parties.

§ 6. When a partnership is dissolved by the withdrawal of any of the partners, notice of dissolution ought to be duly published, or a firm may be bound by a contract made by one partner in the usual course of business and in the name of the firm, with a person who contracted on the faith of the partnership, and who had no notice of the dissolution. The same notice is necessary to protect a retir-

---

§ 2. In what cases does the act of one partner bind all, and in what does it not? § 3. What cases of association are here mentioned that are not partnerships? § 4. How are they to sue and be sued? § 5. What cannot a partner do without the consent of all? What may dissolve a partnership at any time? § 6. Why should notice of dissolution be published when any partner withdraws? How else may he become liable?

ing partner from continued responsibility. And even if due notice is given, yet, if he willingly suffers his name to continue in the firm, or in the title of the firm over the door of the shop or store, he may in certain cases be liable.

§ 7. In some of the states, a partnership may be formed by a number of persons, some of whom are to be responsible only to a limited amount; and their names are not to be used in the firm. Before a partnership of this kind can do business, a writing and certificate signed by the parties stating the terms of partnership, and the amount for which the *special partners* (as they are called) are to be responsible must be recorded. The terms of partnership must also be published in a newspaper.

§ 8. In these *limited* partnerships, as they are termed, the special partners are liable only to the amount stated in the terms of partnership. The other partners, called *general partners,* whose names only are used, and who transact the business, are liable for all the debts contracted, as in ordinary partnerships. If such partnership is to be dissolved by act of the parties before the expiration of the term for which it is formed, notice of dissolution must be filed and recorded, and published in a newspaper. Such is the law in the state of New York; and it is presumed to agree, in its most essential provisions, with the laws of the other states in which these partnerships are authorized.

CHAPTER LX.

Promissory Notes.

§ 1. A PROMISSORY *note* is a written promise to pay a specified sum at a certain time, to a person named, or to his order, or to the bearer. A common form of a note is the following:

---

§ 7. How are limited partnerships formed? § 8. For what amount are the special partners liable? Whose names are used? For what are the general partners liable? If the partnership is to be dissolved by the act of the parties, what is to be done? CHAP. LX. § 1. What is a promissory note? Give a form.

$100. ALBANY, June 9, 1859.

Three months after date, I promise to pay to James Smith, or bearer, one hundred dollars, value received.

JOHN BROWN.

§ 2. A note thus payable to Smith or bearer, or to him or his order, is called *negotiable*, because it may be sold or transferred to any other person, who has the same power to sue for and collect the money, as Smith, the original promisee. If it were made payable to Smith *or order*, he must indorse it by writing his name on the back of it, before it would pass as a negotiable note. The indorsement is considered as the order of Smith to the maker to pay it to any other person. But, though not negotiable, it might be transferred; but the holder must sue in the name of Smith, and Brown might offset any demands which he has against Smith.

§ 3. An indorsement, made by writing the name only on the back of a note, is called a *blank* indorsement. A full indorsement is one which points out the person to whom the note is to be paid. A blank indorsement may be filled up at any time by the holder. For example: A note is payable to "John Jay or order," or to "the order of John Jay," who indorses it in blank which makes it payable to any other holder. Now if any holder or indorsee wishes it paid to any particular person, he fills up the blank by writing a request to that effect above the name of the indorser, thus: "Pay to George Bruce," or "Pay to George Bruce or order;" who, again, may by indorsement order it paid to some particular person. Or, if he should indorse it in blank, or order it paid "to the *bearer*," it would again pass, as at first, by mere delivery.

§ 4. In common business transactions in the country, notes intended to be negotiable are usually made payable to bearer, as in the form given. (§ 1.) The young reader, or other person inexperienced in business, may not know why they are not always so written. The making of a note payable to order protects the holder or owner in case the note should be lost. Take, for example, the note sup-

---

§ 2. What is the effect of inserting "or bearer," or, "or order?" If payable to order, how is it made negotiable? Why is a note called negotiable? If not negotiable, how is it to be sued? § 3. What is a blank indorsement? A full indorsement? What is sometimes done in case of a blank indorsement?

posed in the preceding section, indorsed in blank. Suppose the owner resides in Buffalo, and the maker in Detroit. The owner writes over the name of John Jay, "Pay to George Bruce," also residing in Detroit, to whom it is sent by mail, to be by him presented to the maker for payment. And should the note by accident or fraud fall into the hands of another, it being payable to Bruce only, or to his order, the parties are protected from loss.

§ 5. As a contract is not binding without a valuable consideration, (Chap. LIV, § 6,) the words "value received" are inserted in notes, as evidence of such consideration. But where there is no statute requiring the insertion of these words, a note is good without them. Whether they are inserted or not, the note is presumed to have been given for a valuable consideration ; and the maker, to avoid his obligation to pay it, must make it appear that no value was received.

§ 6. A note made by two or more persons may be joint or joint or several. When it is written, "We promise to pay," it is only a joint note, and all must be sued together. If written, "We jointly and severally promise to pay," they may be sued either jointly or separately. Also if written "I promise to pay," it is treated as a joint and several note. A note written, "We promise," and signed, A. B., principal, and C. D., security, is the joint note of both ; and if written, "I promise," and signed in the same manner, it is the joint and several note of both.

§ 7. Any person having in possession a negotiable note, though a mere agent, is deemed the true owner, and may sue it in his own name, without showing title. The *bona fide* holder can recover upon the paper, though it came to him from a person who had stolen or robbed it from the true owner ; provided he took it innocently in the course of trade for a valuable consideration before it was due, and with due caution. But if suspicion is cast upon the title of the holder, by showing that the instrument has got into

---

§ 4. Show, by example, the benefit of making a note payable to order instead of to bearer. § 5. Why are the words "value received" inserted ? Is a note without these words collectable ? § 6. In what different ways may notes signed by two or more persons be written, to be joint, or joint or several ? § 7. By whom may a negotiable note be sued ? In what case can a holder of a note recover upon it, though he received it of a person who had stolen it ?

circulation by force or fraud, then the holder must show the consideration he gave for it.

§ 8. Ordinarily, a person can not convey to another a valid title to property which is not lawfully his own; and hence the purchaser of stolen goods must give them up to the lawful owner. The exception to this rule, in the case of promissory notes, seems to be founded in reason and good policy. The use of negotiable paper in commercial transactions is of great public convenience; and it is proper that, for the sake of trade, protection should be given to the holder of such paper who receives it fairly in the way of business, though it has been paid, if he received it before it fell due.

§ 9. But it is equally material for the interests of trade, that the owner should have due protection. Hence if a person takes a note from a stranger without inquiring how he came by it; or does not take it in the usual course of business, or for some responsibility incurred on the credit of the note, he takes it at his peril. But the owner, in order to place his right to relief beyond question, ought to use diligence in apprising the public of the loss of the note.

§ 10. A person buying a note after it has become due, takes it at his peril. Although the holder may sue it in his own name, the maker may offset any demands which he had against the promisee before it was transferred, as in the case of notes not negotiable. (§ 2.) But when notes in which no day of payment is expressed comes under this rule, is a question to be determined by circumstances. In New Jersey and Pennsylvania, the words "without defalcation or discount," or words to that effect, must be inserted in notes, or they may be met by offsets as notes that are bought after due.

§ 11. A note made payable in some commodity is not negotiable. If it is not paid according to the conditions therein expressed, the maker becomes liable to pay in cash. But in either case, if it passes to a third person, he can sue

---

§ 8. To what rule is this an exception? Why is this exception? § 9. On the other hand, what is required to protect the owner? What should the owner do? § 10. What is the risk in buying a note after it has become due? How is it when no day of payment is expressed? What regulation exists in New Jersey and Pennsylvania? § 11. What is the law respecting notes payable in some commodity?

it only in the name of the promisee or payee; and it may be met by offsets as other notes not negotiable, (§ 2,) and notes bought after due. (§ 10.)

§ 12. Notes payable *on demand*, or in which no time of payment is mentioned, are due immediately, and no demand of payment is necessary. But a note payable *at sight*, or at a specified time after sight, must be presented for payment before it can be sued. If the words "with interest" are omitted, interest commences at the time the note becomes due. If payable on demand, it will draw interest from the time when payment is demanded.

§ 13. After the day on which a note is made payable, the maker has three days in which to make payment, which are called *days of grace*. Hence, a note payable on the first day of the month is not due and suable until the fourth. If, however, the last day of grace falls on Sunday, or the fourth of July, or any other day recognized by law as a holiday, or day of public rest, the last day of grace would be a day earlier. If the fourth of July or any other holiday should come on Saturday, the note would be due on Friday. Or if such day should fall on Monday, the last day of grace would be Saturday.

§ 14. To hold the indorser of a note responsible, payment must be demanded of the maker on the last day of grace. As to the time of day when the demand should be made, it is considered that the maker is entitled to the latest convenient time within the customary business hours of the place where the note is presented.

§ 15. If payment has been demanded and refused, notice thereof must be given to the indorser; and one entire day is allowed the holder to give the notice. If the demand is made on Saturday, it is sufficient to give notice on Monday. If the indorser resides in the same town, he may be notified personally by the holder, or by a messenger sent to his dwelling-house, where notice may be given personally, or left in a way likely to bring it to his knowledge. If the parties reside in different towns, notice may be sent by

---

§ 12. When do notes payable on demand, or in which no time of payment is mentioned, become due and suable? Notes payable at sight, or after sight? If the words "with interest" are omitted, when does interest commence? If payable on demand, when? § 13. What are days of grace? How do they affect a note? § 14. To bind an indorser, when must payment be demanded? § 15. If payment is refused, how and when is the indorser to be notified?

mail; in which case, the notice must be put into the post-office, as early as the next day after the last day of grace, so as to be forwarded as soon as possible thereafter: or notice may be sent by a private conveyance or a special messenger.

§ 16. If, in consequence of the removal of the maker before the note becomes due, or from any other cause, his residence is unknown, the holder must make endeavors to find it, and make the demand there; though, if he has removed out of the state, it is sufficient to present the note at his former place of residence. If the maker has absconded, that will, as a general rule, excuse the demand.

§ 17. Notes, on being transferred, are guarantied by indorsement. If a person simply writes his name on the back, he is liable as indorser only. If he guarantees "the payment of the note," he is generally considered liable as an original promisor. If he guaranties the note "good," or "collectable," the maker, and the indorsers also, if any, must be sued, before the guarantor is liable. Strict notice to a guarantor is not required to bind him, as in the case of an indorser. But to hold him liable in case immediate notice is not given, or the note is not immediately sued, it must be shown that he has not suffered injury from want of notice, or that the note was not collectable of the maker or indorsers when due. But the kind of liability incurred, whether that of indorser, original promisor, or surety, by indorsing a note or guarantying payment, is not the same in all the states. There are sundry other points in the law relating to promissory notes, on which the statutes and judicial decisions are not uniform in all the states.

---

§ 16. In case the maker's residence is unknown, how is payment to be demanded? § 17. State the effect of the different modes of guarantying notes.

CHAPTER LXI.

Bills of Exchange; Interest; Usury.

§ 1. A BILL *of exchange* is a written order or request to a person in a distant place, to pay a third person a certain sum of money. The following is a common form :

$1,000. NEW-YORK, August 10, 1859.

Twenty days after date, (or at sight, or ten days after sight,) pay to the order of John Stiles, one thousand dollars, value received, and charge the same to account of

To GEORGE SCOTT, THOMAS JONES.

New Orleans, La.

§ 2. Bills drawn on persons in foreign countries, are called *foreign* bills of exchange; those drawn on persons in distant places in our own country, are called *inland* bills of exchange. To persons in mercantile business they are of great convenience, as will be seen from the following example of their nature and operation.

§ 3. A, in New-York, has $1,000 due him from B, in New Orleans. A draws an order on B for that sum, and C, who is going to New Orleans, pays A the money, takes the order, and receives his money again of B. Thus A is accommodated by receiving his debt against B, and C has avoided the risk of carrying the money from place to place. A, who draws the order, or bill, is called the *drawer*. B, to whom it is addressed, is the *drawee*; C, to whom it is made payable, is the *payee*. As the bill is payable to C, or his order, he may, by indorsment, direct the bill to be paid to D; in which case C becomes the *indorser*, and D, to whom the bill is indorsed, is called the *indorsee* or *holder*.

§ 4. If, when a bill is presented to the drawee, he agrees to pay it, he is said to *accept* the bill, and writes his acceptance upon it. An acceptance may, however, be by parol. The acceptor of a bill is the principal debtor; the drawer, the surety. The acceptor is bound, though he accepted

---

CHAP. LXI. § 1. What is a bill of exchange? Give a form. § 2. What are foreign bills of exchange? Inland? § 3. Give an example of its operation and effect? § 4. How is a bill accepted? How is the acceptor liable? How is payment demanded?

without consideration, and for the sole accommodation of the drawer. But payment must be demanded on the last day of grace; and, if refused, notice of non-payment must be given to the drawer, as in the case of an indorsed promissory note. (Chap. LX, § 15.)

§ 5. No precise time is fixed by law at which bills payable at sight or a certain number of days after sight, must be presented to the drawee for acceptance; though an unreasonable delay might discharge the drawer. A bill payable on a certain day after date, need not be presented before the day of payment, but if presented before due, and acceptance is refused, it is dishonored; and notice must be given immediately to the drawer. If a bill has been accepted, payment must be demanded of the acceptor, when the bill falls due; and if no place is appointed for payment, the demand must be made at his house or residence, or upon him personally.

§ 6. A check upon a bank, (Chap. XXIV, § 3,) is another kind of negotiable paper. It partakes more of the nature of a bill of exchange than of a promissory note. It is not a direct promise to pay; but it is an undertaking, by the drawer, that the drawee shall accept and pay; and the drawer is answerable only when the drawee fails to pay. A check payable to bearer passes by delivery; and the bearer may sue on it as on an inland bill of exchange.

§ 7. When a foreign bill of exchange is to be presented for acceptance or payment, demand is usually made by a *notary public;* and in case of refusal, his certificate of the presentment of the bill and of the refusal, is legal proof of the fact in any court. This certificate is called *protest,* which means, *for proof.* A protest may be noted on the day of the demand; though it may be drawn up in form at a future period. Notaries are appointed in all towns and cities of commercial importance.

§ 8. A protest of an inland bill of exchange is not generally deemed necessary in this country; though it is the practice to have bills, drawn in one state on persons in another, protested by a notary. No protest is legal evidence

---

§ 5. When must bills payable at sight, or a certain day after sight, or after date, be presented for acceptance? When presented for payment? § 6. What is the nature of a bank check? § 7. What is the business of a notary public? Define *protest*.

in court, except in the case of a foreign bill. Yet it is expedient, in many cases of inland bills, to employ notaries when evidence is to be preserved, because they are easily found when wanted as witnesses. In some states, bills drawn in one state and payable in another, are deemed foreign bills ; and their protest as such is required. Notes payable at banks are also protested for non-payment.

§ 9. *Interest* is a premium paid for the use of money, or a profit per cent. received for money lent, or on an unpaid demand. Thus a person lends $1,000 to another person, who pays for the use of it six per cent. a year, or $6 for every hundred, as interest. The rate of interest is fixed by a law of the state.

§ 10. The established lawful rates of interest in the several states are as follows : *Six* per cent. in all but the following : In New-York, Michigan, Wisconsin, Minnesota, *seven* per cent. ; in Alabama and Texas *eight* per cent. ; in Louisiana, *five* per cent. ; bank interest *six;* in California, *ten* per cent. But there may be taken by special agreement, in Florida and Louisiana, *eight* per cent. ; in Mississippi, Arkansas, Ohio, Missouri, Iowa, *ten ;* in Texas and Wisconsin, *twelve;* in Minnesota and California, any rate. In Illinois and Michigan, for money loaned, it may be *ten.* In Mississippi, for the *bona fide* use of money *eight* per cent.

§ 11. A rate of interest beyond that which is established by law, is *usury.* Not only can no more be collected on any contract or obligation than the legal rate, but in most of the states there is some forfeiture for taking usurious interest. In a few, the obligation is void, and the payment of no part of the debt can be enforced by law ; in others, twice or thrice the excess above the lawful interest is forfeited ; and in some, only the excess paid can be recovered.

---

§ 8. What is said of protesting inland bills of exchange? § 9. What is interest? § 10. Give the rates of interest in the different states. What is it in this state? § 11. What is usury? What is the forfeiture for taking usury in this state?

CHAPTER LXII.

Crimes and Misdemeanors.

§ 1. The statutes of each state define the crimes of which its laws take cognizance. The definitions given in this chapter, agree substantially, it is presumed, with those of similar crimes in every state in the union. The statutes also prescribe the penalties, which are not precisely the same in all the states. Nor is there in any state an equal measure of punishment inflicted in all cases for the same offense. The laws usually declare the longest and the shortest terms of imprisonment, and the highest and lowest fines, leaving the exact measure of punishment, except for crimes punishable by death, to the discretion of the judges, to be fixed according to the aggravation of the offense.

§ 2. The laws of the several states differ in respect to the number of crimes made punishable by death. In some states the penalty of death is annexed to the crime of murder only. Treason is punishable by death; but as this offense is defined and made punishable by the laws of the United States, not all the states take cognizance of it. If committed in such states, it is tried in the courts of the United States. In New York, murder, treason, and arson in the first degree, are punishable by death. Few states make more than these crimes thus punishable. In two or three states, the penalty of death has been abolished, and imprisonment for life substituted.

§ 3. Crimes punishable by death, are called *capital* crimes, and their punishment is called *capital* punishment. The word capital is from the Latin *caput*, which means head; and so has come to signify the highest or principal. Hence, probably, the application of the word capital to the principal crimes receiving the highest punishment, which was

---

Chap. LXII. § 1. Are the penalties for crimes the same in all the states? Is the measure of punishment always the same for the same offense, in any state? Who fixes the measure of punishment? § 2. What crimes are punishable by death in this state? § 3. Why are crimes punishable by death called *capital* crimes? Define capital.

formerly practiced extensively in other countries by behead ing or *decapitating* the criminals.

§ 4. *Treason* is defined by statute to be, levying war in any state against the people of the state ; or a combination of two or more persons, attempting by force to usurp or overturn the government of the state ; or in adhering to enemies of the state while separately engaged in war with a foreign enemy, and giving them aid and comfort.

§ 5. *Murder* is the killing of a person deliberately and maliciously, and with intent to effect death ; or killing a person in committing some other crime, though not with a design to effect death ; or in killing a person purposely and without previous deliberation. The less aggravated cases of murder, are in some states distinguished as murder in the second degree, and punished by imprisonment for a long term, or for life.

§ 6. *Manslaughter* is killing a person either upon a sudden quarrel, or unintentionally while committing some unlawful act. The statutes of New York define four different degrees of manslaughter.

§ 7. *Arson* is maliciously burning any dwelling-house, shop, barn, or any other building, the property of another. Arson in the first degree, which is burning an inhabited dwelling *in the night time*, is in some states punishable with death.

§ 8. *Homicide* signifies mankilling. It is of three kinds : felonious, justifiable, and excusable. When felonious, it is either murder or manslaughter. *Justifiable* homicide is that which is committed in the necessary defense of one's person, house, or goods, or of the person of another when in danger of injury ; or that which is committed in lawfully attempting to take a person for felony committed, or to suppress a riot, or to keep the peace. *Excusable* homicide is the killing of a person by accident, or while lawfully employed, without any design to do wrong. In the two last cases there is no punishment.

§ 9. Intentionally *maiming* another by cutting out or dis-

§ 4. Define treason. § 5. What is murder ? Are there different degrees of murder in this state ? § 6. Define manslaughter. How many degrees of manslaughter in this state ? § 7. What is arson ? Define arson in the first degree. How is this degree punishable in this state ? § 8. What is homicide ? When is it felonious ? What is justifiable and excusable homicide ?

abling the tongue or any other member or limb; inveigling or *kidnapping; decoying* and taking away children; *exposing children* in the street to abandon them; committing or attempting an assault with *intent to kill*, or to commit any other felony, or in resisting the execution of a legal process; *administering poison* without producing death; *poisoning any well* or spring of water; are all felonies, and punishable as such.

§ 10. *Burglary* is maliciously and forcibly breaking into and entering in the night time, any dwelling-house or other building, with intent to commit a crime. Breaking into and entering a house by day, is considered a minor degree of burglary.

§ 11. *Forgery* consists in falsely making, counterfeiting, or altering any instrument of writing, with intent to defraud. The word *counterfeiting* is generally applied to making false coin or bank notes, or in passing them; or in having in possession any engraved plate, or bills unsigned, which are intended to be used for these purposes.

§ 12. *Robbery* is the taking of personal property from another in his presence and against his will, by violence, or by putting him in fear of immediate injury to his person. Knowingly to send or deliver, or to make for the purpose of being sent, a letter or writing, threatening to accuse any one of crime, or to do him some injury, with intent to extort or gain from him any money or property, is considered an *attempt to rob*, for which the offender may be imprisoned.

§ 13. *Embezzlement* is fraudulently putting to one's own use what is intrusted to him by another. To buy or receive property knowing it to have been embezzled, is to be guilty of the same offense. Embezzling is usually punishable in the same manner as larceny of the same amount.

§ 14. *Larceny* is theft or stealing. The stealing of property above a certain amount in value is called *grand larceny*, and is a state prison offense. If the value of the property stolen is of less amount, the offense is called *petit larceny*, and is punished by fine or imprisonment in jail or both.

---

§ 9. What is maiming? Kidnapping? What other crimes are here mentioned as felonies? § 10. What is burglary? Why is the crime deemed greater when committed in the night time? § 11. Define forgery and counterfeiting? § 12. Define robbery, and an attempt to rob. § 13. What is embezzlement? How is it punishable? § 14. What is larceny? What is *grand*, and what is *petit* larceny?

§ 15. *Perjury* is willfully swearing or affirming falsely to any material matter, upon an oath legally administered. *Subornation of perjury* is procuring another to swear falsely; punishable as perjury.

§ 16. *Bribery* is promising or giving a reward to a public officer, to influence his opinion, vote or judgment. A person *accepting* such bribe, is punishable in the same manner, and forfeits his office, and, in some states, may never hold another public trust. This offense is not in all the states punishable by imprisonment in the state prison.

§ 17. *Dueling* is a combat between two persons with deadly weapons. Killing another in a duel is murder, and punishable with death. If death does not ensue, imprisonment. Challenging, or accepting a challenge to fight, or to be present as a second, imprisonment. Dueling is not a punishable offense in every state.

§ 18. Aiding or attempting to aid a prisoner committed for felony, to *escape from confinement*, or forcibly rescuing a prisoner charged with crime, from the custody of a public officer, is a crime. If the offense for which the prisoner is committed is less than felony, the punishment is imprisonment in jail, or fine, or both.

§ 19. *Bigamy* is the crime of having two or more wives, and is also called *polygamy*. But bigamy literally signifies having *two* wives, and polygamy any number more than one. These words, in law, are applied also to women having two or more husbands. A person having a lawful husband or wife living, and marrying another person, is guilty of bigamy. An unmarried person, also, who shall marry the husband or wife of another, is punishable in like manner.

§ 20. *Incest* is the marrying or cohabiting together as husband and wife, of persons related to each other within certain degrees.

§ 21. *Opening a grave* and removing a dead body for any unlawful purpose, or purchasing such body knowing it to have been unlawfully disinterred, is a crime. This offense

---

§ 15. What is perjury? What is subornation of perjury? § 16. Define bribery. § 17. What is dueling? Is dueling murder in this state? § 18. Is aiding a prisoner to escape a crime? § 19. What is bigamy? What is the difference between bigamy and polygamy? § 20. What is incest? § 21. In what case is opening a grave a crime? How is it punishable in this state?

is in some states punishable by imprisonment in a county jail, or by fine, and not in a state prison.

§ 22. Persons sometimes advise or are knowing to the commission of felonies, but are not actually engaged in committing them. Such are *accessories.* He who advises or commands another to commit a felony, is called an *accessory before the fact,* and is punished in the same manner as the principal. If he conceals the offender after the offense has been committed, or gives him any aid to prevent his being brought to punishment, he is an *accessory after the fact,* and may be imprisoned or fined.

§ 23. *Assault and Battery* is unlawfully to assault or threaten, or to strike or wound another. Besides being liable to fine and imprisonment, the offender is liable also to the party injured for damages.

§ 24. A *riot* is the assembling together of three or more persons, with intent forcibly to injure the person or property of another, or to break the peace; or agreeing with each other to do such unlawful act, and making any movement or preparation therefor, though lawfully assembled. When riotous persons are thus assembled, and are proceeding to commit offenses, any judge, justice, sheriff, or other ministerial officer, may in the name of the state, command them to disperse. If they refuse, the peace officers are required to call upon all persons near to aid in taking the rioters into custody. Persons refusing to assist may be fined.

§ 25. A sheriff or other officer voluntarily suffering a prisoner charged with or convicted of an offense, to *escape* from his custody, is guilty of a misdemeanor. To *rescue* a prisoner thus charged or convicted, is punishable in a similar manner. It is also a misdemeanor to assist a criminal, with a view to effect his escape, though he does not escape from jail.

§ 26. A person taking upon himself to act as a public officer, and taking or keeping a person in custody unlawfully or without authority, is *false imprisonment;* for which the offender may be fined or imprisoned.

---

§ 22. Who are accessories to crime? § 23. Define assault and battery. § 24. What is a riot? How may riots be suppressed? § 25. What grade of offense is it for an officer to rescue a prisoner or voluntarily to suffer him to escape? § 26. What is false imprisonment?

§ 27. The offenses mentioned in the last four sections, being of a lower grade than those defined in the preceding sections, and not being punishable in a state prison, are usually called *misdemeanors*, and are punishable by fine or imprisonment in a county jail. There are numerous other misdemeanors and immoralities, as profane cursing and swearing, betting and gaming, horse racing, disturbing religious meetings, sabbath-breaking, trespasses and injury to property, and many disorderly practices, all of which are punishable in a like manner.

LAW OF NATIONS.

CHAPTER LXIII.

Origin and Progress of the Law of Nations; the Natural, Customary, and Conventional Laws of Nations.

§ 1. The *law of nations* consists of those rules by which intercourse between nations is regulated. In its present improved state, the law of nations has not long existed. Ancient nations were little governed by the principles of natural justice. Little respect was paid by one nation to the persons and property of the citizens of another. Robbery on land and sea was not only tolerated, but esteemed honorable; and prisoners of war were either put to death, or reduced to slavery. By this rule of national law, commerce was destroyed, and perpetual enmity kept up between nations.

§ 2. Within the last three or four centuries, essential improvement in the law of nations has been made. By the

§ 27. What grade of offense are the four offenses last named? What other misdemeanors are mentioned in this section? Can you name any other? Chap. LXIII. § 1. Of what consists the law of nations? What was its early character?

light of science and Christianity, the rights and obligations of nations have come to be better understood, and more generally regarded. Commerce also has done much to improve the law, by showing that the true interests of a nation are promoted by peace and friendly intercourse.

§ 3. Hence we find the nations of Europe and America recognizing the same rules of international law. And as the light and power of Christianity shall increase, the law of nations will undergo still further improvements. And it is to be hoped, that, as one of these improvements, the practice of settling national disputes by war will be abolished, and the more rational and humane course be adopted, of referring difficulties which the parties are incapable of adjusting, to some disinterested power for adjudication.

§ 4. There are, in every nation or state, courts of justice to try and punish offenders ; but there is no tribunal before which one nation can be brought to answer for the violation of the rights of another. Every nation, however small and weak, is independent of every other. Therefore, when injuries are committed by one upon another, the offended party, unless it chooses quietly to endure the wrong must seek redress, either by appealing to the sense of justice of the party offending, or by a resort to force.

§ 5. Every nation has a right to establish such government as it thinks proper ; and no other nation has a right to interfere with its internal policy. To this rule, however, some writers make an exception. They hold that the natural right of a state to provide for its own safety, gives it the right to interfere where its security is seriously endangered by the internal transactions of another state. But it is admitted that such cases are so very rare, that it would be dangerous to reduce them to a rule.

§ 6. So cases seldom arise in which one nation has a right to assist the subjects of another in overturning or changing their government. It is generally agreed, that such assistance may be afforded consistently with the law of nations, in extreme cases ; as when the tyranny of a

---

§ 2. By what means has it been improved? § 3. What particular further improvement is desirable? § 4. What is said of the independence of nations? How, then, is redress for injuries obtained? § 5. What right has a nation in respect to its government? To this rule, what exception do some make?

government becomes so oppressive, as to compel the people to rise in their defense, and call for assistance. When the subjects of any government have carried their revolt so far as to have established a new state, and to give reasonable evidence of their ability to maintain a government, the right of assistance is unquestionable. But it is not clear that, prior to this state of progress in a revolution, the right to interpose would be justifiable.

§ 7. There is a sense, however, in which nations are not wholly independent. Mankind in the social state, as we have seen, are dependent upon each other for assistance. (Chap. I, § 2.) Such is, in a measure, the mutual dependence of nations. Although the people of every nation have within themselves the means of maintaining their individual and national existence, their prosperity and happiness are greatly promoted by commerce with other nations. And as laws are necessary to govern the conduct of the individual citizens of a state, so certain rules are necessary to regulate the intercourse of nations.

§ 8. It has been observed, also, that the law of nature is a perfect rule for all moral and social beings, and ought to be universally obeyed. Equally binding is this law upon nations. It requires each nation to respect the rights of all others, and to do for them what their necessities demand, and what it is capable of doing, consistently with the duties it owes to itself. And the general good of mankind is as really promoted by the application of this law to the affairs of nations, as by its application to the affairs of individuals.

§ 9. The law of nature applied to nations or states as moral persons, is called the *natural law of nations.* It is also called the *necessary law of nations*, because nations are morally bound to observe it; and sometimes the *internal law of nations*, from its being binding on the conscience.

§ 10. Although the law of nature, as expressed in the law of revelation, is a correct rule of human conduct; yet, as much of this law consists of general principles from

---

§ 6. In what cases may one nation assist another in changing its government? § 7. In what respect are nations mutually dependent? § 8. By what law ought all nations to be governed? What does this law require? § 9. By what names is this law when applied to nations or states called? Why is it so called?

which particular duties can not always be deduced, positive human enactments are necessary to define the law of nature and revelation. So an important part of the law of nations necessarily consists of positive institutions. Hence some writers have divided international law under these two principal heads: the *natural* law of nations, and the *positive*.

§ 11. The *positive law of nations* is founded on usage or custom and agreement, and may be considered as properly divided into the *customary* law of nations, and the *conventional*. The *customary law of nations* consists of certain maxims, or is founded on customs and usages which have been long observed and tacitly consented to by nations, and have thereby become binding upon all who have adopted them, so far as their observance does not require a violation of the law of nature.

§ 12. A *conventional law of nations* is one that has been established by a treaty or league. The word *convention* usually signifies an assembly of persons met for some benevolent, political, or ecclesiastical purpose. It also signifies a treaty, or agreement between nations; and such agreement or contract, though made without a formal meeting, is deemed conventional.

§ 13. As the law of nature is liable to misconstruction, and as the law of usage or custom is vague and uncertain, *conventional* law, because more definite, has been found to afford greater security to the rights of commerce. Hence the practice, now so common among nations, of regulating their intercourse by negotiation. By treaties, the rights of the contracting parties are placed beyond dispute.

§ 14. But it may be said, if each nation is independent of every other, and if there is no constituted authority to enforce the fulfillment of treaty stipulations, the rights guarantied by treaties are still insecure. But few governments are so devoid of a sense of honor as, by a palpable violation of treaty obligations, to incur the odium and condemnation of all mankind. Self-respect and the fear of provoking a war, have generally proved sufficient incentives to the observance of treaties.

---

§ 10. For what reasons do some writers divide it into the *natural* and *positive* laws of nations? § 11. Define the positive law of nations. How is it divided? Define the customary law of nations. § 12. What is a conventional law of nations? Define *convention*. § 13. What is the advantage of conventional law? § 14. By what consideration is the observance of treaties induced?

§ 15. The obligations of nations are sometimes called *imperfect*. A *perfect obligation* is one that can be enforced—one that exists where there is a right to compel the party on whom the obligation rests to fulfill it. An *imperfect obligation* gives only the right to demand the fulfillment, leaving the party pledged to judge what his duty requires, and to do as he chooses, without being constrained by another to do otherwise.

CHAPTER LXIV

The Jurisdiction of Nations; their mutual Rights and Obligations; the Rights of Embassadors, Ministers, &c.

§ 1. The seas are regarded as the common highway of nations. The main ocean, for navigation and fishing, is open to all mankind. Every state, however, has jurisdiction at sea over its own subjects in its own public and private vessels. The persons on board such vessels are protected and governed by the laws of the country to which they belong, and may be punished by these laws for offenses committed on board of its public vessels in foreign ports.

§ 2. The question how far a nation has jurisdiction over the seas adjoining its lands, is not clearly settled. It appears to be generally conceded, that a nation has a right of exclusive dominion over navigable rivers flowing through its territory; the harbors, bays, gulfs, and arms of the sea; and such extent of sea adjoining its territories as is necessary to the safety of the nation, which is considered by some to be as far as a cannon shot will reach, or about a marine league.

§ 3. It is the duty of a nation in time of peace, to allow

---

§ 15. What is a perfect obligation? An imperfect obligation? Why are the obligations of nations called imperfect? Chap. LXIV. § 1. What rights have nations on the seas? By what laws are persons at sea governed? § 2. Over what waters flowing through its territory has a nation jurisdiction? To what distance on the sea?

the people of other states a passage over its lands and waters, so far as it can be permitted without inconvenience, and with safety to its own citizens. Of this the nation is to be its own judge. The right of passage is only an *imperfect right*, because the obligation to grant the right is an *imperfect obligation.* (Chap. LXIII, § 15.)

§ 4. In general, it is the duty of a nation to allow foreigners to enter and settle in the country. On being admitted into a state, the state becomes pledged for their protection, and they become subject to its laws; and in consideration of the protection they receive, they are obliged to aid in defending it, and in supporting its government, even before they are admitted to all the rights of citizens.

§ 5. But no state is bound to shelter criminals fleeing into it from a foreign state. They can be tried only in the state whose laws they have violated. It is therefore the duty of the government to surrender a fugitive on demand of the proper authorities of the state from which he fled, if, after due examination by a civil magistrate, there shall appear sufficient grounds for the charge. The surrender of criminals is sometimes provided for in treaties.

§ 6. The rule which makes foreigners amenable to the laws of the state in which they remove, does not apply to embassadors. They are not responsible to the laws of the country to which they are sent, even when guilty of crime. When their conduct is dangerous to the government and its citizens, all that can be done is, either to deprive them of liberty by confinement, or to send them home and demand their punishment. As every nation has a right to treat and communicate with all others, it ought not to be deprived of the services of its representative. Hence, the persons and property of all public ministers are held sacred and inviolable.

§ 7. Embassadors are entitled to the same protection in the countries through which they pass in going to, and returning from the government to which they are sent. And

---

§ 3. What right have other nations to a passage over its lands and waters? Why is this an imperfect right? § 4. What are the mutual rights and duties of a state and foreign immigrants? § 5. What is its duty in respect to foreign criminals? § 6. What is said of the responsibility of embassadors? For bad conduct, how are they punishable? Why are they not amenable to the laws of the foreign state?

to insure them a safe passage, some governments have given them passports to be shown if required. A *passport* is a written license from the authority of a state granting permission or safe conduct for one to pass through its territory. Passports, though named in our law, are not known in practice, being deemed unnecessary.

§ 8. If a minister at a foreign court treats the sovereign with disrespect, the fact is sometimes communicated to the government that sent him, with a request for his recall. Or, if the offense is a more serious one, the offended sovereign refuses intercourse with him while his master's answer is awaited. Or, if the case is an aggravated one, he expels him from the country.

§ 9. Ministers at foreign governments, in their negotiations or business correspondence with those governments, sometimes consider themselves ill treated, and their own nation dishonored, and take their leave and return home; or the minister informs his sovereign, who either recalls him, or takes such other measure as he thinks the honor and interest of his nation demand.

§ 10. The peculiar condition of a country, the nature of the business upon which an embassador is sent, or the personal character of the embassador, may be such as to justify a government in refusing to receive him. But to preserve the friendly relations of the two countries, satisfactory explanations ought to be made, or good reasons offered for the refusal.

§ 11. A minister can not bind his sovereign to any treaty or agreement, conclusively, under the authority of an ordinary credential, or letter of attorney. He can not do so without a special power, containing express authority so to bind his principal. Ministers act under secret instructions which they are not bound to disclose. Even the treaties signed by plenipotentiaries, (a word signifying full power,) are, according to present usage, of no force, until ratified by their governments.

§ 12. Consuls are not entitled to the privilege enjoyed by

---

§ 7. What rights have they in countries through which they pass? What is a passport? § 8. How are embassadors dealt with for disrespectful conduct at a foreign court? § 9. What do ministers do when they are ill-treated? § 10 If a government, for good cause, refuses to receive a minister, what is its duty? § 11. What power has a minister in making treaties?

ministers, but are subject to the laws of the country in which they reside. Their principal duties have been described. (Chap. XL, § 9.) The office of consul has been found to be one of great utility; hence, every trading nation has a consul in every considerable commercial port in the world. As in the case of ministers, consuls carry a certificate of their appointment, and must be acknowledged as consuls by the government of the country in which they reside, before they can perform any duties pertaining to their office.

CHAPTER LXV.

Offensive and Defensive War; Just Causes and Objects of War; Reprisals; Alliances in War.

§ 1. Wars are offensive and defensive. The use of force to obtain justice for injuries done, is *offensive war.* The making use of force against any power that attacks a nation or its privileges, is *defensive war.* A war may be defensive in its principles, though offensive in its operation. For example: one nation is preparing to invade another; but before the threatened invasion takes place, the latter attacks the former as the best mode of repelling the invasion. In this case, the party making the attack acts on the *defensive.* (§ 10.) The contending parties are called *belligerents.* The word *belligerent* is from the Latin *bellum,* war, and *gero,* to wage or carry on. Nations that take no part in the contest, are called *neutrals.*

§ 2. War ought never to be undertaken without the most cogent reasons. In the first place, there must be a *right* to make war, and *just grounds* for making it. Nations have no right to employ force any further than is necessary for their own defense, and for the maintenance of their

---

§ 12. To what laws are consuls subject? What is their business? Chap LXV. § 1. Define offensive and defensive war. What are the contending parties called? Who are neutrals? § 2. What are the proper characteristics of a war?

rights. Secondly, it should be made from *proper motives*, the good of the state, and the safety and common advantage of the citizens. Hence, there may be, according to the law of nations, just cause of war, when it would be inexpedient to involve the nation in such a calamity.

§ 3. The numerous objects of a lawful war may be reduced to these three: (1.) To recover what belongs to us, or to obtain satisfaction for injuries. (2.) To provide for our future safety by punishing the offender. (3.) To defend or protect ourselves from injury by repelling unjust attacks. The first and second are objects of an *offensive* war; the third is that of a *defensive* war.

§ 4. Injury to an individual citizen of a state, by the subjects of another state, is deemed a just cause of war, if the persons offending, or the government of the state to which they belong, do not make reparation for the injury; for every nation is responsible for the good behavior of its subjects. But, although this would, according to the law of nations, afford justifiable cause of war, neither the honor nor the true interest of a nation requires that war should always be made for so slight a cause.

§ 5. Generally, the injury sought to be redressed should be serious, and satisfaction be demanded and refused, before recourse should be had to arms. Where there is a question of right between the parties, the government making war should have no reasonable doubt of the justice of its claim. And even when no such doubt exists, it would be the duty of such government to prevent a war, if possible, by proposals of compromise. It is believed that war ought in no case to be made, until attempts have been made to effect an adjustment of difficulties by compromise, or by offers to submit them for arbitration.

§ 6. One of the means by which satisfaction is sought without making war, is that of *reprisals*. (Chap. XXXVI, § 4, 5.) If a nation has taken what belongs to another, or refuses to pay a debt, or to make satisfaction for an injury, the offended nation seizes something belonging to the former or to her citizens, and retains it, or applies it to her own

---

§ 3. What are objects of a lawful war? § 4. When is a personal injury to the citizens of one state by those of another deemed just cause of war? § 5. What ought a government to do before resorting to war to redress injuries?

advantage, till she obtains satisfaction : and when there shall be no longer any hope of satisfaction, the effects thus seized are confiscated. To *confiscate* is to adjudge property to be forfeited, and to appropriate it to the use and benefit of the state. But as the loss in this case would fall upon unoffending citizens, it is the duty of their government to grant them indemnity.

§ 7. But to justify reprisals by the law of nations, the grounds upon which they are authorized must be just and well ascertained. If the right of the party demanding satisfaction is doubtful, he must first demand an equitable examination of his claim, and next be able to show that justice has been refused, before he can justly take the matter into his own hands. He has no right to disturb the peace and safety of nations on a doubtful pretension. But if the other party refuses to have the matter brought to the proof, or to accede to any proposition to terminate the dispute in a peaceable manner, reprisals become lawful.

§ 8. By treaties of alliance, nations sometimes agree to assist each other in case of war with a third power. It is a question not clearly settled, whether the government that is to afford the aid is bound to do so when it deems the war to be unjust. The reasonable conclusion seems to be, that, in cases simply doubtful, the justice of the war is to be presumed ; and the government pledging its aid is bound to fulfill its engagement. The contrary doctrine would furnish a nation with too ready a pretext for violating its pledge. In cases only of the clearest injustice on the part of its ally, can a nation rightfully avoid a positive engagement to afford assistance.

§ 9. But when the object of the war is hopeless, or when the state under such engagement would, by furnishing the assistance, endanger its own safety, it is not bound to render the aid. But the danger must not be slight, remote, or uncertain. None but extreme cases would afford sufficient cause for withholding the promised assistance.

§ 10. When the alliance is defensive, the treaty binds

---

§ 6. How is satisfaction sometimes sought without making war ? How are reprisals made ? Define confiscate. § 7. To justify reprisals, what is necessary ? § 8. How far is a nation bound by a treaty of alliance to assist another in war ? § 9. In what cases is it not bound to render the aid ?

each party to assist the other only when engaged in a defensive war, and unjustly attacked. By the conventional law of nations, the government that first declares, or actually begins the war, is considered as making *offensive* war; and though it should not be the first actually to apply force, yet if it first renders the application of force necessary, it is the aggressor; and the other party, though the first to apply force, is engaged in a *defensive* war. (§ 1.)

CHAPTER LXVI.

Declaration of War; its Effect upon the Person and Property of the Enemy's subjects; Stratagems in War; Privateering.

§ 1. When a nation has resolved on making war, it is usual to announce the fact by a public declaration. In monarchical governments, the power to declare war, which of course includes the right of determining the question whether it shall be made, is vested in the king. In the United States, this power is, by the constitution, given to the representatives of the people, for reasons elsewhere stated. (Chap. XXXVI, § 3.)

§ 2. It was usual, formerly, to communicate a declaration of war to the enemy. According to modern practice, a formal declaration to the enemy is not required. Any manifesto or paper from an official source, announcing that the country is in a state of war, is considered sufficient. The recalling of a minister has alone been regarded as a hostile act, and followed by war, without any other declaration. But such cases have not been frequent. Under ordinary circumstances, the recall of a minister is not an offensive act.

§ 3. The government of a state acts for and in behalf of all its citizens; and its acts are binding upon all. Hence,

---

§ 10. What if the alliance is defensive? Is the government that first applies force always the aggressor? Chap. LXVI. § 1. How is war usually announced? By what authority? § 2. Is a declaration communicated to the enemy? What is deemed sufficient?

when war is declared, it is not merely a war between the two governments; all the subjects of the government declaring it become enemies to all the subjects of that against which it is declared.

§ 4. Whether, on the occurrence of a war in any state, the subjects of the enemy found within the state may be detained as prisoners of war, and their movable property confiscated; or whether they are entitled to a reasonable time to retire with their effects, is a question upon which writers of public law are not agreed. Few civilized nations, at the present day, would deny such persons a reasonable time to retire with their property. Of houses and lands, all admit that only the income is subject to confiscation. The privilege spoken of, instead of being left to uncertainty, is now, with great propriety, generally secured by treaty.

§ 5. When war is declared, all intercourse between the two countries at once ceases. All trade between the citizens, directly or indirectly, is strictly forbidden; and all contracts with the enemy made during the war are void.

§ 6. Although a state of war makes all the subjects of one nation enemies of all those of the other, they cannot lawfully engage in offensive hostilities without permission of their government. If they have no written commission as evidence of such permission, and if they should be taken by the enemy, they would not be entitled to the usual mild treatment which other prisoners of war receive, but might be treated without mercy as lawless robbers and banditti.

§ 7. As the object of a just war is to obtain justice, a nation, when it has declared war, has a right to use all necessary means, and no other, for attaining that end. A just war gives the right to take the life of the enemy; but there are limits to this right. If an enemy submits, and lays down his arms, we can not justly take his life. And justice and humanity forbid that women, children, feeble old men, and sick persons, who make no resistance, should be maltreated.

---

§ 3. When war is declared, who are involved in it? § 4. How does war in a state affect the persons and property of the enemy's subjects found within such state? § 5. How is trade between the two countries affected by the war? § 6. What is necessary to make offensive hostilities lawful? In what case would such permission be beneficial? § 7. How far does a just war give the right to take the life of the enemy?

§ 8. Prisoners of war are not to be treated with cruelty. They may be confined, and even fettered, if there is reason to apprehend that they will rise against their captors, or make their escape. Prisoners of war are detained to prevent their returning to join the enemy, or to obtain from their government a just satisfaction as the price of their liberty. Prisoners may be kept till the end of the war. Then, or at any time during the war, the government may exchange them for its own soldiers taken prisoner by the enemy; or a ransom may be required for their release. It is the duty of the government to procure, at its own expense, the release of its citizens.

§ 9. Ravaging a country, burning private dwellings, or otherwise wantonly destroying property, is not justifiable, except in cases of absolute necessity. But all fortresses, ramparts, and the like, being appropriated to the purposes of war, may be destroyed.

§ 10. Stratagems and deceit to obtain advantage of an enemy, are, to some extent, justified by the law of nations; but in general they are dishonorable and wrong.

§ 11. Spies are sometimes sent among an enemy, to discover the state of his affairs, to pry into his designs, and carry back information. This is a dishonorable office; spies, if detected, are condemned to death.

§ 12. The rights of a nation in war at sea are essentially different from those in war upon land. The object of a maritime war is to destroy the commerce and navigation of the enemy, with a view of weakening his naval power. To this end, the capture or destruction of private property is necessary, and is justified by the law of nations. Hence, for the purpose of attack as well as defense, every nation of considerable power or commercial importance, keeps a *navy*, consisting of a number of war vessels, ready for service.

§ 13. Besides these national ships of war, there are armed vessels owned by private citizens, and called *priva-*

§ How are prisoners of war to be treated? What is said about the exchange and ransom of prisoners? § 9. What kinds of property may not, and what may, be destroyed? § 10. What is said of stratagems? § 11. Of spies? § 12. In what kind of war is the destruction of private property lawful? On what ground?

teers. Their owners receive from the government a commission to go on the seas, and to capture any vessel of the enemy, whether it is owned by the government or by private citizens, or whether it is armed or not. And to encourage privateering, the government allows the owner and crew of a privateer to keep the property captured as their own.

§ 14. To prevent the abuse of this right, the owners are required to give security, that the cruise shall be conducted according to instructions and the usages of war ; that the rights of neutral nations shall not be violated ; and that the captured property shall be brought in for adjudication.

§ 15. When a prize is brought into a port, the captors make a writing, called *libel*, stating the facts of the capture, and praying that the property may be condemned ; and this paper is filed in the proper court. If it shall be made to appear that the property was taken from the enemy, the court condemns the property as *prize*, which is then sold, and the proceeds are distributed among the captors.

§ 16. All prizes, whether taken by a public or private armed vessel, primarily belong to the sovereign ; and no person has any interest in a prize, except what he receives from the state : and due proof must in all cases be made before the proper court, that the seizure was lawfully made. In this country, prizes are proved and condemned in a district court of the United States, which, when sitting for that purpose, is called a *prize court.*

CHAPTER LXVII.

Rights and Duties of Neutral Nations ; Contraband Goods ; Blockade ; Right of Search ; Safe Conducts and Passports ; Truces ; Treaties of Peace.

§ 1. A NEUTRAL nation is bound to observe a strict impartiality toward the parties at war. If she should aid one

---

§ 13. What are privateers ? What are their owners authorized to do ? How is privateering encouraged ? § 14. How is the abuse of this right prevented ? § 15. State the proceedings of the captors and the court, in cases of capture ? § 16. Who has the primary right to all prizes ? How do the citizens get any interest in them ?

party to the injury of the other, she would be liable to be herself treated as an enemy. A loan of money to one of the belligerents, or supplying him with other means of carrying on a war, if done with the view of aiding him in the war, would be a violation of neutrality. But an engagement made in time of peace to furnish a nation a certain number of ships, or troops, or other articles of war, may afterward, in time of war, be fulfilled.

§ 2. A nation is not bound, however, on the occurrence of a war, to change its customary trade, and to cease supplying a belligerent with articles of trade which such belligerent was wont to receive from her, although the goods may afford him the means of carrying on the war. So if a nation has been accustomed to lend money to another for interest, and the latter should become engaged in war with a third power, the neutral would not break her neutrality if she should continue to lend her money. The wrong in any case lies in the *intention* to aid one to the detriment of the other.

§ 3. This rule, it is believed, is universally admitted in cases of belligerents going themselves to a neutral country to make their purchases. But whether a neutral nation is at full liberty to *carry the goods* in the cases mentioned, is not so certain. A nation in a just war has a right to deprive her enemy of the means of resisting or injuring her, and therefore may lawfully intercept every thing of a warlike nature which a neutral is carrying to such enemy.

§ 4. Articles which a neutral nation is not allowed to carry to an enemy, are called contraband goods. What these are, it is impossible to say with precision, as some articles may in certain cases be lawfully carried, which would be justly prohibited under other circumstances. Among the articles usually contraband, are arms, ammunition, materials for ship-building, naval stores, horses, and sometimes even provisions.

§ 5. Contraband goods, when ascertained to be such, are confiscated to the captors as lawful prize. Formerly

---

Chap. LXVII. § 1. To what is a neutral nation bound? What kind of aid to an enemy is unlawful? § 2. How is the trade of a neutral affected by war? With what may she still supply a belligerent? § 3. What is said of the right of a neutral to carry the goods in such cases? § 4. What are prohibited articles called? What goods are contraband?

the vessel also was liable to be condemned and confiscated; but the modern practice, it is said, exempts the ship, unless it belongs to the owner of the contraband articles, or the carrying of them is connected with aggravating circumstances.

§ 6. One of the rights of a belligerent nation which a neutral is bound to regard, is the right of blockade. *Blockade* is a blocking up. A war blockade is the stationing of ships of war at the entrance of an enemy's ports, to prevent all vessels from coming out or going in. The object of a blockade is to hinder supplies of arms, ammunition, and provisions from entering, with a view to compel a surrender by hunger and want, without an attack. A neutral vessel attempting to enter or depart, becomes liable to be seized and condemned. Towns and fortresses also may be shut up by posting troops at the avenues.

§ 7. A simple decree or order declaring a certain coast or country in a state of blockade, does not constitute a blockade. A force must be stationed there, competent to maintain the blockade, and to make it dangerous to enter. And it is necessary that the neutral should have due notice of the blockade, in order to subject his property to condemnation and forfeiture. According to modern usage, if a place is blockaded by sea only, trade with it by a neutral nation may be carried on by inland communication. And a neutral vessel, loaded before the blockade was established, has a right to leave the port with her cargo.

§ 8. To prevent the conveyance of contraband goods, the law of nations gives a belligerent nation the *right of search;* that is, the right, in time of war, to search neutral vessels, to ascertain their character, and what articles are on board. A neutral vessel refusing to be searched by a lawful cruiser, would thereby render herself liable to condemnation as a prize. Private merchant vessels only are subject to search; the right does not extend to public ships of war.

§ 9. The property of an enemy found on board of a neutral vessel, may be seized, if the vessel is beyond the limits

---

§ 5. What is done with contraband goods? In what cases is the vessel also confiscated? § 6. What is a blockade? Its object? How does it affect neutrals? § 7. What is necessary to a lawful blockade? In case a place is blockaded by sea only, how may trade be carried on with it? § 8. What is the right of search? What vessels are subject to search?

of the jurisdiction of the nation to which she belongs; but the vessel is not confiscated; and the master is entitled to freight for the carriage of the goods. The *property of neutrals* found in an enemy's vessels, is to be restored to the owners.

§ 10. A neutral is forbidden by the law and practice of nations, to permit a belligerent to arm and equip vessels of war within her forts. Nor may the citizens of a nation fit out any vessel, or enlist, to go beyond the limits of their own country to assist any people in war against another with whom they are at peace.

§ 11. It is sometimes agreed to suspend hostilities for a time. If the agreement is only for a short period, for the purpose of burying the dead after battle, or for a parley between the hostile generals; or if it regards only some particular place, it is called a cessation or *suspension of arms;* if for a considerable time, and especially if general, it is called a *truce.* By a partial truce, hostilities are suspended in certain places, as between a town and the general besieging it; and generals have power to make such truces. By a general truce, hostilities are to cease generally, and in all places, and are made by the governments or sovereigns. Such truces afford opportunities for nations to settle their disputes by negotiation.

§ 12. A truce binds the contracting parties from the time it is made; but individuals of the nation are not responsible for its violation before they have had due notice of it. And for all prizes taken after the time of its commencement, the government is bound to make restitution. During the cessation of hostilities, each party may, within his own territories, continue his preparations for war, without being charged with a breach of good faith.

§ 13. War is generally terminated, and peace secured, by *treaties of peace.* The manner of making treaties has been described. (Chap. XL, § 5.) A treaty of peace puts an

§ 9. In what case is the property of an enemy in a neutral vessel liable to seizure? What is done with the property of neutrals found in an enemy's vessel? § 10. What may not a neutral permit in her ports? What may not her citizens do? § 11. For what purposes are hostilities sometimes suspended? When is the suspension called a suspension of arms? In what cases a truce? What is the difference between a partial and a general truce? § 12. How are the contracting parties and their citizens affected by a truce? § 13. How is peace generally secured?

end to the war, and leaves the contracting parties no right to take up arms for the same cause.

§ 14. The parties to a treaty of peace are bound by it from the time of its conclusion, which is the day on which it is signed ; but, as in the case of a truce, persons are not held responsible for any hostile acts committed before the treaty was known ; and their government is bound to order and enforce the restitution of property captured subsequently to the conclusion of the treaty.

§ 15. War is sometimes terminated by *mediation.* A friend to both parties, desirous of stopping the destruction of human life, kindly endeavors to reconcile the parties. The friendly sovereign who thus interposes, is called *mediator.* Many desolating wars might have been early arrested in this way, or wholly prevented, had there always been among friendly powers a disposition to reconcile contending nations.

---

§ 14. When do treaties of peace take effect between the parties ? § 15. How is the service of mediation performed ?

SYNOPSIS OF THE STATE CONSTITUTIONS.

MAINE.

The District of Maine, formerly belonging to the state of Massachusetts, adopted in convention, October 29, 1819, the present constitution, and was admitted into the Union as a state, March 15, 1820. The constitution has received several alterations.

Electors. All male citizens, having had a residence in the state three months, except paupers, persons under guardianship, and Indians not taxed.

Legislature. The house of representatives consists of one hundred and fifty-one members, apportioned among the counties according to population; and the number apportioned to each county are apportioned among the towns according to the population. A representative must have been a citizen of the United States five years, resided in the state one year, and in the town or district he is chosen to represent, three months. Senate, not less than twenty, nor more than thirty-one members, elected in districts by majority. If a senator is not elected by the electors, the house and the senators elected choose one from the two candidates having the highest numbers of votes. Age, twenty-five years, otherwise qualified as representatives.

A majority constitutes a *quorum.* Bills vetoed by the governor become laws when re-passed by two-thirds majorities. Also bills become laws if not returned by the governor within five days, unless their return is prevented by adjournment, in which case they will become laws unless returned within three days after the next meeting.

Executive. The governor is elected annually, by majority. If no person has a majority, the house, from those voted for (not exceeding four) having the highest numbers of votes, elects two, of whom the senate elects a governor. Age, thirty years, a native citizen, resident of the state five years. An executive council of seven, chosen annually by the legislature on joint ballot. Power of appointment is exercised by the governor and council. No lieutenant-governor.

Secretary of state, treasurer, and attorney-general, are chosen annually by joint ballot of both houses.

Judiciary. A supreme judicial court, and such other courts as the legislature may establish. Judges of the judicial court are appointed by the governor and council for seven years ; judges and registers of probate are elected in the counties for four years.

Officers may be removed by impeachment, and by the governor and council on address of both houses of the legislature.

Amendments to the constitution may be proposed by two-thirds of both branches, and ratified by the electors at the next annual election.

NEW HAMPSHIRE.

THE first constitution of this state was adopted in 1784 ; the present one in 1792, and has been amended.

Electors. All male citizens, except paupers and persons excused from paying taxes at their own request, resident in the state six months, and in the town three months.

Legislature—called *general court.* Senate, twelve members, elected annually in single districts ; thirty years of age ; inhabitants of the state seven years, and inhabitants of their respective districts. Representatives are apportioned among the towns according to ratable male polls, (male tax-payers ;) state residence, two years. Senators and representatives must be of the Protestant religion. *Quorum*, a majority.

Bills passed against the veto by two-thirds majorities—also become laws if not returned within five days, unless the return is prevented by adjournment.

Executive. The governor is elected annually by majority. If no person has a majority, the two houses elect one of the two highest. Age, thirty years; inhabitant of the state, seven years, and a Protestant. Council of five, one in each district, elected annually by majority. Power of appointment and of pardon exercised by the governor and council. No lieutenant-governor.

Secretary of state, treasurer, and commissary-general appointed by joint ballot of both houses.

Judiciary. Judicial officers are appointed by the governor and council; justices of the peace for five years, judges of the higher courts during good behavior. Judges disqualified at seventy years of age.

Attorney-general, solicitors, sheriffs, coroners, registers of probate, and naval and the higher militia officers, are appointed by the governor and council. County treasurers and registers of deeds are elected in the counties.

Amendments. The sense of the people is taken every seven years; and if a majority favor a revision, the legislature calls a convention; and any alterations proposed by the convention must be approved by two-thirds of the qualified electors who vote thereon.

VERMONT.

This state was admitted into the Union in 1791, with a constitution formed in 1777; the present one was adopted in 1793, and has been several times amended.

Electors. Citizens having resided in the state one year, of quiet and peaceable behavior, are entitled to all the privileges of freemen, by taking an oath that, in giving their votes, they will so do it as they believe will conduce to the best good of the state.

Legislature. Senate, thirty members, elected annually; apportioned among the counties according to population, each county to have at least one senator; age, thirty years; freemen of the county. Representatives are elected in towns, each town being entitled to at least one representative; resident of the state two years, of the town one year.

Quorum, a majority. For raising a tax, two-thirds of the members elected must be present.

Bills vetoed by the governor may be again passed by simple majorities. Bills not returned by the governor within five days become laws, unless their return is prevented by adjournment.

Executive. The governor is elected annually by majority. If no person has a majority, the legislature chooses one of the three highest. Resident of the state four years. A lieutenant-governor.

A secretary of state, chosen by the two houses; a treasurer, elected as governor and lieutenant-governor.

Judiciary. A supreme court and county courts; the judges chosen annually by the senate and house; justices of the peace are elected in the towns; judges of probate in districts; assistant judges of county courts, sheriffs, high bailiffs, and state's attorneys, in their respective counties.

Amendments. A council of thirteen censors, chosen every seven years, examines into the different departments, and have power to call a convention to amend the constitution

---

MASSACHUSETTS.

The constitution of this state was formed in 1780. It has been several times amended.

Electors. Every male citizen, except paupers and persons under guardianship, having resided in the state one year, in the town or district six months; and having paid a tax within two years, or is legally exempt from taxation.

Legislature—styled *general court.* Senate, forty members, chosen in districts, and apportioned according to population; residents of the state five years, and inhabitants of the districts they represent. Representatives are apportioned among the towns and cities. Every town or city containing 1,200 inhabitants, is entitled to one, and an additional one for every 2,400 additional inhabitants. Residence one year in the towns they represent.

Bills passed against the veto by two-thirds majorities—or

become laws if not returned within five days, unless the legislature by adjournment, prevent their return.

Executive. The governor is chosen annually, by majority. If no candidate has a majority, the house elects two of those voted for, (not exceeding four,) having the highest numbers of votes, of which two the senate elects a governor. He must have resided in the state seven years, and declare himself to be of the Christian religion. A council of nine, elected annually by joint ballot of the two houses, act with the governor in pardons and appointments, and in directing the affairs of state generally. Counselors must have resided in the state five years.

The secretary, treasurer, receiver-general, commissary-general, notaries public, and naval officers, are chosen annually by the legislature.

Judiciary. A supreme judicial court and a court of common pleas, held in every county of the state, and courts held by justices of the peace. All judicial officers are appointed by the governor and council ; justices of the higher courts during good behavior, justices of the peace for seven years. The former are removable by the governor and council, or address of the legislature.

The attorney-general, the solicitor-general, sheriffs, coroners, and registers of probate, are appointed as justices.

Amendments agreed to by a majority of the senators and two-thirds of the representatives at two successive sessions, are submitted to the qualified voters of the state for ratification.

RHODE ISLAND.

A CHARTER granted in 1663, by Charles II, to the Rhode Island and Providence Plantations, continued, with some modifications, the basis of government of this state, until 1842, when the present constitution was adopted.

Electors. Every male *native* citizen, resident in the state two years, in the town or city six months, and having within a year paid a tax of $1, or has done military duty.

Also every naturalized citizen, resident in the state one year, in the town or city six months, owning real estate worth $134 above all incumbrances, or which rents for $7 a year. Voters in this state must be registered in the town clerk's office, at least seven days before they offer their votes.

Legislature styled *general assembly.* Representatives, not to exceed seventy-two, are apportioned among the towns, no town to have more than one-sixth of the whole house. The senate consists of the lieutenant-governor and one senator from each town or city. The governor, and in his absence, the lieutenant-governor, presides in the senate, and in grand committee, (the two houses united.) *Quorum,* a majority.

Bills when passed by both houses are laws.

Executive. The governor and lieutenant-governor are elected annually by majority. If no candidate has a majority, the two houses in joint assembly (grand committee) elect from the two having the highest numbers of votes.

A secretary, an attorney-general, and a general treasurer, are elected in the same manner as the governor.

Judiciary. A supreme court and such inferior courts as the legislature shall establish. Judges of the supreme court are elected by the two houses in grand committee. The judges hold their offices until their places shall be declared vacant by the general assembly.

Amendments must be agreed to by two successive legislatures, (a majority of all the members elected to each house voting in their favor,) and approved by three-fifths of the electors of the state voting thereon.

CONNECTICUT.

This state was governed under a charter granted by Charles II, in 1662, until 1818, when the present constitution was adopted. This constitution has received numerous amendments.

Electors. Every white male citizen, who has resided in the state a year, and in the town six months, who sustains a good moral character, and is able to read any section of the constitution of the state and of the constitution of the United States.

Legislature—styled *general assembly.* Representatives are apportioned among the towns according to population. Any elector is eligible to either house. Senators, not less than eighteen, nor more than twenty-four, are chosen in districts, the number of which is not to be less than eight, nor more than twenty-four. *Quorum*, a majority.

Bills rejected by the governor may be again passed by a majority of each house. Bills become laws also if not returned by the governor within three days, unless the legislature sooner adjourn.

Executive. A governor and lieutenant-governor are elected annually. Any qualified elector thirty years of age is eligible. Election by majority. In case of a failure to elect, the general assembly chooses a governor from the two having the highest numbers of votes.

A treasurer, a secretary, and a controller of public accounts, are elected as the governor and lieutenant-governor. A sheriff is elected in each county for three years.

Judiciary. A supreme court, a superior court, and such inferior courts as the legislature shall establish. The judges are appointed by the general assembly ; the judges of the supreme and superior courts for eight years ; removable by the governor on address of two-thirds of each house. Judges of probate are chosen annually by the electors in districts ; justices of the peace in the towns.

Amendments are proposed by a majority of the house of representatives, approved by two-thirds of both houses of the next legislature and a majority of the electors at an election.

NEW YORK.

The first constitution of this state was formed in 1777 · the second in 1821, and adopted in 1822 ; the present was formed and adopted in 1846.

Electors. Every white male citizen, resident in the state a year, and in the county four months, and thirty days in the district which the person voted for is to represent. Naturalized persons must have been admitted as citizens ten days before voting. Colored men must have resided in the state three years, own a freehold of $250 in value over incumbrances, and have paid a tax thereon.

Legislature. Senate, thirty-two members elected in single districts for two years. Assembly, one hundred and twenty-eight members, apportioned among the counties. Counties entitled to more than one member are divided into districts and a member is elected in each district. A census is taken, and a new apportionment made every ten years. A majority is a quorum to do business. The final passage of bills requires a majority of all the members. Bills may be passed against the veto by two-thirds majorities. They become laws if not returned within ten days, unless their return is prevented by adjournment.

Executive. A governor is elected for two years; a citizen, thirty years of age; a resident of the state five years. A lieutenant-governor.

Judiciary. A court of appeals, a supreme court, county courts, and courts held by justices of the peace. There are eight judicial districts, in each of which four justices of the supreme court are elected for eight years, two of them every two years. The court of appeals is composed of eight judges, four of whom are elected by the electors of the state for eight years, one every two years, and the other four are of the class of justices of the supreme court whose term has most nearly expired. In each county are held circuit courts and special terms of the supreme court, by one or more justices of the supreme court. General terms of the supreme court are held in the several districts by three or more of the justices. A county court is held by a county judge elected for four years, who is also *surrogate*, called in other states, *judge of probate.* In counties having more than 40,000 inhabitants, a separate officer may be chosen as surrogate. Justices of the peace are elected in the several towns for four years.

Judges of the court of appeals and justices of the supreme court may be removed by the legislature; county judges by the senate on recommendation of the governor.

A secretary of state, a controller, a treasurer, an attorney-general, and a state engineer and surveyor, are chosen for two years; three canal commissioners and three inspectors of state prisons, for three years, one of each every year.

Sheriffs, clerks of counties, coroners, and district attorneys, are elected for three years in the several counties. Sheriffs are ineligible for the next three years.

Amendments must receive the sanction of two successive legislatures, and of a majority of the electors voting thereon at an election.

NEW JERSEY.

NEW JERSEY, as a colony, adopted a constitution in 1776, under which the state was governed until the present constitution, framed in 1844, was adopted.

Electors. White male citizens, who have resided in the state a year, and in the county five months.

Legislature. A senate and general assembly. The senate consists of one senator from each county, elected for three years; one-third of the senators elected every year. Age, thirty years; residence in the state four years, and in the county one year. Members of the general assembly, not to exceed sixty, are apportioned among the counties according to population. Residence in the state two years, in the county one year. A majority is a *quorum.*

The final passage of bills requires a majority of the members elected. The same majorities may pass bills disapproved by the governor. Bills become laws if not returned by the governor within five days, unless their return is prevented by adjournment.

Executive. The governor is elected for three years, and is ineligible for the next three years. He must be thirty years of age; have been twenty years a citizen, seven years a resident of the state. The pardoning power is exercised by the governor in conjunction with the chancellor and the judges of the court of errors and appeals. No lieutenant-governor.

The state treasurer, and the keeper and inspectors of the state prison are appointed annually by joint assembly of the two houses. The secretary of state, attorney-general, and prosecutors of the pleas, are appointed by the governor and senate, for five years.

Judiciary. A court of errors and appeals; a court of chancery; a prerogative court; a supreme court; circuit courts; and inferior courts. The court of errors and appeals consists of the chancellor, the justice of the supreme court, and six judges, or a majority of them. The court of chancery consists of the chancellor, who is also the ordinary, or surrogate-general, and judge of the prerogative court, to which appeals are made from the orphans' court. The supreme court consists of a chief justice and four associates. The circuit courts are held in every county by one or more justices of the supreme court, or a judge appointed for that purpose. Chancellor and justices of the supreme court hold for seven years; judges of the court of errors and appeals for six years; and all are appointed by the governor and senate. The inferior court of common pleas shall not have more than five judges, one to be appointed every year by the senate and assembly.

Justices of the peace, from two to five, are elected in each township and city ward, for five years.

Sheriffs and coroners are elected annually in their respective counties, and may be re-elected until they shall have served three years; after which they are ineligible for three years.

Amendments must be agreed to by two successive legislatures, a majority of all the members elected to each house concurring, and be ratified by the electors at an election held for that purpose. Amendments, (if more than one,) must be submitted separately; and not oftener than once in five years.

PENNSYLVANIA.

A CONSTITUTION was adopted in 1776; another in 1790; the present one in 1838.

Electors. White freemen, having resided in the state one year, in the election district ten days, and paid a tax within two years ; if between twenty-one and twenty-two years, they need not have paid the tax. An elector having removed from the state and returned, may vote after six months residence in the state, and ten days in the district, and the payment of taxes.

Legislature—called *general assembly.* Representatives are chosen annually, and apportioned every seven years among the counties according to the number of taxable inhabitants ; number not less than sixty, nor more than one hundred. Age, twenty-one ; residence in the state three years, one in the district. Senators are chosen for three years, (one-third every year,) in districts, not more than two in any district, unless the taxable inhabitants in any city or county entitle it to elect more ; but no city or county may elect more than four. The whole number may not be less than one-fourth nor greater than one-third of the number of representatives. Twenty-five years ; state residence, four years ; district, one year.

Quorum, a majority of each house. Bills passed against the veto by two-thirds majorities. Bills not returned by the governor within ten days, become laws, unless their return is prevented by adjournment.

Executive. The governor is elected for three years, and may not hold the office more than six years in nine Age, thirty years ; a citizen and inhabitant of the state, seven years. No lieutenant-governor.

A secretary is appointed by the governor during pleasure. A treasurer is chosen annually by joint assembly.

Judiciary. Supreme court, the judges elected for fifteen years ; courts of oyer and terminer and general jail delivery in the counties, held by judges of the supreme court and court of common pleas ; a court of common pleas in each judicial district, which may not include more than five counties, the presiding judge to hold his office for ten years, the associates for five years ; a court of quarter sessions and orphans' court for each county, held by judges of the common pleas ; a register's court for each county, composed of the register of wills and judges of the common pleas ; and courts held in the several townships, wards, and boroughs, by justices of the peace or aldermen elected by the voters therein, for five years. Judges of the supreme court are elected by the people of the state at large; others are chosen in the districts or counties over which they preside.

Sheriffs and coroners are elected in their counties for three years. Sheriffs may not be twice chosen in any term of six years.

Amendments must be agreed to by majorities of all the members of two successive legislatures, and ratified by a majority of the electors voting thereon. Amendments must be voted on separately; and none may be submitted to the electors oftener than once in five years.

DELAWARE.

THE first constitution of this state was adopted in 1776; the present, in 1831, and has been amended.

Electors. White males twenty-two years of age, having resided in the state one year, in the county one month, and within two years paid a county tax assessed at least six months before the election. If twenty-one, and under twenty-two years of age, they may vote without having paid any tax.

Legislature—called *general assembly.* Representatives are chosen in counties for two years; must be twenty-four years of age; have been citizens and inhabitants of the state three years, of the county one year. Senators are elected in the counties for four years; the number not to be greater than one-half, nor less than one-third of the number of representatives. A senator must be twenty-seven years of age; have been a citizen and an inhabitant of the state three years, of the county, one year; and possess a freehold estate in the county of two hundred acres of land, or real and personal property, or either, worth £1,000, at least.

A majority of each house is a quorum. Bills are not submitted to the governor.

Executive. The governor is elected for four years, and is

not eligible a second time. Thirty years of age ; a citizen and inhabitant of the United States twelve years, of the state, six years. No lieutenant-governor.

A secretary of state, appointed by the governor during his continuance in office ; a state treasurer, biennially, by a concurrent vote of the two houses. [By this mode of election, the two houses do not meet and vote jointly, but they vote separately, as in passing laws.]

Judiciary. Five judges appointed by the governor, of whom one is chancellor, and holds the court of chancery. Of the other four, one is chief-justice, and the other three are associate justices, of whom one resides in each county.

The superior court, and the court of general sessions of the peace and jail delivery, consist of the chief-justice and two associates. The court of oyer and terminer consists of all the judges except the chancellor. The court of errors and appeals issues writs of error to the superior court, receives appeals from the court of chancery, and determines finally all matters in error in the judgments and proceedings of the superior court ; and when thus acting, it consists of the chancellor and two of the other judges. In other cases, it is differently constituted. The orphans' court in each county is held by the chancellor and the associate judge residing in the county. The register's court in each county is held by the register of the county.

Judges of the courts are appointed by the governor during good behavior ; and they may be removed by him on the address of two-thirds of all the members of each branch of the general assembly.

In pursuance of the power vested in the legislature to establish inferior courts, a court of common pleas is established in each county.

Justices of the peace in each county are appointed by the governor for seven years, and may be removed as the judges.

The attorney-general, registers, and prothonotaries are appointed for five years, removable in like manner.

The sheriff and the coroner of each county are elected by the citizens thereof ; but the legislature may vest their appointment in the governor. The sheriff may not be chosen twice in any term of six years.

Amendments are proposed by two-thirds of each house,

with the approbation of the governor, and ratified by three-fourths of each branch of the next general assembly. Or, a convention to amend may be called by the legislature, in pursuance of the sense of the people expressed at a previous election.

MARYLAND.

The constitution of this state adopted in 1776, continued until 1851, when the present one was adopted.

Electors. White male citizens, having resided a year in the state, and six months in the county.

Executive. The governor is elected for four years ; must be thirty years of age ; have been a citizen five years, a resident of the state five years, and for three years a resident of the district from which he is elected. In case of vacancy, the general assembly elects a resident of the same district for the residue of the term. If the vacancy happens during the recess of the legislature, the president of the senate serves until the next session. No lieutenant-governor.

A secretary of state is appointed by the governor and senate during the official term of the governor. A controller of the treasury is elected by the electors of the state for two years ; and a treasurer and a state librarian are chosen by the legislature on joint ballot at each session.

Legislature. A senate and a house of delegates, styled *general assembly.* Senators, one from each county and the city of Baltimore, are elected for four years, one-half every two years. Age, twenty-five years ; residence, three years in the state, one in the county. Delegates are eligible at twenty-one ; otherwise qualified as senators ; elected for two years, apportioned among the counties according to population ; the city of Baltimore to have four more delegates than the most populous county, and no county to have less than two delegates ; the whole number not to be more than eighty, nor less than sixty-five.

A majority constitutes a quorum. Bills must pass by majorities of all the members elected ; and when so passed and sealed with the great seal, the governor is required to sign them in the presence of the presiding officers and chief clerks of both houses.

Judiciary. A court of appeals, consisting of four judges, one of whom is elected in each judicial district for ten years. One is designated by the governor and senate as chief-justice. They must be thirty years of age, and have been citizens of the state five years. They are disqualified at seventy. There are eight judicial circuits, in each of which, except the fifth, is elected a judge, for ten years, who holds circuit courts in the counties within his circuit.

There are, in the city of Baltimore, courts peculiar to that city.

Justices of the peace and constables, are elected for two years in each ward of the city of Baltimore, and in each election district in the several counties.

A sheriff and a state's attorney are elected in each county and the city of Baltimore, the former for two, and the latter for four years. Sheriffs are ineligible for the next two years.

Amendments may be made only by a convention, called by the legislature in pursuance of a vote of the people to be taken after each United States census.

VIRGINIA.

A CONSTITUTION was adopted in 1776 ; another in 1830 ; the present in 1851.

Electors. White male citizens, having resided in the state two years, and in the county, city or town where they offer to vote, one year. Votes are given openly, or *viva voce.* Dumb persons only vote by ballot.

Legislature. Senate and house of delegates. Delegates, one hundred and fifty-two in number, are elected biennially, and apportioned among the several counties and election districts according to population. The senate consists of fifty members, elected in single districts for four years, one-half every two years. Apportionments are made every ten years. Delegates are eligible at the age of twenty-one years ; senators at the age of twenty-five.

Quorum, a majority. Bills to become laws, do not require the governor's approval.

Executive. The governor is elected for four years, and is ineligible for the next term. He must be thirty years of age, a native citizen of the United States, and have been a citizen of the state five years. A lieutenant-governor.

A secretary of state, a treasurer, and an auditor of public accounts, are elected for two years in joint assembly ; an attorney general is elected for four years by the people at every election for governor.

Judiciary. The state is divided into twenty-one judicial circuits, ten districts, and five sections, in each of which division, one judge is elected by the people ; the circuit judges for eight years, the judges of the supreme court of appeals for twelve years. A circuit judge holds circuit courts in the several counties composing his district. The judges of the circuits constituting a section, and the judge of the supreme court of appeals for that section, hold district courts in such section. The supreme court of appeals consists of the five judges elected in the sections, and three of whom may hold a court. Judges may be removed by the legislature.

A county court is held monthly in each county, by not less than three, nor more than five justices of the peace, except when the law requires a greater number. Each county is divided into districts, in each of which four justices are elected for four years. The justices so elected choose one of their own body as presiding justice of the county court.

In each county are elected, a clerk of the county court and a surveyor, for six years ; an attorney for four years ; a sheriff for two years ; and constables and overseers of the poor as may be prescribed by law.

Amendments. The constitution does not provide for its amendment. The last two constitutions were framed by conventions authorized by acts of the legislature, and ratified by the electors.

NORTH CAROLINA.

This state adopted a constitution in 1776, which was amended in 1835.

Legislature. A senate and a house of commons, called the *general assembly.* The senate consists of fifty members, chosen biennially, in single districts, which are laid off in proportion to the average amount of taxes paid by the citizens during the five years preceding. Senators must have resided within their respective districts a year, and possess not less than three hundred acres of land. The house of commons is composed of one hundred and twenty members, chosen biennially, and apportioned among the counties, according to population, three-fifths of the slaves being added to the number of free persons. They must have resided a year in the counties they represent, and possess one hundred and twenty acres of land.

Bills passed by both houses become laws without being presented to the governor.

Executive. A governor is elected every two years, and is eligible only four years in any term of six years. He must be thirty years of age; must have been a resident of the state five years, and must have in the state a freehold of the value of £1,000. No lieutenant-governor.

There is a council of seven persons to advise the governor; a secretary of state, and a treasurer, all chosen by joint vote of the two houses at each session, for two years; and an attorney-general for four years, unless for certain reasons the term shall be altered.

Judiciary. A supreme court, superior courts, courts of admiralty, and justices' courts. The judges are appointed by the general assembly, and hold during good behavior. Justices of the peace, within their respective counties, are recommended to the governor by the representatives of the general assembly. They are commissioned by the governor, and hold during good behavior.

Electors. White freemen, inhabitants of the state one year, who have paid taxes. Voters for senators are required also to own a freehold of fifty acres.

Amendments. A convention may be called by a majority of two-thirds of all the members of each house of the general assembly. Or, amendments may be proposed by majorities of three-fifths of all the members of both houses; and they take effect when agreed to by two-thirds majorities of the whole representation in the next assembly, and ratified by the qualified voters of the state.

SOUTH CAROLINA.

The first constitution of this state was formed in 1775; the present in 1790. Its principal amendments were made in 1808.

Legislature. A senate and a house of representatives, styled *general assembly.* The house consists of one hundred and twenty-four members, elected for two years in districts, and apportioned according to the number of white inhabitants and the amount of taxes paid therein. Residence in the state three years: and if a resident of the election district, a freehold of five hundred acres of land and ten negroes, or a real estate worth £150 sterling, clear of debt; if a non-resident of the district, a clear freehold of £500 sterling. Senators, forty-five, elected by districts, for four years, one-half every two years; each district, except one, having one senator. Age, thirty years, state residence, five years. If a resident in the district, a clear freehold of £300 sterling; if a non-resident, a freehold in the district of £1,000.

Bills passed by both houses are laws without being presented to the governor.

Executive. The governor and lieutenant-governor are chosen by the legislature for two years. Age, thirty years: state residence, ten years; a clear freehold in the state of £1,500 sterling. A governor is ineligible for the next four years.

Commissioners of the treasury, secretary of state, and surveyor-general, are elected by joint ballot of both houses for four years, and ineligible for the next four years.

Judiciary. Such superior and inferior courts of law and equity as the legislature may establish. The judges are appointed by the legislature during good behavior.

Electors. White male citizens, resident in the state two years, and owning a freehold of 50 acres of land, or a town lot, which he has owned six months; or, not having such freehold, or town lot, resident in the election district six months, and having paid a tax the preceding year of three shillings sterling.

Amendments may be made by a convention called by two-thirds of all the members of both branches. Alterations may also be made by like majorities of two successive legislatures.

GEORGIA.

The first constitution was formed in 1777; the second in 1785; the present in 1798, and amended in 1839, and 1844.

Legislature. Senate and house, together styled *general assembly.* The members of both houses are elected biennially. Representatives are apportioned among the counties according to population, including three-fifths of the slaves. Age, twenty-one years; citizenship, seven years; state residence, three years; county, one year. Senators are elected in districts. Age, twenty-five years; citizenship, nine years; state residence, three years; district, one year.

Bills are passed against the veto by two-thirds majorities. Bills not returned by the governor within five days are laws, unless their return is prevented by adjournment.

Executive. The governor is elected for two years; must be thirty years of age; have been a citizen of the United States twelve years, of the state, six years. No lieutenant-governor.

Secretary of state, treasurer, and surveyor-general, are elected for two years.

Judiciary. A supreme court for the correction of errors, to consist of three judges chosen by the legislature for six years, one every two years ; a superior court, whose judges are elected in their several circuits for four years ; inferior courts, one in each county, consisting of five judges, elected by the people ; courts held by justices of the peace elected for four years.

Sheriffs are elected for two years, but may not be twice elected in four years.

Electors, white male citizens and inhabitants of the state, having resided in the county six months, and paid all the taxes required of them, and which they had an opportunity of paying the preceding year.

Amendments may be made by two successive legislatures, two-thirds of both houses concurring.

FLORIDA.

THIS state was admitted into the union with its present constitution, by act of congress, March 3, 1845.

Executive. The governor is elected for four years, and is ineligible for the next term. Age, thirty years ; citizenship ; state residence five years. No lieutenant-governor.

A secretary of state, elected by the people for four years ; a treasurer and a controller of public accounts for two years.

Legislature. A senate and a house of representatives, styled, the *general assembly*. Representatives are apportioned among the counties according to the number of free whites and three-fifths of the slaves ; the number not to exceed sixty. They are elected biennially. Age, twenty-one ; citizenship ; state residence, two years ; county, one year. Senators are elected in districts, at least one in each district, for four years, one-half every two years ; the number to be not less than one-fourth, nor more than one-half of the number of representatives. Age, twenty-five years ; other qualifications the same as those of representatives.

Bills become laws against the veto by majorities of all the members elected.

Judiciary. A supreme court, courts of chancery, circuit courts, and justices of the peace. The supreme court consists of three judges elected by the people for six years. The state is divided into four circuits, and a judge elected in each judicial circuit for six years, who presides in the courts held in his circuit. Justices of the peace for each county are appointed or elected, as the general assembly may direct.

An attorney-general is chosen by joint vote of the two houses, for four years.

Electors. White male citizens, residents of the state two years, of the county, six months; enrolled in the militia, unless by law exempted from serving. The general assembly is required to provide for registering the qualified electors of each county.

Amendments. A convention may be called by the general assembly, two-thirds of each house concurring. Alterations may be made by like majorities of two successive legislatures.

ALABAMA.

This state was admitted into the union in 1819, with its present constitution.

Legislature—called the *general assembly.* Representatives are apportioned among the counties according to the free white population; chosen biennially; must be twenty-one years of age, residents of the state two years, and of the county, city or town they represent, one year. Senators are chosen in single districts for four years, one-half of them every two years; must be twenty-seven years of age; residence the same as representatives. The number of representatives may not exceed one hundred; the number of senators may not exceed thirty-three.

Bills negotiated by the governor, may be passed by majorities of all the members elected. If not returned within five days, vetoed bills become laws unless their return is prevented by adjournment.

Electors. White male citizens, having resided in the state one year, in the county, city, or town, three months.

Executive. The governor is elected for two years, and eligible four years in any term of six years. He must be thirty years of age, a native citizen of the United States, and have been a resident of the state four years. No lieutenant-governor.

A secretary of state is chosen biennially, and a treasurer and a controller of public accounts are chosen annually, by joint vote of both houses.

Judiciary. A supreme court; circuit courts to be held in each county; and inferior courts of law and equity, to be established by the general assembly. Judges of the supreme court and chancellors are chosen by the legislature for six years; judges of the circuit and inferior courts by the people for the same term. A competent number of justices of the peace, and a sheriff, are elected in each county.

An attorney-general for the state, and the requisite number of solicitors are elected by joint vote of the general assembly, for four years.

Amendments are proposed by one legislature, approved by the electors at the next election for representatives, and ratified by the next legislature; two-thirds majorities being required in both cases.

MISSISSIPPI.

In 1817, this state was admitted into the union with a constitution adopted the same year. The present constitution was formed in 1832.

Electors. White male citizens, residents of the state one year, of the county, four months. An elector who happens to be in any county, city, or town, other than that of his residence, or who may have removed to any such place within four months preceding an election, may vote for such officers as he could have voted for in the county of his residence, or from which he removed.

Legislature. Representatives, not less than thirty-six, nor more than one hundred, are elected for two years in the several counties, among which they are apportioned according to the number of white inhabitants. They must have been residents of the state two years, one of the county. Senators, not less than one-fourth, nor more than one-third of the number of representatives, are elected by districts for four years. Age, thirty years; state residence, four years; district one year.

Bills are passed against the veto by two-thirds majorities. Bills must be returned within six days, or they become laws, unless their return is prevented by adjournment.

Judiciary. A high court of errors and appeals, consisting of three judges, one in each district, elected for six years; a circuit court to be held in each county at least twice a year, the judges to be elected in their respective judicial districts for four years; a superior court of chancery, the chancellor to be elected by the electors of the whole state for six years; a court of probate in each county, the judge to be elected for two years; a competent number of justices of the peace and constables, chosen in each county for two years. Other inferior courts may be established by the legislature.

An attorney-general is chosen by the electors of the state, and a competent number of district-attorneys in their respective districts. A sheriff and one or more coroners are elected in each county for two years.

Executive. The governor is elected for two years; must be thirty years of age; have been a citizen twenty years, a resident of the state five years; and may not hold the office more than four years in six. No lieutenant-governor.

A secretary of state, a treasurer, and an auditor of public accounts, are elected for two years.

Amendments are proposed by two-thirds of both branches of the legislature, and ratified by the people at the next election.

LOUISIANA.

THIS state was admitted into the union in 1812, with a constitution formed the same year. In 1845, a second, and in 1852 the present constitution was adopted.

Legislature—styled *general assembly.* Representatives are apportioned among the several parishes, (corresponding to counties in other states,) and are elected for two years; the number not to exceed one hundred, nor to be less than seventy. Senators, in number thirty-two, are apportioned among the districts according to population, and are elected for four years, one-half every two years. Every qualified elector is eligible to a seat in either house.

Vetoed bills are passed by majorities of two-thirds of all the members. They become laws if not returned within ten days, unless their return is prevented by adjournment; in which case they will become laws if not sent back within three days after the commencement of the next session.

Executive. The governor is elected for four years, and is ineligible the next four. Age, twenty-eight years; citizenship, and residence in the state four years. A lieutenant-governor.

A secretary of state and a treasurer are elected by the electors, the former for four years, the latter for two years.

Judiciary. A supreme court and such inferior courts as the legislature may establish, and justices of the peace. The supreme court is composed of a chief-justice and four associate justices; the former elected by the electors of the state at large, the latter in their respective districts. They are elected for ten years, one of the five every two years. Judges of the inferior courts are elected in their respective parishes or districts. Justices of the peace are elected for two years by the electors in each parish, district, or ward.

An attorney-general and a requisite number of district-attorneys, are elected for four years; the former by the electors of the whole state, the latter in their respective districts.

A sheriff and a coroner are elected in each parish for two years.

Electors. White males, having been citizens two years, residents of the state one year, and of the parish six months An elector removing from one parish to another, may vote in the former until he shall have become a voter in the latter.

Amendments are proposed by two-thirds of all the members of each house, and ratified by a majority of the electors voting thereon at the next general election.

TEXAS.

TEXAS, formerly a part of Mexico, declared itself independent in 1835. By a joint resolution of congress, approved December 29, 1845, this independent republic was admitted as a state into the union.

Electors. White male citizens who have resided in the state one year, and the last six months in the district, city, or town in which they offer to vote. If an elector happens to be in any other county within his district, he may there vote for any district officer; and he may vote any where in the state for state officers.

Legislature. Representatives, not less than forty-five, nor more than ninety, are apportioned among the counties according to the free population, and are elected for two years. They must have been residents of the state two years, of the county, city, or town they represent, one year. Senators, no less than nineteen, nor more than thirty-three, are elected in districts for four years, one-half every two years; must be thirty years of age; inhabitants of the state three years, of the district one year.

Bills negatived by the governor become laws when passed by two-thirds of both houses; bills not returned within five days become laws. Two-thirds of each house constitutes a quorum.

Judiciary. A supreme court, district courts, and such inferior courts as the legislature may establish. The supreme court consists of a chief-justice and two associates, and has appellate jurisdiction chiefly. It holds sessions once a year in not more than three places in the state. District courts are held by the judge of each judicial district at one place in each county at least twice a year. The judges of both the supreme and district courts are elected by the people for six years.

A convenient number of justices of the peace, one sheriff, one coroner, and a sufficient number of constables, are elected in each county for two years. The sheriff is eligible only four years in six.

Executive. The governor is elected for two years ; is eligible four years in every six. Age, thirty years ; state residence, three years ; a citizen of the United States, or a citizen of the state of Texas at the time of the adoption of the constitution. A lieutenant-governor.

A treasurer, a controller of public accounts, and an attorney-general are elected by the people for two years. A secretary of state is appointed by the governor and senate, to hold during the official term of the governor.

Amendments are proposed by two-thirds majorities of the legislature, approved by the electors, and ratified by majorities of two-thirds of the next legislature.

ARKANSAS.

In 1836, this state was admitted into the union with its present constitution, which was slightly amended in 1845.

Electors. White male citizens, residents of the state six months, and actual residents of the county.

Legislature—styled *general assembly.* Representatives, not more than one hundred, nor less than fifty-four, are apportioned among the counties according to the number of free white male inhabitants, and are elected for two years. Age, twenty-five years ; residents of the counties they represent. Senators are chosen in single districts for four years, one-half every two years ; the number to be not less than seventeen, nor more than thirty-three. Age, thirty years, inhabitants of the state one year, and actual residents of the district they represent.

General elections are *viva voce*, until otherwise directed by law. Bills are passed against the veto by majorities of all the members. Bills not returned within three days become laws, unless their return is prevented by adjournment.

Executive. The governor is elected for four years, and is ineligble more than eight in twelve years. Age, thirty years ; residence in the state four years. No lieutenant-governor.

A secretary of state for four years, and an auditor and a treasurer for two years, are elected by a joint vote of both houses.

Judiciary. A supreme court, circuit courts, county courts, and justices of the peace. The supreme court is composed of three judges, elected by the legislature for eight years ; one every four years, one every six, and one every eight years. In each circuit a judge is elected by the legislature for four years. There is in each county a county court held by justices of the peace. Justices are elected in the townships for two years.

An attorney of state is elected in each judicial district for two years.

A sheriff, a coroner, a treasurer and a county-surveyor, are elected in each county for two years.

Amendments may be made by two successive legislatures, by two-thirds majorities.

MISSOURI.

This state was admitted into the union in 1821. The present constitution was adopted in 1820, and has been several times amended.

Legislature—styled the *general assembly.* Representatives are apportioned among the counties on the basis of the white population, and are elected for two years. Age, twenty-four years ; state residence, two years ; county or district one year ; payment of state or county tax. Senators, not to be less than twenty-five, nor more than thirty-three, are chosen in single districts for four years, one-half every two years. Age, thirty years ; residence in the state, four years ; in the district, one year ; payment of a state or county tax.

Sessions of the legislature are limited to sixty days. Bills vetoed by the governor must be passed by majorities of all the members to become laws. Bills not returned by the governor within four days become laws, unless their return is prevented by adjournment.

Electors. White male citizens, having resided in the state one year, in the county or district three months.

Executive. The governor is elected for four years, and is ineligible the next four ; must be thirty years of age ; have been a citizen of the United States ten years, and of the state five years. A lieutenant-governor.

A secretary of state, an auditor of public accounts, a treasurer, an attorney-general, and a register of lands, are elected by the people for four years.

Judiciary. A supreme court, circuit courts, justices of the peace, and such other tribunals as the general assembly shall establish. The three judges of the supreme court are elected by the electors of the state for six years. A judge in each of the circuits is elected by the electors thereof for six years. Justices of the peace are elected in the townships.

Amendments may be proposed every fourth year by a majority of the whole of each house ; and they take effect when ratified by the electors of the state.

TENNESSEE.

THIS state was admitted into the union with its first constitution in 1796. The present one was formed in 1835.

Legislature—styled *general assembly.* Representatives are apportioned among the counties or districts according to the number of qualified voters in each, and are not to exceed seventy-five until the population of the state shall be 1,500,000, and may never exceed ninety-nine. They must be citizens of the state three years, and residents of the county they represent one year. Senators are apportioned as representatives ; the number not to exceed one-third of the number of representatives ; must be thirty years of age ; in other respects qualified as representatives. Both are elected biennially.

Bills passed by both houses are laws without having been presented to the governor. *Quorum*, two-thirds of each house.

Executive. The governor is elected for two years ; and may not hold the office more than six in any term of eight years. He must be thirty years of age, and have been a citizen of the state seven years. No lieutenant-governor.

A secretary of state for four years, and a treasurer for two years, are chosen by joint vote of the general assembly.

Electors. White males having been citizens of the county six months ; also male persons of color, twenty-one years of age, who are competent witnesses in a court of justice against a white man.

Judiciary. A supreme court, such inferior courts as the legislature may establish, and justices' courts. The supreme court consists of three judges, one in each of the grand divisions of the state, elected for twelve years. Judges of inferior courts are elected for eight years. For the election of justices of the peace, each county is divided into districts of convenient size, in each of which are elected two justices and one constable. A district containing a county town, may elect three justices and two constables.

Attorneys for the state are elected by joint assembly for six years.

In each county are elected one sheriff, and one trustee for two years ; and one register for four years. The justices of the peace of each county elect one coroner and one ranger for two years.

Amendments are proposed by majorities of all the members elected, approved by two-thirds of all the members of the next legislature, and ratified by the people.

KENTUCKY.

The first constitution of this state was adopted in 1790; and the state was admitted with the same in 1792. Another was adopted in 1799; and the present in 1850.

Legislature—styled *general assembly.* The house of representatives consists of one hundred members, elected for two years; apportioned among the counties in proportion to the qualified voters. Age, twenty-four years; state residence, two years; county, one year. When a city or town has a sufficient number of voters, it may elect one or more representatives. Senate, thirty-eight members, one elected in each district for four years; one-half every two years. Age, thirty years; residence in the state six years, in the district, one year.

Bills vetoed by the governor, if again passed by majorities of all the members elected, are laws; also if not returned by him within ten days, unless the return is prevented by adjournment; in which case they become laws, unless sent back within three days after the commencement of the next session.

Executive. The governor is elected for four years, and is ineligible the next four. Age, thirty-five years; residence in the state six years. A lieutenant-governor.

A treasurer for two years; and an auditor of public accounts, a register of the land-office, and an attorney-general for four years, are chosen by the electors.

Judiciary. A supreme court, styled court of appeals, consisting of four judges, one to be elected in each district for eight years, in such rotation that one may be elected every two years. Should the number be changed, the principle of electing one every two years is to be preserved. A circuit court to be held in each county by a district judge, one to be elected in each of the twelve judicial districts, for six years. The number of districts may be increased, but may not exceed sixteen until the population shall exceed 1,500,000. A county court in each county, consisting of a presiding judge and two associates, elected for four years. Other inferior courts may be established by law.

Justices of the peace in each county are elected in districts, two in each district for four years, and a constable for four years. A state's attorney for each judicial district; a sheriff in each county, for two years, and several other county officers.

Electors. White male citizens who have resided in the state two years; in the county, town, or city, one year; and in the precinct in which they offer to vote, sixty days.

Amendments by conventions only are provided for. No convention may be called by the legislature, until a majority of all the voters of the state shall have voted at two successive elections in favor of calling a convention.

OHIO.

THE first constitution of this state was adopted in 1802, preparatory to her admission into the union; the present one, in 1851.

Legislature—styled *general assembly.* Senators and representatives are elected biennially in their respective counties or districts, in which they must have resided a year. The ratio of representation in the house is ascertained by dividing the whole population of the state by the number one hundred; the quotient being the ratio for the next ten years. The ratio for a senator is ascertained by dividing the whole population by thirty-five. Senators are elected in districts. The representation of fractions of population is provided for.

Bills are not submitted to the governor. Quorum, not less than a majority.

Executive. A governor, a lieutenant-governor, a secretary of state, a treasurer, and an attorney-general, are elected for two years; and an auditor for four years.

Judiciary. A supreme court consisting of five judges chosen by the electors of the state at large for five years, one, every year. The number may be altered by law. A district court in each of the nine common pleas districts, composed of a supreme court judge and the judges of the court of common pleas of the respective districts, and held in each county within a district, or in at least three places in each district. One or more of these judges hold a court of common pleas in every county in the district. A county probate judge is elected for three years.

Justices of the peace, a competent number, are elected in each township for three years.

A sheriff is elected in each county for two years, but may hold only four years in any period of six years.

Electors. White male citizens who have resided in the state one year, and in the county, township, or ward, such time as the law shall prescribe.

Amendments are proposed by three-fifths of all the members elected to each house, and ratified by a majority of the voters who vote thereon at an election. Or a majority of two-thirds of all the members of each house may submit to the electors the question of calling a convention ; and if a majority of the electors vote for a convention, the legislature shall provide for calling the same. Every twentieth year, the question of calling a convention is to be submitted to the electors.

INDIANA.

THIS state formed a constitution and was admitted into the union, in 1816. The present constitution was adopted in 1851.

Electors. White male citizens, having resided in the state six months. Also foreigners who have resided in the United States one year, in the state six months, and have declared their intention to become citizens.

Legislature—styled *general assembly.* The number of senators may not exceed fifty ; the number of representatives may not exceed one hundred ; both to be chosen in their respective counties or districts, senators for four years, one-half every two years ; representatives for two years. Both are apportioned according to the number of white male inhabitants twenty-one years of age, every six years. They must have been citizens of the state two years ; of the county or district, one year. Senators must be twenty-five years of age.

Quorum, two-thirds. Bills must be finally passed by majorities of all the members elected. The same majorities enact a bill disapproved by the governor. If he does not return a bill within three days, it is a law, unless its return is prevented by adjournment ; in which case it will be a law, unless he shall, within five days after the adjournment, file the bill, with his objections, in the office of the secretary of state, who shall lay the same before the general assembly at the next session, as if it had been returned by the governor. Bids may not be presented to the governor within two days previous to the adjournment.

Executive. The governor is elected for four years ; and is eligible only four years in eight. Age, thirty years ; citizenship, five years ; state residence, five years. A lieutenant-governor.

A secretary of state, an auditor, and a treasurer, are elected for two years, and are eligible four years in six.

Judiciary. A supreme court, circuit courts, and such inferior courts as the general assembly may establish. Judges of the supreme court, not less than three nor more than five, one in each district, are elected by the electors of the state at large, for six years. Circuit courts consist of a judge for each judicial circuit, chosen by the electors thereof, for six years ; and a prosecuting attorney for the circuit, for two years. Justices of the peace are elected for four years in the townships.

There are elected in each county, a clerk of the circuit court, an auditor, a recorder, a treasurer, a sheriff, a coroner, and a surveyor ; the first three for four years ; the others for two years. The sheriff and treasurer are eligible only four years in eight ; the first three eight years in twelve.

Amendments must be agreed to by two successive legislatures, a majority of all the members of each house concurring, and ratified by the electors of the state.

ILLINOIS.

Illinois was admitted into the union in 1818. The present constitution is dated August 31, 1847.

Legislature—styled *general assembly*. Representatives are elected for two years; must be twenty-five years of age; inhabitants of the state three years, and of the county or district, one year; and have paid a state or county tax. The number is never to exceed one hundred. The districts are not limited to a single representative. The senate consists of twenty-five members, elected in single districts, for four years, one-half every two years; must be thirty years of age; citizens of the United States; inhabitants of the state five years, of the county or district, one year; and have paid a county or state tax. Apportionments of senators and representatives are made after each census, taken in 1855, and every ten years thereafter.

Quorum, two-thirds. Bills passed against the veto by a majority of all the members elected to each house. If not returned within ten days, they are laws, unless their return is prevented by adjournment; in which case they must be returned on the first day of the next legislative session, or they will be laws.

Executive. The governor is elected for four years, and is eligible four years in eight. Age, thirty-five years; citizenship, fourteen years; state residence, ten years. A lieutenant-governor.

A secretary of state and an auditor of public accounts are elected for four years, and a treasurer for two years.

Judiciary. A supreme court of three judges, one to be chosen in each of the three grand divisions, for nine years, one every three years; the one oldest in commission to be chief-justice. The legislature may provide for their election by the whole state. Circuit judges are elected for six years, one in each of the nine judicial districts, the number of which may be increased, if necessary. A circuit court is to be held two or more terms annually in each county

A judge of the county court is elected in each county for four years, and has also probate jurisdiction.

Justices of the peace are elected in each county by districts for four years. Inferior local courts may be established in the cities by the legislature.

A state's attorney is elected in each judicial circuit, for four years; or in each county, if the legislature shall so direct. In each county a clerk of the circuit court is elected for four years and a sheriff for two years, who is eligible only once in four years; a supreme court clerk by the electors of each grand division.

Electors. White male citizens having resided in the state one year. A poll or capitation-tax of not less than fifty cents, nor more than a dollar, may, in case of necessity, be laid upon every voter under sixty years of age.

Amendments must be proposed by two-thirds majorities of all the members of one legislature, approved by majorities of all the members of the next legislature, and ratified by the electors at the next general election. Or, the legislature, by two-thirds majorities of all the members, may submit to the people the question of calling a convention; and if a majority of the electors voting for representatives shall vote for a convention, an act for calling one shall be passed.

MICHIGAN.

THIS state was admitted into the union in 1836. The present constitution was adopted in 1850.

Legislature. The senate has thirty-two members, elected in single districts, for two years. Representatives, not less than sixty-four, nor more than one hundred, are elected also in single districts, for two years. An apportionment of members is made every ten years. Any qualified elector holding no other office, is eligible to either house.

The final passage of bills requires a majority of all the members elected to each house. Majorities of two-thirds of all the members pass bills against the veto. Bills not returned within ten days, are laws unless their return is

12*

prevented by adjournment. Bills passed within the last five days of a session, may be signed by the governor and filed by him in the office of the secretary of state within five days after the adjournment; and the same become laws.

Executive. The governor is elected for two years; must be thirty years of age; have been a citizen of the United States five years, and a resident of the state two years. A lieutenant-governor.

Judiciary. A supreme court, circuit courts, a probate court, and justices of the peace. For six years, and until the legislature shall otherwise provide, the circuit judges are to be judges of the supreme court. After six years, a supreme court may be organized, consisting of a chief-justice and three associate justices, chosen by the electors for eight years, and so classed that only one of them shall go out of office at a time. A circuit judge is elected in each of the eight judicial circuits for six years. The number of circuits may be increased. The probate judge of each county is elected for four years.

Justices of the peace, not exceeding four, are elected in each township, for four years.

Electors. White male citizens who have resided in the state three months, and in the township or ward ten days; also foreigners after a residence of two and a half years in the state, and a declaration of their intention to become citizens; and civilized males of Indian descent.

A secretary of state, a superintendent of public instruction, a treasurer, a commissioner of the land-office, an auditor-general, and attorney-general, are elected for two years.

In each county are elected a sheriff, a county clerk, a county treasurer, a register of deeds, and a prosecuting attorney, all for two years. The sheriff can hold only four years in six. The board of supervisors may unite the offices of clerk and register in one office.

Amendments are proposed by two-thirds of all the members of each branch, and ratified by a majority of the electors voting thereon at the next general election. Every sixteenth year the question of a general revision of the constitution by a convention shall be submitted to the electors of the state.

WISCONSIN.

This state was admitted into the union by an act of congress, May 29, 1848.

Electors. White male citizens, or foreigners who have declared their intention to become citizens, having resided in the state one year; also civilized persons of Indian descent, not members of any tribe.

Legislature. A senate and an assembly. Members of the assembly are elected annually; the number not to be less than fifty-four, nor greater than one hundred. The number of senators may not be less than one-fourth, nor greater than one-third of the number of members of assembly. Senators are chosen for two years, half every year. Members of both houses are elected in single districts, apportioned every five years; and must have resided in the state a year, and be qualified electors of the districts.

Bills are passed over the veto by majorities of two-thirds. Quorum, a majority,

Executive. The governor is elected for two years. Any citizen of the United States and qualified elector of the state, is eligible to the office of governor or lieutenant-governor.

A secretary of state, a treasurer, and an attorney-general, are elected for two years.

Sheriffs, coroners, registers of deeds, and district-attorneys, are elected in counties, for two years. Sheriffs are ineligible for the next two years.

Judiciary. A supreme court, circuit courts, courts of probate, and justices of the peace. Inferior courts, with limited civil jurisdiction, may be established by law in the several counties. By the constitution, the judges of the circuit courts were to be judges of the supreme court for five years, and until the legislature should otherwise provide. A separate supreme court may be organized, to consist of a chief-justice and two associate justices elected by the electors of the state for six years; one only to be elected at a time. The circuit judges also, one in each judicial circuit, are elected for six years. The supreme court shall hold at least one term annually at the seat of government, and at such other places as the legislature may provide. A circuit court is to be held at least twice a year in each county.

A judge of probate is chosen in each county for two years; but the office may be abolished, and probate powers conferred on inferior county courts. Justices of the peace are elected in the several towns, cities, and villages, for two years.

Amendments are to be approved by a majority of the whole of each house of two successive legislatures, and ratified by the people. Also the legislature may submit to the people the question of calling a convention to revise or change the constitution.

IOWA.

THE state of Iowa was admitted into the union by an act of congress approved December 28, 1846.

Electors. White male citizens, resident in the state six months, and in the county twenty days.

Legislature. The two houses are called the *general assembly.* Representatives are elected in their respective districts for two years; their number to be not less than thirty-nine, nor exceed seventy-two. They must be inhabitants of the state one year, and residents of the county or district thirty days. Senators, in number not less than one-third, nor more than one-half of the number of representatives, are elected for four years, one-half every two years. Age, twenty-four years; otherwise qualified as representatives.

Two-thirds majorities of the members present, pass bills vetoed by the governor. Bills not returned within three days also become laws, unless their return is prevented by adjournment.

Executive. The governor is elected for four years; must have been a citizen of the United States and a resident of the state, two years; and must be thirty years of age. No lieutenant-governor. In case of vacancy in the office of governor, the office devolves upon the secretary of state until the vacancy is filled.

A secretary of state, an auditor of public accounts, and a treasurer, are elected for two years.

Judiciary. A supreme court, district courts, and such inferior courts as the legislature may establish. The supreme court consists of a chief-justice and two associates, elected by joint vote of the two branches, for six years. It has appellate jurisdiction only in all cases of chancery, and constitutes a court for the correction of errors at law. Each district court consists of a judge elected by the voters of the district, for five years, at the township elections. A prosecuting attorney and a clerk of the district court, are elected in each county at the general election, for two years.

Amendments are provided for only by a convention. The legislature may provide for a vote of the people, and if a majority of the votes are in favor of a convention, an election of delegates is to be held within six months.

CALIFORNIA.

The constitution of this state was adopted November 13, 1849; and the state was admitted by act of congress, September 9, 1850.

Electors. White male citizens of the United States, and white male citizens of Mexico having elected to become citizens of the United States under the treaty of peace, who have resided in the state six months, and in the county or district thirty days.

Legislature. Senate and assembly. Members of assembly, the number to be not less than thirty, nor greater than eighty, are chosen annually by districts. Senators, not to be less than one-third nor more than one-half of the number of members of assembly, are elected by districts for two years, one-half every year. Members of both houses must have resided in the state two years, and in their respective districts one year, and be qualified voters. They are apportioned every five years.

Bills, rejected by the governor, must be passed by a majority of two-thirds of each house, to become a law. Bills become laws if not returned by the governor within ten days, unless the legislature shall sooner adjourn.

Executive. A governor and a lieutenant-governor are elected for two years. Age, twenty-five years, and two years' residence in the state.

A secretary of state, a controller, a treasurer, an attorney-general, and a surveyor-general, are elected for two years, by joint vote of the two houses.

Judiciary. A supreme court, district courts, county courts, justices of the peace, and such municipal and other inferior courts as the legislature may establish. The supreme court consists of three judges elected by the electors of the state for six years, one every two years; the senior justice in commission to be chief-justice. District judges are elected in their respective districts for six years. A judge of the county court is elected in each county for four years, and performs also the duties of judge of probate. The number of justices of the peace elected in each county, city, town, or village, is fixed by law.

The election of sheriffs, coroners, county clerks and certain other officers, is provided for by law.

Amendments must be agreed to by majorities of all the members of the two houses of two successive legislatures, and ratified by the people. The legislature may, by two-thirds majorities, submit to the people the question of calling a convention for a general revision of the constitution.

MINNESOTA.

This state was admitted into the union in 1858.

Electors. White male citizens having resided in the United States one year, and in the state four months. Also foreigners who have so resided, and declared their intention to become citizens; and persons of mixed white and Indian blood, and of Indian blood, under certain regulations.

Legislature. A senate and a house of representatives. The first legislature consisted of thirty-seven senators and eighty representatives.

Executive. A governor and a lieutenant-governor are elected for two years.

A secretary of state, a treasurer, and an attorney-general, are elected for two years, and a state auditor for three years.

Judiciary. The judicial power is vested in a supreme court, district courts, courts of probate, justices of the peace, and such other courts inferior to the supreme court, as the legislature may establish by a two-thirds vote.

CONSTITUTION OF THE UNITED STATES.

We, the people of the United States, in order to form a more perfect union, establish justice, insure domestic tranquillity, provide for the common defense, promote the general welfare, and secure the blessings of liberty to ourselves and our posterity, do ordain and establish this Constitution for the United States of America.

ARTICLE I.

Section 1. All legislative powers herein granted shall be vested in a congress of the United States, which shall consist of a senate and house of representatives.

Sec. 2. The house of representatives shall be composed of members chosen every second year, by the people of the several states ; and the electors in each state shall have the qualifications requiste for electors of the most numerous branch of the state legislature.

No person shall be a representative who shall not have attained to the age of twenty-five years, and been seven years a citizen of the United States, and who shall not, when elected, be an inhabitant of that state in which he shall be chosen.

Representatives and direct taxes shall be apportioned among the several states which may be included within this union, according to their respective numbers, which shall be determined by adding to the whole number of free persons, including those bound to service for a term of years, and excluding Indians not taxed, three-fifths of all other persons. The actual enumeration shall be made within three years after the first meeting of the congress of the United States, and within every subsequent term of ten years, in such manner as they shall by law direct. The number of representatives shall not exceed one for every thirty thousand, but each state shall have at least one representative; and until such enumeration shall be made, the state of New Hampshire shall be entitled to choose *three;* Massachusetts, *eight;* Rhode Island and Providence Plantations, *one;* Connecticut, *five;* New York, *six;* New Jersey, *four;* Pennsylvania, *eight;* Delaware, *one;* Maryland, *six;* Virginia, *ten;* North Carolina, *five;* South Carolina, *five;* and Georgia, *three.*

When vacancies happen in the representation from any state, the executive authority thereof shall issue writs of election to fill such vacancies.

The house of representatives shall choose their speaker and other officers, and shall have the sole power of impeachment.

Sec. 3. The senate of the United States shall be composed of two senators from each state, chosen by the legislature thereof, for six years; and each senator shall have one vote.

Immediately after they shall be assembled in consequence of the first election, they shall be divided as equally as may be, into three classes. The seats of the senators of the first class shall be vacated at the expiration of the second year; of the second class at the expiration of the fourth year; and of the third class at the expiration of the sixth year; so that one-third may be chosen every second year; and if vacancies happen, by resignation or otherwise, during the recess of the legislature of any state, the executive thereof may make temporary appointments, until the next meeting of the legislature, which shall then fill such vacancies.

No person shall be a senator who shall not have attained to the age of thirty years, and been nine years a citizen of the United States, and who shall not, when elected, be an inhabitant of that state for which he shall be chosen.

The vice-president of the United States shall be president of the senate, but shall have no vote, unless they be equally divided.

The senate shall choose their other officers, and also a president pro tempore, in the absence of the vice-president, or when he shall exercise the office of president of the United States.

The senate shall have the sole power to try all impeachments: when sitting for that purpose, they shall be on oath or affirmation. When the president of the United

States is tried, the chief-justice shall preside ; and no person shall be convicted without the concurrence of two-thirds of the members present.

Judgment, in cases of impeachment, shall not extend further than to removal from office, and disqualification to hold and enjoy any office of honor, trust, or profit, under the United States ; but the party convicted shall, nevertheless, be liable and subject to indictment, trial, judgment and punishment, according to law.

SEC. 4. The times, places and manner of holding elections for senators and representatives, shall be prescribed in each state by the legislature thereof ; but the congress may at any time, by law, make or alter such regulations, except as to the places of choosing senators.

The congress shall assemble at least once in every year ; and such meeting shall be on the first Monday in December, unless they shall, by law, appoint a different day.

SEC. 5. Each house shall be the judge of the elections, returns and qualifications of its own members ; and a majority of each shall constitute a quorum to do business ; but a smaller number may adjourn from day to day, and may be authorized to compel the attendance of absent members, in such manner, and under such penalties, as each house may provide.

Each house may determine the rules of its proceedings, punish its members for disorderly behavior, and, with the concurrence of two-thirds, expel a member.

Each house shall keep a journal of its proceedings, and from time to time publish the same, excepting such parts as may, in their judgment, require secrecy ; and the yeas and nays of the members of either house, on any question, shall at the desire of one-fifth of those present, be entered on the journal.

Neither house, during the session of congress, shall, without the consent of the other, adjourn for more than three days, nor to any other place than that in which the two houses shall be sitting.

SEC. 6. The senators and representatives shall receive a compensation for their services, to be ascertained by law, and paid out of the treasury of the United States. They shall, in all cases, except treason, felony and breach of the peace, be privileged from arrest during their attendance at the session of their respective houses, and in going to and returning from the same; and for any speech or debate in either house, they shall not be questioned in any other place.

No senator or representative shall, during the time for which he was elected, be appointed to any civil office under the authority of the United States, which shall have been created, or the emoluments whereof shall have been increased during such time; and no person holding any office under the United States, shall be a member of either house during his continuance in office.

Sec. 7. All bills for raising revenue shall originate in the house of representatives; but the senate may propose, or concur with, amendments, as on other bills.

Every bill which shall have passed the house of representatives and the senate, shall, before it become a law, be presented to the president of the United States; if he approve, he shall sign it; but if not he shall return it, with his objections, to that house in which it shall have originated, who shall enter the objections at large on their journal, and proceed to reconsider it. If after such reconsideration, two-thirds of that house shall agree to pass the bill, it shall be sent, together with the objections, to the other house, by which it shall likewise be reconsidered, and, if approved by two-thirds of that house, it shall become a law. But, in all such cases, the votes of both houses shall be determined by yeas and nays, and the names of the persons voting for and against the bill shall be entered on the journal of each house respectively. If any bill shall not be returned by the president within ten days (Sundays excepted) after it shall have been presented to him, the same shall be a law, in like manner as if he had signed it, unless the congress, by their adjournment, prevent its return, in which case it shall not be a law.

Every order, resolution, or vote, to which the concurrence of the senate and house of representatives may be necessary, (except on a question of adjournment,) shall be presented to the president of the United States, and before the same shall take effect, shall be approved by him, or, being disapproved by him, shall be repassed by two-thirds of the senate and house of representatives, according to the rules and limitations prescribed in the case of a bill.

Sec. 8. The congress shall have power:

To lay and collect taxes, duties, imposts, and excises to pay the debts and provide for the common defense, and general welfare of the United States ; but all duties, imposts, and excises shall be uniform throughout the United States :

To borrow money on the credit of the United States :

To regulate commerce with foreign nations, and among the several states, and with the Indian tribes :

To establish a uniform rule of naturalization, and uniform laws on the subject of bankruptcies throughout the United States :

To coin money ; to regulate the value thereof, and of foreign coin ; and fix the standard of weights and measures :

To provide for the punishment of counterfeiting the securities and current coin of the United States :

To establish post offices and post roads :

To promote the progress of science and useful arts, by securing for limited times, to authors and inventors, the exclusive right to their respective writings and discoveries :

To constitute tribunals inferior to the supreme court :

To define and punish piracies and felonies committed on the high seas, and offences against the law of nations :

To declare war ; grant letters of marque and reprisal ; and make rules concerning captures on land and water :

To raise and support armies ; but no appropriation of money to that use shall be for a longer term than two years :

To provide and maintain a navy :

To make rules for the government and regulation of the land and naval forces :

To provide for calling forth the militia to execute the laws of the union, suppress insurrections, and repel invasions :

To provide for organizing, arming and disciplining the militia, and for governing such part of them as may be employed in the service of the United States ; reserving to the states respectively, the appointment of the officers, and the authority of training the militia, according to the discipline prescribed by congress :

To exercise exclusive legislation in all cases whatsoever, over such district (not exceeding ten miles square) as may, by cession of particular states, and the acceptance of congress, become the seat of the government of the United States, and to exercise like authority over all places purchased by the consent of the legislature of the state in which the same shall be, for the erection of forts, magazines, arsenals, dock-yards, and other needful buildings: And,

To make all laws which shall be necessary and proper for carrying into execution the foregoing powers, and all other powers vested by this constitution in the government of the United States, or in any department or officer thereof.

Sec. 9. The migration or importation of such persons as any of the states now existing shall think proper to admit, shall not be prohibited by the congress prior to the year one thousand eight hundred and eight; but a tax or duty may be imposed on such importation, not exceeding ten dollars for such person:

The privilege of the writ of habeas corpus shall not be suspended unless when, in cases of rebellion or invasion, the public safety may require it.

No bill of attainder or ex post facto law shall be passed.

No capitation or other direct tax shall be laid, unless in proportion to the census or enumeration hereinbefore directed to be taken.

No tax or duty shall be laid on articles exported from any state. No preference shall be given, by any regulation of commerce or revenue, to the ports of one state, over those of another; nor shall vessels bound to or from one state be obliged to enter, clear, or pay duties in another.

No money shall be drawn from the treasury, but in consequence of appropriations made by law; and a regular statement and account of the receipts and expenditures of all public money shall be published from time to time.

No title of nobility shall be granted by the United States; and no person holding any office of profit or trust under them shall, without the consent of the congress, accept of any present, emolument, office, or title of any kind whatever, from any king, prince, or foreign state.

Sec. 10. No state shall enter into any treaty, alliance, or confederation; grant letters of marque and reprisal; coin money; emit bills of credit; make anything but gold and silver coin a tender in payment of debts; pass any bill of attainder, ex post facto law, or law impairing the obligation of contracts; or grant any title of nobility.

No state shall, without the consent of the congress, lay any imposts or duties on imports or exports, except what may be absolutely necessary for executing its inspection laws; and the net produce of all duties and imposts laid by any state on imports or exports, shall be for the use of the treasury of the United States; and all such laws shall be subject to the revision and control of the congress. No state shall, without the consent of congress, lay any duty of tonnage, keep troops or ships of war in time of peace, enter into any agreement or compact with another state, or with a foreign power, or engage in war unless actually invaded, or in such imminent danger as will not admit of delay.

ARTICLE II.

SECTION 1. The executive power shall be vested in a president of the United States of America. He shall hold his office during the term of four years, and, together with the vice-president, chosen for the same term, be elected as follows:

Each state shall appoint, in such manner as the legislature thereof may direct, a number of electors equal to the whole number of senators and representatives to which the state may be entitled in the congress; but no senator or representative, or person holding an office of trust or profit under the United States, shall be appointed an elector.

The electors shall meet in their respective states, and vote by ballot for two persons, of whom one at least shall not be an inhabitant of the same state with themselves. And they shall make a list of all the persons voted for, and of the number of votes for each, which list they shall sign and certify, and transmit, sealed, to the seat of the government of the United States, directed to the president of the senate. The president of the senate shall, in the presence of the senate and house of representatives, open all the certificates, and the votes shall then be counted. The person having the greatest number of votes shall be the president, if such number be a majority of the whole number of electors appointed; and if there be more than one who have such majority, and have an equal number of votes, then the house of representatives shall immediately choose by ballot one of them for president; and if no person have a majority, then, from the five highest on the list, the said house shall, in like manner, choose the president. But in choosing the president, the votes shall be taken by states, the representation from each state having one vote; a quorum for this purpose shall consist of a member or members from two-thirds of the states, and a majority of the states shall be necessary to a choice. In every case, after the choice of the president, the person having the greatest number of votes of the electors, shall be the vice-president. But if there should remain two or more who have equal votes, the senate shall choose from them, by ballot, the vice-president.

[By the 12th article of amendment, the above clause has been repealed.]

The congress may determine the time of choosing the electors, and the day on which they shall give their votes, which day shall be the same throughout the United States.

No person, except a natural born citizen, or a citizen of the United States at the time of the adoption of this constitution, shall be eligible to the office of president; neither shall any person be eligible to that office who shall not have attained to the age of thirty-five years, and been fourteen years a resident within the United States.

In case of the removal of the president from office, or of his death, resignation, or inability to discharge the powers and duties of the said office, the same shall devolve on the vice-president, and the congress may, by law, provide for the case of removal, death, resignation, or inability, both of the president and vice-president, declaring what officer shall then act as president; and such officer shall act accordingly, until the disability be removed, or a president shall be elected.

The president shall, at stated times, receive for his services a compensation, which shall neither be increased nor diminished during the period for which he shall have been elected; and he shall not receive, within that period, any other emolument from the United States, or any of them.

Before he enter on the execution of his office, he shall take the following oath or affirmation:

"I do solemnly swear (or affirm) that I will faithfully execute the office of President of the United States; and will, to the best of my ability, preserve, protect, and defend the constitution of the United States.

SEC. 2. The president shall be commander-in-chief of the army and navy of the United States, and of the militia of the several states, when called into the actual service of the United States ; he may require the opinion, in writing, of the principal officer in each of the executive departments, upon any subject relating to the duties of their respective offices ; and he shall have power to grant reprieves and pardons for offenses against the United States, except in cases of impeachment.

He shall have power by and with the advice and consent of the senate, to make treaties, provided two-thirds of the senators present concur : and he shall nominate, and by and with the advice and consent of the senate, shall appoint ambassadors, other public ministers and consuls, judges of the supreme court, and all other officers of the United States whose appointments are not herein otherwise provided for, and which shall be established by law : but the congress may, by law, vest the appointment of such inferior officers as they think proper, in the president alone, in the courts of law, or in the heads of departments.

The president shall have power to fill up all vacancies that may happen during the recess of the senate, by granting commissions which shall expire at the end of their next session.

SEC. 3. He shall from time to time give to the congress information of the state of the union ; and recommend to their consideration such measures as he shall judge necessary and expedient. He may, on extraordinary occasions, convene both houses, or either of them ; and in case of disagreement between them, with respect to the time of adjournment, he may adjourn them to such time as he shall think proper. He shall receive ambassadors and other public ministers. He shall take care that the laws be faithfully executed ; and shall commission all the officers of the United States.

SEC. 4. The president, vice-president, and all civil officers of the United States, shall be removed from office on impeachment for, and conviction of, treason, bribery, or other high crimes and misdemeanors.

ARTICLE III.

Section 1. The judicial power of the United States shall be vested in one supreme court, and in such inferior courts as the congress may, from time to time, ordain and establish. The judges both of the supreme and inferior courts, shall hold their offices during good behavior ; and shall, at stated times, receive for their services a compensation which shall not be diminished during their continuance in office.

Sec. 2. The judicial power shall extend to all cases in law and equity, arising under this constitution, the laws of the United States and treaties made, or which shall be made, under their authority ; to all cases affecting ambassadors, other public ministers, and consuls ; to all cases of admiralty and maritime jurisdiction ; to controversies to which the United States shall be a party, to controversies between two or more states ; between a state and citizens of another state ; between citizens of different states ; between citizens of the same state claiming lands under grants of different states ; and between a state, or the citizens thereof ; and foreign states, citizens or subjects.

In all cases affecting ambassadors, other public ministers and consuls, and those in which a state shall be a party, the supreme court shall have original jurisdiction. In all the other cases before mentioned, the supreme court shall have appellate jurisdiction, both as to law and fact, with such exceptions, and under such regulations, as the congress shall make.

The trial of all crimes, except in cases of impeachment, shall be by jury ; and such trial shall be held in the state where the said crimes shall have been committed ; but when not committed within any state, the trial shall be at such place or places as the congress may by law have directed.

Sec. 3. Treason against the United States shall consist only in levying war against them, or in adhering to their enemies, giving them aid and comfort. No person shall be convicted of treason, unless on the testimony of two witnesses to the same overt act, or on confession in open court

The congress shall have power to declare the punishment of treason; but no attainder of treason shall work corruption of blood, or forfeiture, except during the life of the person attainted.

ARTICLE IV.

SECTION 1. Full faith and credit shall be given, in each state, to the public acts, records, and judicial proceedings of every other state. And the congress may, by general laws, prescribe the manner in which such acts, records and proceedings shall be proved, and the effect thereof.

SEC. 2. The citizens of each state shall be entitled to all the privileges and immunities of citizens in the several states.

A person charged in any state with treason, felony, or other crime, who shall flee from justice, and be found in another state, shall, on demand of the executive authority of the state from which he fled, be delivered up, to be removed to the state having jurisdiction of the crime.

No person held to service or labor in one state, under the laws thereof, escaping into another, shall, in consequence of any law or regulation therein, be discharged from such service or labor; but shall be delivered up on claim of the party to whom such service or labor may be due.

SEC. 3. New states may be admitted by the congress into this union; but no new state shall be formed or erected within the jurisdiction of any other state, nor any state be formed by the junction of two or more states, or parts of states, without the consent of the legislatures of the states concerned, as well as of the congress.

The congress shall have power to dispose of, and make all needful rules and regulations respecting the territory or other property belonging to the United States; and nothing in this constitution shall be so construed as to prejudice any claims of the United States, or of any particular state.

SEC. 4. The United States shall guaranty to every state in this union, a republican form of government; and shall protect each of them against invasion, and on application of the legislature, or of the executive (when the legislature cannot be convened) against domestic violence.

ARTICLE V.

The congress, whenever two-thirds of both houses shall deem it necessary, shall propose amendments to this constitution, or on the application of the legislatures of two-thirds of the several states, shall call a convention for proposing amendments; which, in either case, shall be valid to all intents and purposes, as part of this constitution, when ratified by the legislatures of three-fourths of the several states, or by conventions in three-fourths thereof, as the one or the other mode of ratification may be proposed by the congress: Provided, that no amendment which may be made prior to the year one thousand eight hundred and eight, shall in any manner affect the first and fourth clauses in the ninth section of the first article; and that no state, without its consent, shall be deprived of its equal suffrage in the senate.

ARTICLE VI.

All debts contracted, and engagements entered into, before the adoption of this constitution, shall be as valid against the United States under this constitution, as under the confederation.

This constitution, and the laws of the United States which shall be made in pursuance thereof, and all treaties made or which shall be made under the authority of the United States, shall be the supreme law of the land, and the judges in every state shall be bound thereby, any thing in the constitution or laws of any state to the contrary notwithstanding.

The senators and representatives before mentioned, and the members of the several legislatures, and all executive and judicial officers, both of the United States, and of the several states, shall be bound, by oath or affirmation, to support this constitution; but no religious test shall ever be required as a qualification to any office or public trust under the United States.

ARTICLE VII.

The ratification of the conventions of nine states shall be sufficient for the establishment of this constitution between the states so ratifying the same.

Done in convention, by the unanimous consent of the states present, the seventeenth day of September, in the year of our Lord one thousand seven hundred and eighty-seven, and of the Independence of the United States of America, the twelfth. In witness whereof we have hereunto subscribed our names.

GEORGE WASHINGTON,
President, and Deputy from Virginia.

New Hampshire.—John Langdon, Nicholas Gilman.
Massachusetts.—Nathaniel Gorham, Rufus King.
Connecticut.—Wm. Samuel Johnson, Roger Sherman.
New-York.—Alexander Hamilton.
New Jersey.—William Livingston, David Brearly, William Paterson, Jonathan Dayton.
Pennslyvania.—Benjamin Franklin, Robert Morris, Thomas Fitzsimmons, James Wilson, Thomas Mifflin, George Olymer, Jared Ingersoll, Gouverneur Morris.
Delaware.—George Read, Gunning Bedford, Jr., John Dickinson, Richard Bassett, Jacob Broom.
Maryland.—James M'Henry, Daniel of St. Thomas Jenifer, Daniel Carroll.
Virginia.—John Blair, James Madison, Jr.
North Carolina.—William Blount, Richard Dobbs Spaight, Hugh Williamson.
South Carolina.—John Rutledge, Charles Pinckney, Pierce Butler, Charles Cotesworth Pinckney.
Georgia.—William Few, Abraham Baldwin.
Attest: WILLIAM JACKSON, *Secretary.*

AMENDMENTS.

ARTICLE 1. Congress shall make no law respecting an establishment of religion, or prohibiting the free exercise thereof; or abridging the freedom of speech or of the press; or the right of the people peaceably to assemble, and to petition the government for a redress of grievances.

ART. II. A well regulated militia being necessary to the security of a free state, the right of the people to keep and bear arms shall not be infringed.

ART. III. No soldier shall, in time of peace, be quartered in any house without the consent of the owner, nor in a time of war, but in a manner to be prescribed by law.

ART. IV. The right of the people to be secure in their per sons, houses, papers and effects, against unreasonable searches and seizures, shall not be violated; and no warrant shall issue, but upon probable cause, supported by oath or affirmation, and particularly describing the place to be searched, and the person or things to be seized.

ART. V. No person shall be held to answer for a capital or otherwise infamous crime, unless on a presentment or indictment of a grand jury, except in cases arising in the land or naval forces, or in the militia when in actual service, in time of war or public danger; nor shall any person be subject, for the same offense, to be twice put in jeopardy of life or limb, nor shall be compelled, in any criminal case, to be a witness against himself; nor be deprived of life, liberty or property, without due process of law; nor shall private property be taken for public use, without just compensation.

ART. VI. In all criminal prosecutions, the accused shall enjoy the right to a speedy and public trial, by an impartial jury of the state and district wherein the crime shall have been committed, which district shall have been previously ascertained by law, and to be informed of the nature and cause of the accusation; to be confronted with the witnesses against him; to have compulsory process for obtaining witnesses in his favor, and to have the assistance of counsel for his defense.

ART. VII. In suits at common law, where the value in controversy shall exceed twenty dollars, the right of trial by jury shall be preserved, and no fact tried by a jury shall be otherwise reëxamined in any court of the United States, than according to the rules of the common law.

ART. VIII. Excessive bail shall not be required, nor excessive fines imposed, nor cruel and unusual punishments inflicted.

ART. IX. The enumeration in the constitution of certain rights, shall not be construed to deny or disparage others retained by the people.

ART. X. The powers not delegated to the United States, by the constitution, nor prohibited by it to the states, are reserved to the states respectively, or to the people.

ART. XI. The judicial power of the United States shall not be construed to extend to any suit in law or equity, commenced or prosecuted against one of the United States by citizens of another state, or by citizens or subjects of any foreign state.

ART. XII. The electors shall meet in their respective states and vote by ballot for president and vice-president, one of whom, at least, shall not be an inhabitant of the same state with themselves; they shall name in their ballots the person voted for as president, and in distinct ballots the person voted for as vice-president, and they shall make distinct lists of all persons voted for as president, and of all persons voted for as vice-president, and of the number of votes for each, which lists they shall sign and certify, and transmit sealed to the seat of the government of the United States, directed to the president of the senate;—the president of the senate shall, in the presence of the senate and house of representatives, open all the certificates, and the votes shall then be counted;—the person having the greatest number of votes for president, shall be the president, if such number be a majority of the whole number of electors appointed; and if no person have such majority, then, from the persons having the highest numbers, not exceeding three, on the list of those voted for as president, the house of representatives shall choose immediately, by ballot, the president. But in choosing the president, the votes shall be taken by states, the representatives from each state having one vote; a quorum for this purpose shall consist of a member or members from two-thirds of the states, and a majority of all the states shall be necessary to a choice. And if the house of representatives shall not choose a president whenever the right of choice shall devolve upon them, before the fourth day of March next following, then the vice-president shall act as president, as in the case of the death or other constitutional disability of the president. The person having the greatest number of votes as vice-president, shall be the vice-president, if such number be a majority of the whole number of electors appointed, and if no person have a majority, then, from the two highest numbers on the list, the senate shall choose the vice-president; a quorum for the purpose shall consist of two-thirds of the whole number of senators, and a majority of the whole number shall be necessary to a choice. But no person constitutionally ineligible to the office of president shall be eligible to that of vice-president of the United States.

INDEX.

www.ingramcontent.com/pod-product-compliance
Lightning Source LLC
LaVergne TN
LVHW020240110826
845151LV00003B/985

* 9 7 8 1 4 2 5 5 2 9 3 2 1 *